GERMAN INFLUENCE
IN THE
ENGLISH ROMANTIC PERIOD

T0381756

The attempt to describe the effects of The Tales &c Wonderful is doubtful. A. M.ʳ G. Lewis Esq.ʳ M.P.

TALES of WONDER!

SOME EFFECTS OF *DIABLERIE*

GERMAN INFLUENCE

IN THE

ENGLISH ROMANTIC PERIOD

1788–1818

WITH SPECIAL REFERENCE
TO SCOTT, COLERIDGE, SHELLEY
AND BYRON

BY

F. W. STOKOE

CAMBRIDGE
AT THE UNIVERSITY PRESS
MCMXXVI

CAMBRIDGE UNIVERSITY PRESS
Cambridge, New York, Melbourne, Madrid, Cape Town,
Singapore, São Paulo, Delhi, Mexico City

Cambridge University Press
The Edinburgh Building, Cambridge CB2 8RU, UK

Published in the United States of America by Cambridge University Press, New York

www.cambridge.org
Information on this title: www.cambridge.org/9781107662742

First published 1926
First paperback edition 2013

A catalogue record for this publication is available from the British Library

ISBN 978-1-107-66274-2 Paperback

PREFACE

IT is proposed to examine here in what manner and to what extent interest in German literature was excited in England at the end of the eighteenth and at the beginning of the nineteenth century; and to trace this interest more particularly in the work of certain English writers of the period. Our investigation extends approximately from 1790 to 1820[1]; before the former of these dates the existence of German literature as a subject of study and a source of pleasure and enlightenment had received next to no public recognition in Great Britain, beyond that contained in Henry Mackenzie's paper on the German drama: by 1820 the long torpor which succeeded the first extravagant enthusiasm for certain products of German literature is yielding to a renewed and more intelligent realisation of the importance of Germany for Western culture; the way is prepared for Carlyle, and in general for the acquisition by the English public of more reliable and more valuable information about Germany and its literature.

Within these limits we shall note an increasing knowledge of German literature, and on the whole an increasing admiration for it, amounting to enthusiasm in particular cases. It must be acknowledged, however, that the enthusiasm is frequently misdirected, that a sane appreciation by English students of the relative values of German works is confined chiefly to a few of the more comprehensive thinkers of the day; and that the general cultured estimate of German literature during this period is erratic and uncritical. This may be chiefly due to the fact, which is mentioned in the Introductory Chapter and will be confirmed in later chapters, that the considerations which first recommend the literature of Germany to the attention of the English public are not, properly speaking, literary at all; it

---

[1] Where the opinions of individual writers is the subject of study this limit (1820) may be considerably exceeded, though their chief concern with German literature lies mainly within it. The periodical literature has been consulted more closely up to 1817, where we may place the beginning of the revival of interest in the products of German intellect and imagination. (v. chap. III.)

was the attraction of the new, the exotic, the revolutionary, which first roused English readers from their profound indifference to the German point of view—roused them either to sympathy or dislike, for unwise admiration was balanced by ill-judged antagonism. Between the two, periodical criticism tended to lose its balance and become hysterical. The first critical appreciation of German thought and literature must be looked for in a few minds, whose excellence destined them sooner or later to occupy a dominant position in English literature; and it is thanks to these that the German influence on English Romanticism was on the whole beneficent.

It may be well to inquire at the outset of our investigation, what meaning we are to attach to the word *influence*, when applying it to the action of one literature upon another, or of a foreign literature or author on a given writer; and further, how far our concern here is with the question of German influence on English literature generally or on individual English writers.

Influence is a modification of consciousness by action from without; and such action, to become effective, must have had the way prepared for it by previous tendencies in the consciousness concerned. The foreign example serves to justify and encourage the expression of the native aptitude. It supplies a precedent for departure in an untried direction. In the case of the general influence of literatures upon one another, it should not be difficult to discover, by following the trend of literary endeavour before and after the impact of a foreign influence, what changes of direction may be probably attributed to the latter. To measure these results is the task of the literary historian whose investigations extend for some distance on either side of the period of influence; for us, primarily and sufficiently concerned with the detail of the moment of impact, inquiry will turn on the channels through which influence becomes effective, on their formation, on the changes and development which they undergo; it is in fact mainly our business to supply and order the materials which the general historian requires as a basis for his estimate.

These remarks apply, *mutatis mutandis*, to the more particular case of foreign influence on a writer. Here the channels of influence can be more accurately traced, the reaction to it more precisely noted. One effect of such reaction, that of direct imitation of foreign writers or direct borrowing from them, has necessarily received a large share of the attention of previous investigators in our field of research. It constitutes, indeed, the bulk of the direct evidence of influence, and is obviously valuable as an indication of its extent. But inquiry is faced here with a peculiar difficulty, which has been too frequently overlooked or too negligently dealt with: how can we be confident that a likeness between an English and a foreign writer is due to imitation?

Where the counterfeit has retained the verbal form of its original the problem of course does not exist; we can entertain no reasonable doubt as to the source, for instance, of some of Coleridge's unacknowledged loans. Further, when situations or characters of a foreign work unite a number of features not necessarily related, and these reappear in similar juxtaposition in the work of an English writer probably acquainted with the former, we may safely allege imitation; as in the case of Fenella in *Peveril of the Peak*. Such well-defined instances are, however, infrequent; and we are not justified in proceeding with similar assurance where ideas, incidents, personages, belong to what might be called the common stock of the literary imagination, to the general fund of notions and images; here further evidence must be adduced before we claim the resemblance to be due to imitation. We must show, for instance, that the idea is not probably native to the soil in which it grows, that its appearance proclaims it exotic or of recent transplantation; or, on the other hand, we must bring evidence that the author was, at the time of writing, probably under the impression of a perusal of the alleged original—had been observed, as it were, wandering in a suspicious manner among his neighbour's flower-beds.

The amount of evidence requisite to constitute a strong probability of imitation will of course vary greatly with the degree of resemblance. In many instances it will be found impossible to bring forward anything amounting to proof; but if we mark clearly the degree of probability in doubtful cases, our results will be such that valid inference may be drawn from them.

Mathematical certainty is indeed unattainable in this branch of knowledge, where the problems are rather of a qualitative than of a quantitative order. Demonstration must aim here, not at certainty, but at conviction; and where conviction is unattainable, must sift the lesser probabilities and present them in a right subordination.

It may be thought that this statement of principles is unnecessary, that these or similar considerations are assumed as the basis of any study in comparative literature. But this is not the case in fact. It has been my business to read a very large amount of printed matter, dealing with the influence of German literature in England; and a standard of the kind suggested, by which facts may be tried and arranged, is nowhere, to my recollection, defined, and is rarely implied; it is on the contrary painfully clear that the necessity of a standard of any kind has scarcely presented itself to the consciousness of many of the writers. The accumulation of facts proceeds uncritically; their interpretation is handled without skill or judgment, and frequently in defiance of rudimentary common-sense. The method, bad in itself, is often applied without even the saving grace of accuracy in the statement of matters of fact. The student is confronted with a litter of details, not sorted according to their values, and not to be utilised safely until they have been individually verified. The subject will necessarily recur when we come to the discussion of debatable points of our inquiry. Whether, as may be suspected, this condition of affairs is not peculiar to this small corner of the field of comparative literature may be decided by those who have worked in it elsewhere.

In examining the state of English opinion concerning German literature at the end of the eighteenth and the beginning of the nineteenth century we observe fluctuations, indeed, but mark an advance on the whole towards steady and intelligent interest in the subject from an initial indifference to it. The means by which this change was brought about are to be studied here in two main directions: in the public journals, and in the lives and writings of those who came more or less directly under the spell of German literature, and whose attitude towards it was of importance either on account of their eminence as English writers, or because of the exceptional extent of their knowledge of German literature and of their powers of propaganda.

From a review of the periodicals of the time we may infer something of the stages by which the general reading public woke to the consciousness of the significance of the foreign body of thought, and what elements in the latter it selected for particular approval or reprobation. From the study of individual writers we may gather information as to the qualities in the foreign literature which chiefly appealed to livelier imaginations and more cultured and discriminating minds. The formation in England of an enlightened public opinion about German literature was a slow process, and its development at any moment was of course outrun by certain individual thinkers; though at a given stage it might leave the earlier of these behind. Thus about 1820 the sedulous reader of the more cultured type of periodicals probably had a better general idea of the relative values of German literature than had, say, Coleridge in 1800; whereas in 1800 the latter was incomparably better informed in this respect than the cultured review-reader of the day.

After a general introduction, our inquiry begins with an account of a paper read in 1788 before the Royal Society of Edinburgh by Henry Mackenzie. His subject, the German Drama, was of a nature so unusual at that time and in those surroundings that it is worth mentioning here on that score alone; it marks moreover conveniently for our purpose the beginning of a new era in the relations of the English public to German literature[1], and helped, no doubt, to hasten the change.

In the next place, an attempt will be made to shape what hints the periodical literature of the time affords us into a sketch of the state and variations of the public mind on the subject of

---

[1] There were naturally many intermediate steps between the almost complete indifference to German literature in England prior to 1750 and the interest in it discernible towards 1795. Mackenzie's paper was but one of these steps, though a more decisive one than most. But before Mackenzie *Werther* had had its translations; one of them had reached its seventh edition in 1788. Hans Schwarz (*Henry Mackenzie*, p. 129, see Bibliographical Note to chap. II) mentions a *Sketch of the Origin and Progress of Dramatic Poetry in Germany* which appeared in the Edinburgh Magazine, August 1786. And there had been for many years a thin trickle of miscellaneous translation from German (v. J. L. Haney, *German Literature in England before 1790*).

German literature; some account of two of its propagandists in England, William Taylor of Norwich and Henry Crabb Robinson, may fitly be given here.

Having made some acquaintance with the general estimate of German literature, we shall proceed to examine the attitude of individual writers, whose opinion of it can be followed in some detail, and occasionally (as in letters and diaries) be surprised, as it were, off its guard.

Most of the facts dealt with in this book were previously known and have been discussed in books, articles and university dissertations. Apart from the consideration that in this form they are not always easily accessible, it is hoped that their verification and restatement, with a discussion and appreciation of their relative importance, may contribute to a better understanding of their significance.

I gladly take this opportunity of heartily thanking Professor Karl Breul, for his constant encouragement and help in my work; and Professor J. G. Robertson for valuable criticism and advice in its later stages. The book is the outcome of research principally carried out by me as holder of the Tiarks Scholarship for two years (1915–17). The delay in bringing the work to a conclusion has been due to economic factors.

On pp. 188 ff. will be found Bibliographical Notes referring to the individual chapters, giving in full the titles, etc. of books referred to in the text or notes. On pp. 196 ff. a General Bibliography contains an alphabetical list of works which bear rather generally on the subject than particularly on the separate chapters.

F. W. S.

February, 1926

CONTENTS

CHAPTER I

General Introduction

THE hundred years preceding the outbreak of the French Revolution have some claim to be called the Age of Reason; the direction of men's intellectual endeavour in England, France and Germany during this century was on the whole towards a restatement of the results of human experience on strictly rational lines, an attempt to answer the riddle of the universe by translating all its terms into the language of systematic common-sense. A certain gallantry cannot be denied to those adventurers who set out to disprove the existence of mystery; but in a world whose very substance is mystery, they could not progress, even apparently, towards their goal without an artificial restriction of their subject-matter.

The speculation of the eighteenth century turned particularly to the study of man in his social aspects and, more generally, of that approximate order in phenomena taken in the mass which is the resulting average of individual eccentricities. It was an age that rejoiced in generalisations—in politics, in ethics, in criticism, in religion. It did not realise that these generalisations no more corresponded to the realities of existence than a map reproduces the geological formation of the country-side it charts. Thought ran in a broadening stream, and ran shallow. The consciousness of European mankind sways with a pendulum movement between extremes; its momentum drove it now towards the limit of the Social Idea; but already this movement, which appeared to the expectant generations which shared the impulse as an indefinitely extensible line of progress, suffered the disturbance of an attraction towards the inverse direction, the weightier elements becoming first aware of the pull. With Rousseau begins the rush towards the pole of the Individual Idea, the impetus which reached its point of exhaustion near the close of the first quarter of the nineteenth century.

The trend of thought that dominated almost all that was most youthfully alive and vitally active in Europe at the end of the eighteenth and beginning of the nineteenth century is most clearly marked in the intellectual movement called Romanticism. The Romantics are conscious that they have broken with the tradition of the immediate past; they are conscious that the future is on their side; but they are aware too that they have to overcome the resistance of the inert mass—of the ageing generations, who can no longer respond quickly to the call of new ideals, who tend to drift on in the direction once entered upon, though its goal be no longer a reality to them; of the intellectually and emotionally dull, who follow without question tradition or the pompous assurance of authority; in a word, of that vast body of conservatism or dormant intelligence in our civilisation which helps to withhold it at once from swift achievement and from swift disaster.

When a group or a society is preparing for departure in an untried direction, the pioneers of the new movement become aware of a larger fraternity than that of state and race; and this is the fructifying moment of foreign influence in literature and thought. Romanticism, conscious of a vast purpose and slender means, looked round it for support, looked beyond the narrow frontiers of nationality for allies to help it in its fight with the enemy at home.

The influence of French literature had predominated in England and Germany in the earlier eighteenth century. Over England, indeed, was showing the unpromising dawn of a new era in the "Nature" poetry of Thomson, Collins, Gray, in the subjective effusions of Young; and Germany, in reflecting the faint gleam, did something to disperse its own darkness and torpor, to shake off the incubus of French classical and pseudo-classical formalism. Though incapable of spontaneous effort, of any considerable originality, Germany in Gottsched's time began to feel the shame of its intellectual helotism, to be vaguely conscious of the vast intellectual and creative potentialities which, within sixty years, were to place it at a bound in the first rank of cultured nations. The long trance which had befallen its intellectual life was perhaps in a sense an advantage: like a man who has long lain in heavy sleep, it sprang up refreshed and with the keen enterprising consciousness of early morning. We hardly realise even now, perhaps, the nature of the task that Germany accomplished; in less than two centuries it has changed from the likeness of a stammering boor to one of the leading intellectual forces in Europe; it has produced literature of the highest type in such abundance that we forget how short the period of effective literary activity has been; and from it have emanated almost all the elements of the philosophical synthesis which enables us to apprehend, to some extent, the conditions of the new world which science has thrust upon us.

The middle years of the eighteenth century in Germany are dominated by two figures. In one of these, Lessing, are epitomised the best qualities of the age which was drawing to an end; the extreme, courageous, and highly skilled use of the reasoning faculty, the acceptance of the conclusions to which it leads, provided him with a basis of critical values, and the vivid intelligence with which he applied them—sometimes indeed misapplied them, for his aesthetic criticism is frequently preposterous in its assumptions—endowed his work with a brightness disturbing to the half-truths, prejudices, and other darkness-loving denizens of the unswept corners of our minds. The Aufklärung of which Lessing was the most brilliant exponent brought, as it were, the past up to date. The other great literary figure of the time, Klopstock, foreshadowed, though incompletely, the new age. His poetry sounds an extremely personal note which was enthusiastically greeted by his younger contemporaries; but his personality, no less than Lessing's, seems to belong to the past. His leading characteristic is perhaps sentiment; he exemplifies the reverse of the medal whose clear-cut obverse is presented by Lessing. For since the emotional side of humanity may be denied in theory but in practice will seek satisfaction, we have the curious spectacle of the most rationalising of generations melting into tears or dissolving into vapours on what appears to us slight provocation; the Age of Reason was also the age of sentiment, which is generalised passion. A succeeding generation, following a new ideal of individual expression, did not forget at once the ageing poet who, if he had little understanding for that ideal, had helped it to find expression by shattering the outworn poetic convention of the preceding age.

Werther and Lotte, watching the splendour of the storm, in admiration almost past articulate speech, look at one another, and breathe simultaneously the word: "Klopstock!"

The justification of the individual; the assertion of the rights of the individual against the exaggerated claims of the Social Idea; in the extreme case, the rebellion of the individual against society—these are of the essence of the new doctrine. Rousseau flung the gauntlet in the face of a self-complacent social order; he denounced it as degenerate, corrupt, corrupting: "Tout est bien sortant des mains de l'Auteur des choses, tout dégénère entre les mains de l'homme." Over against that idol of the age, the social man clipped of his idiosyncrasies, generalised, conformed to pattern, Rousseau set up the ideal of the free-born, the natural man, the man previous to a social and political order, the individualistic idol. France attended at first chiefly to the political side of his message, and prepared for revolution. But Germany was gathering itself for a mightier liberation, and the youngest generation there thrilled in response to the voice which cried for nature and sincerity in a wilderness of convention and hypocrisy. Herder, the wiser, more temperate leader of a rather fantastic band, sought individuality in the primitive utterance of peoples, in folk-song, popular epic, sacred myth. Gifted with historical intelligence, with a capacity for synthesis lacking in the analytical and emotional Rousseau, he did not place his ideal of humanity in some unattainable prehistoric or fabulous condition of independence, but in the fully-developed genius of the race. In the history of peoples, in their culture and art, he perceived the unfolding of this genius in more or less favourable circumstances, according as outward influences fostered or thwarted the innate impulses of growth.

On this view it was time that the direction of Germany's intellectual development should change. Lessing's clear cool thought had indeed already grasped what Herder's intuition now passionately felt: that the French genius and the Teutonic genius were not only not akin, but scarcely reconcilable; and if Germany could not—at the moment there was little evidence that she could—evolve a literature from her unaided consciousness, if imitation there must be, then let her turn to the kindred genius of England, to the primitive literatures of other peoples, and to her own past. Herder thus anticipated and strengthened the impulse towards those three among the dominant pre-occupations of Romanticism—Shakespeare, folk-song and medieval Germany.

Herder's enthusiasms were somewhat sobered and controlled by his historical philosophy; his audacity was not the mere ebullition of youthful spirits, but an intelligent, a reasoned audacity. It was otherwise with the group of young men who acknowledged his leadership. For philosophy, historical or other, they had little inclination, perhaps little capacity; sobriety and control they deemed unworthy of the natural man; their audacity was not reasoned, nor particularly intelligent. Of Herder's doctrine, they took whatever lighter material might serve as fuel to their flaming emotionalism. Shakespeare's apparent disorder, his apparent subordination of the theme to the individual; the untutored savagery of naïve ages in folk-song: these chimed with their mood, were valued as the distinguishing marks of *Genie*, that indispensable if insufficiently defined qualification of the aspiring literary youth of the early seventies, when the Geniezeit, one of the most curious and irresponsible of literary movements, broke like a storm over Germany. It was a storm at once destructive and fructifying; bursting with sudden violence in the dawn, it swept away the accumulated dust and wilted foliage of the Age of Reason, and cleared the air for the coming day.

The Geniezeit, in spite of its name, was not fertile in genius; it appears in retrospect as chiefly an exacerbation of self-consciousness in revolt against the limitations that circumstances imposed upon its need of display; its literary output, with few exceptions, is negligible; and of these exceptions, the three most notable are the outcome of a phase in the development of poets whose relation to the Sturm und Drang movement was transient. *Götz von Berlichingen*, *Werther* and *Die Räuber* may be credited to Sturm und Drang, since they all, and particularly the last, owe something of their form or tone, or both, to the Geniezeit, to its manner, to the formulation of its outlook and its literary theory; had these not been achieved, their out-

lines must have been presumably less sharp, their fury less com-
pelling; at the same time, these first-fruits of genius are in their
essence perhaps rather a refutation than an illustration of the
tenets of the Geniezeit. By virtue of his very limitations, Bürger
in his ballads belongs to it more exclusively, exemplifies it more
precisely. Its delight in the devastating extravagance of emotion, which in Klinger's *Zwillinge*, where it is almost untram-
melled by form, degenerates into bombast and absurdity, has
poignant reality in *Lenore*, in the agonised rush and flurry of
passion fretted like flooding torrents caught in a rugged channel.

Long ere Sturm und Drang had raged itself to the sleep of
exhaustion, Goethe had discovered that the unbridled assertion
of personality however genial is "sound and fury, signifying
nothing"; that the development of self can be attained only by
the limitation of self. In this there lay no necessary contradiction with the Individual Idea, but a possibility of its reconciliation with the Social Idea: Faust finds the greatest scope for his
individuality in the service of others. Goethe was not caught
away to the limit of the pendulum movement of his age; he
hovered about the centre, the synthesis of extremes attainable
to others only singly, and unreconciled.

The discovery which Goethe had made by virtue of his close
and true relation to the actuality of experience had come to
Schiller likewise, though by a different, a systematically built
road. He had the speculative nature for which not experience
but the conclusions to be drawn from it are of chief interest.
His reaction from the crude spontaneity of his Sturm und Drang
period was, like Goethe's, acute; and in the conscious pursuit
of an ideal of form in which all undue stress of the personal
should be eliminated, it may be held that they were mutually
encouraged to excesses of restraint. We have not infrequently
the sense that freer movement is hindered by their anxiety lest
a perfection of gesture be missed, lest an arrangement of classical folds be disturbed. It needed the utmost ardour of divine
fire to animate images so arbitrarily statuesque; at supreme
moments the miracle occurred. *Tasso* and *Iphigenie* have not the
spontaneity of *Götz* and *Werther*; the rant of Moor's robber-
band is more agreeably absurd than the somewhat pompous

emphasis of Wallenstein and his circle; but the agony of human good-will caught in the meshes of human error can move these self-consciously impassive masks to a tragic grimace.

While Goethe and Schiller, in the last decade of the eighteenth and the first of the nineteenth century were defining and consolidating their position, which by virtue of their personal, intellectual and literary qualities was to some extent both dominating and isolated in the literary activities of their time and country, these were concentrating about a movement which, though related to Sturm und Drang on the one hand and to the later Goethe and Schiller on the other, had a momentum and direction which were to carry it to destinies and conclusions peculiarly its own.

Two main literary groups may be distinguished in Germany at this time. One is composed of elements whose chief bond is contemporaneity, personal friendship, local proximity—the illustrious Weimar group, with the four greater lights, Goethe, Schiller, Herder, Wieland, ageing men of assured fame and settled views. The other group, welded by a more essential unity of purpose and consciousness of spiritual kinship, was approaching the problems of life and consciousness with a self-confidence worthy of the Geniezeit; but it brought intellectual powers to its task which promised very different results.

The first Romantic School in Germany woke to consciousness in a world where mental confusion and uncertainty accompanied the breaking-up of the social order of the Age of Reason and the discredit which had befallen its ideals. Consciousness was stirred in European mankind at depths where the rationalistic formulae no longer held good; it was recognised, if not consciously yet effectively, that to call man a rational being is to name him by that one of his attributes which soonest vanishes under the stress and pressure of circumstance. It belonged to Romanticism, especially to German Romanticism, to strive to plumb the mysterious depths upon which rational consciousness rests like a brittle film, a phenomenon of surface tension. The importance of the rôle of the subconscious in the totality of the individual was recognised, and an attempt was made to formu-

late the relation of the subconscious to the conscious self, a
daring and in the main a rightly directed attempt. The progress
of a century in psychological science has justified the endeavour
of Romanticism; and perhaps more than another century must
elapse before Romantic speculation on the mystery of personality can be rightly appraised in all its aspects; for if the direction
of twentieth-century thought coincides more and more closely
in essentials with some tendencies of Romantic thought, its
vanguard has not yet approached the furthest-flung outposts of
Romantic inquiry.

We have at least, however, come to accept the Romantic view
that the origin of emotions, of impulses, of the inspiration of art,
lies in the subconscious. To the Romantics, the kinds of human
endeavour, the arts, the sciences, philosophy, ethics, were as the
extremities of radiating lines from a common source of power;
the further you trace back these lines of force, from manifestation to their source in the individual, the clearer becomes the
fact that they converge at the centre; the artist, the scientist,
the philosopher, the prophet, express variously the same central
truth, and with less divergence in their methods and a closer
interdependence than is usually supposed. This theory—or let
us rather say, this emotional and intellectual conviction—they
worked out in some of its far-reaching implications. It had
practical results of no small importance; with the Romantic
School in Germany we associate names but indirectly connected
with literature, those, for instance, of the metaphysician Fichte,
of the theoretical scientist Schelling, of the moralist Schleier-
macher, of the philologists Grimm. For the Romantics realised
to some extent their vision of literature, as something not of the
nature of a restricted cult, not sharply divided from other forms
of intellectual activity, not isolated from the main currents of
life, but on the contrary peculiarly relevant to them all. Friedrich Schlegel, in the preface to his *Geschichte der alten und neuen
Literatur*, defining literature as the *Inbegriff des intellektuellen
Lebens einer Nation*, sums up not only his own but the Romantic
attitude towards it, though possibly with a personal restriction
in fixing the intellectual frontier as the limit of literary interest.
It was this wider conception of literature that enabled the

Romantic School to rebuild literary criticism on so bold and generous a plan.

There was close communion and co-operation between artist and thinker in those fortunate days, especially perhaps in the earlier of them, which witnessed the expansion and disruption of the first Romantic School. Viewed as a purely literary phenomenon the latter is, however, disappointing. In tracing the convergent lines of art and philosophy to their source, in regarding them as expressions of the same power, it troubled, it would seem, the clearest manifestation of either. Early Romantic art tends to be too philosophical, Romantic science to become involved in literary imaginations. The most immediately acceptable results of the first Romantic School lie in the region where literature effects a compromise between the scientific and the imaginative—in criticism.

The later generations of German Romanticists were less preoccupied with the theory of art, though the essential unity of all forms of art and life, the secret correspondences which link together the phenomena of mind and matter, were taken by them for granted. The new realisation of subconscious activities affecting human feeling and conduct had drawn their attention away from the daylight world to lands as strange as "the misty mid region of Weir." Since the society about them, however subject in fact to the sway of the Unknown, observed in the main a certain humdrum common-sense in its behaviour, they transported the figures of their imagination to more congenial spheres, where the subconscious might manifest its immanence without ridicule or a too flagrant contradiction with experience, to the lands of Faerie and legend, to a medieval past which, if it never existed in the form in which Romanticism conceived it, is nevertheless in that form a most attractive playground for the imagination. It needed the rare genius of E. T. A. Hoffmann to make the commonplaces of contemporary society the effective background for the play of the terrifying omnipresent forces of mystery.

The Romantic School in Germany produced no considerable dramatic literature, if we except the work of Heinrich von Kleist. Over the whole period of the supremacy of the Romantic

School, the German drama has little or nothing to show between the excellence of Kleist, Schiller, Goethe, and the confections of Iffland, Kotzebue and the writers of the Schicksalstragödien. The Schicksalstragödie may be said to derive some of its elements from Romanticism; mystery and terror are chief items in its recipe; but here they do not spring from a necessity of temperament and outlook, but are grossly added for effect, for a crude piquancy of flavour. In one Schicksalstragödie however we do find the Romantic spirit manifested; in Grillparzer's *Ahnfrau* the mechanism of fatality is built up and set in motion with sincerity and conviction, and crushes its victims with an effect of genuine, if rather clumsy and grotesque, horror. But the spell of Romanticism held Grillparzer for a moment only and before his power as a dramatist was fully developed. We cannot but suspect that there lay in the nature of the Romantic movement, in the eagerness with which its curiosity turned from appearances to origins, in its pre-occupation with the wonder of individual experience, its subjectivity, a principle inimical to dramatic creation.

Its lyrical output is more noteworthy. Yet, if we might sum up in one generalisation and judgment the variety of our impressions with regard to the Romantic lyric—with a reservation to be mentioned later—we should name it the record of sentiment, of mood, rather than of emotion, of passion, and hold that it falls short of the highest lyrical quality. A comparison with the lyrics of Goethe's youth and early manhood will point the significance of the distinction. Tieck and Eichendorff lack neither spontaneity nor grace; but whereas the images offered to our consciousness by Goethe's early poems contain and manifest the golden moments of a heightened realisation, of a lover's ecstasy—the love is not necessarily attached to a personal object —the "mondbeglänzte Zaubernacht" of Tieck, the woods, the nightingales, the far-heard post-horns of Eichendorff are rather the musical accompaniment of gentle, permanent yearning for dreamy solitude and vague adventure. The Romantic lyric is musical—in the highest degree musical, if by that we mean that it conveys to the listener an impression of melodious and gliding sound, independently of its sense. Tieck consciously pursued the ideal of realising the close kinship of music and poetry—an obvious relationship which Romanticism, with its unifying theory of origins, could not overlook—by making language deliver its message by its sound, as much as or rather than by its sense associations. The process is, no doubt, part of the magic secret of all greater poetry; but the isolation of this element and the excessive pre-occupation with it often result in a formless fluidity. The great, the imperishable lyric, as Goethe or Heine uttered it in their singing-season, is on the contrary tense, particular, passionate: the utterance of the individual at the culminating moment when emotion has broken down the barriers between thought and feeling, and these are merged in a new and unique apprehension. This realisation of the intensest lyrical moment is rare with the Romantics; the intensity of the emotional crisis being indeed almost unrepresented in the literature of the Romantic School, save in the case of two poets whom we reserved for separate consideration. In the poetry of Novalis and Hölderlin we find something of the intensity which we postulated as indispensable to the highest lyricism. But the proudest flights, though attempted by them, failed perhaps of achievement. The *Hymnen an die Nacht* have something arbitrary in the fixity of their yearning; and Hölderlin's more inevitable longing too rarely teaches him the inevitable form that would contain and express it perfectly.

The Novelle, in which German literature of the nineteenth century was to be conspicuously successful, constituted perhaps the most satisfactory artistic performance of the Romanticists. Tieck, Fouqué, Brentano, Kleist, Hoffmann, Chamisso, produced masterpieces of this delicate art.

Romanticism, as might be expected, was attracted by the opportunities for introspective analysis and synthetic psychology offered by the subjective novel, the novel dealing with the education of a personality in and by life. *Wilhelm Meister* had shown its hero emerging from a nebulous existence of instinct and impulse to a clear, if somewhat arid, conception of the relation of the individual to society. The example was admired, the method adopted or adapted to their purpose by the Romantics, but with results sufficiently different. In the *Heinrich von Ofter-*

dingen of Novalis the hero does not so much emerge from the dreams of instinctive life as penetrate into them more deeply; for weal or disaster, "nach Innen geht der geheimnisvolle Weg."

The Romantic School in Germany, which set out with such illimitable confidence and ardour, directing its course towards the eternal and absolute, was to prove subject to the laws of relative existence; within thirty years the movement was approaching or had reached the exhaustion of its original impulse. The Romantic leaders were growing old, were learning to compromise, were no longer, in fact, Romantic; the winds of circumstance had scattered them, and they had been chiefly effective as a group. We need not follow them further, nor assist at the tragedy of Wilhelm Schlegel's toilet—the battle against old age daily renewed and lost; nor at that of Friedrich exchanging his birthright of intellectual and moral unrest for the sedative pottage of priestly absolution and epicurean self-indulgence. The incapacity shown by the brothers to realise in later years the promise of their youth is typical of the Romantic group[1].

By the side of the greater German literature of the last decades of the eighteenth century and the first quarter of the nineteenth, there flourished a lesser, which has sunk into oblivion, and is of interest now to the literary historian only, and of living interest to him perhaps only in so far as it illustrates the aberrations and retrogressions in the cultural development of our civilisation. We cannot omit all mention of it here. It is, indeed, such literature which is most widely read in its own day, however short that may be—the literature of fashion, of popular taste, of popular stupidity.

The greater literature represents an advance on previous thought, a new view of life; its stimulus is vital, a stimulus to growth, and the reader can respond only by shaking off the sloth in human nature which objects to all effort not indispensable, and continually seeks to lower the standard of the indispensable; the demon who for ever whispers in our ears that the time has come "wo wir was Guts in Ruhe schmausen mögen." The ideas

---

[1] The personal relations of the Romantics are vividly portrayed in Ricarda Huch's *Die Romantik*, which contains moreover a valuable and sympathetic study of the ideas of the School.

most inimical to progress are those which we accept uncondi-
tionally, which have passed into the category of what we take
for granted; it is on these that the effort towards truth is tempted
to repose with misplaced confidence. The minor literature now
referred to deals mainly with that stock of ideas which is one of
the most cherished possessions of human society at any given
time: the sophistries of its accepted morality, the commonplaces of its philosophy, the bathos of its sentiments. But since,
to attract, it must have an air of novelty—for mankind is not
happy in its torpor unless it can persuade itself that it is rapidly
progressing—this literature follows closely on the footsteps of
the masters of thought, ignobly exploiting the regions they have
freshly conquered for a better purpose. Hence the domestic
drama of Lessing, with its attempt to reveal the play of passion
in the surroundings of contemporary middle-class existence, is
followed by that of Iffland and Kotzebue, which rather shows
passion subservient to the requirements of a middle-class
standard of physical and mental comfort. To Götz and Karl
Moor succeed the heroes of Cramer and Vulpius. The combat
of heroic figures against ineluctable fate of the *Braut von Messina*
becomes in the Schicksalsdrama the entanglement of ridiculous
people in the toils of an interfering and malicious destiny.

Not unnaturally, specimens of this depraved literature found
their way as readily to England as works of permanent value—
more easily, indeed, so long as there existed here no body of
educated opinion relative to German literature. Regarded as
characteristic examples of that literature, they were devoured by
the uncultured, and even by the cultured; for, until the work
of the greater writers was better known on this side, the novelties
which had been merely stolen from them and adapted to the
purposes of this debased literature were regarded as its independent conquests; even intelligent readers were too much
dazzled by the new apparatus of ideas to distinguish clearly
between the inherent poverty and the borrowed wonders. This
confusion, particularly general in the early days of German
influence on English literature, had for a time a marked effect on
its direction and intensity.

Romanticism, in England as in Germany, appears as a literary movement in the last decade of the eighteenth century. But in this country it assumed less incontestable sway. Germany, in departing on its new quest, had been held back but feebly by the bonds of tradition, while for the literary consciousness of England unbroken chains of at least respectable achievement stretched back into the glorious past. If some of the links were weak, their multiplicity and serried continuity lent them strength; and they joined and at not too infrequent intervals were riveted to pillars whose mass seemed as enduring as that of earth itself. From Chaucer to Shakespeare, from Shakespeare to Milton, from Milton to Pope, the lines, however erratic, marked a general direction which exercised restraining influence on the successive momentary tendencies. But if they restrained, they could not repress them altogether; and the general direction itself is a compromise between the forces of the past and new impulses.

The Social Idea had celebrated a particularly complete triumph in the Augustan Age of English literature. That age had formulated with peculiar decision its literary code, and the stamp of its approval on certain forms and types of literature and thought gave these precedence long after the age that produced them had passed away, and when the ideas they had been designed to express had given place to others, fresh and fermenting. This new wine had a particularly difficult task in making away with the old bottles.

Thomson, Collins, Gray show in various admixture the contradictions of the transitional period. Complete harmony of form and intention is lacking; hints of Romantic outline are muffled everywhere in the generalising habit. Macpherson and Chatterton did something by their impostures to shatter the spell; but it lay heavy on the former of these at any rate; and it was precisely he, who did little more than dissolve the crystals of classicism in infinite wateriness, who won a European reputation in his day.

The sway of classical tradition could be no more than shaken by raids of this kind; it was not seriously contested till the revolutionary forces, with youth, vigour and genius on their side, were marshalled under great leaders in the open field against it. Till the late nineties, independence of the classical canon could be attained only by favour of some isolating peculiarity of temperament or circumstance, at the price of a kind of exile from the main walks of literature—the detachment of Christopher Smart in the madhouse, of Burns in the remoteness of his social and geographical environment and of his racy dialect, of Blake in that visionary England where he saw the golden builders at work "near mournful ever-weeping Paddington."

We have seen that Herder, long before the day of Romanticism had arrived, called the attention of literary Germany to the monuments of her past. The works of the Minnesänger, the Court and popular epics of the thirteenth century, brought to light by Swiss editors, were beginning once more to engage the attention of the cultivated public. Klopstock saw fit, in re-editing his Odes about this time, to replace the names of classical divinities by others borrowed from Teutonic mythology. In England, too, the records of the non-classical past aroused general interest in the reading public of the eighteenth century, reaching it by way of the publications and comments of Percy, Ritson and Warton. Medievalism became a fashion. Even the soulless, clumsy, creaking machinery of the *Castle of Otranto* scored a success, and the medieval properties were soon to count among those to which the public most surely and kindly reacted.

If a definite date is to be assigned to the birth of Romanticism in England, we might place it at 1797, in the days which witnessed the deep confabulations, the walks, musings, enthusiasms of the Wordsworths and Coleridge at Nether Stowey. Here perhaps was realised for the first time the extent of that difference of outlook which signified a profound change in thought, a reversal of its previous direction. The formula of Romanticism includes a deeper reference to individual experience, and a distrust of that classification of life in purely rational categories which had charmed the preceding age. The intellect must, indeed, use some form of classification in dealing with phenomena; but Romanticism widened its classes indefinitely, not seeking to pack all experience into the narrow limits of a rationalistic system, but framing its certainties in a broad margin of mystery and wonder. The results of this method varied with the temperament of those who used it; for some it was the certainties that mattered more, for others, the unknown in which certainty merged at its edges. The latter type was found more frequently in Romantic Germany than in Romantic England; Romanticism in England being, indeed, considerably tempered by eighteenth century elements.

It was to Germany that those turned who in England were temperamentally drawn to the shadowy boundaries of the known and what lies beyond. The attraction is perhaps a fundamental instinct of human nature, and will be found to flourish wherever the inward bent of the mind is not checked either by a rigid mental training directed to that end, by strong acquisitive propensities, by a vivid sensuous apprehension, or by some other inducement or compulsion to fix the attention on the outer world. The bulk of the public to which the mysterious appealed had not so much discovered the inadequacy of the classical discipline, as escaped culture altogether. For these, the coarsest literary fare sufficed, so long as it was highly flavoured. The finer work of the German Romantic School, though springing from the same elemental wonder, presented its results in a form too quintessential for the appreciation of the general, and remained for the most part unknown in England during the period now under consideration.

Goethe and Schiller represented in much of their work, and especially in their early work, those individualistic tendencies which were becoming predominant in Europe. Neither Goethe nor Schiller was Romantic in the full and extreme sense of the term; they dwelt more lovingly on the brightly lit certainties and sought continually to enlarge the illuminated region by dissipating the shadows at its edges. The process was congenial to the English mind, and these writers, however misapprehended, rousing whatever fierce opposition, did win at an early date some kind of widespread recognition.

It was at first, however, recognition of certain characteristics which no longer figure very prominently in our mental picture of these writers: they were regarded as violent innovators and revolutionaries in the social order, and as such were dear to the ardent youth of the age, mistrusted by cooler or older heads.

It was not till the publication of de Staël's *De l'Allemagne* in 1813 that a fairer estimate of the aims and development of these writers and of German literature generally came to be held among the cultured. Before that time the position of German literature in England was insecure. Among the reading public there was an attitude of expectancy towards it, indeed, but the expectancy was directed to certain aspects to the exclusion of others. It looked to Germany to provide a succession of violent sensations; the unrest of the age produced the craving for these in England as elsewhere, and literature of native growth did not provide them with the abundance and acuteness required. The charnel horror of *Lenore*, the sublime extravagance of *Werther*, the subversive fury of *Die Räuber*—these stimulated palates weary of the insipid pabulum of rationalistic writers; and the appetite was catered for by a swarm of translators, who knew their public well enough to choose their originals not for literary merit, but for the lengths to which they carried the pursuit of the ghostly, the sentimental, the revolutionary.

At the end of the eighteenth century, the reviews represented a body of opinion but little better educated than that of the general reading public. The day of the great literary periodicals does not open till the founding of the Edinburgh Review in 1802; before that the Monthly Review alone may be regarded as attempting with some success to maintain a serious critical standard. In general, the reviewers who deal with German literature in the earlier days of its influx are scarcely more discriminating with regard to it than their readers; their general ignorance of the subject is hardly less complete. Being, however, as craftsmen of literature, more under the sway of the literary tradition, they affect some severity towards the innovations which have captivated the popular taste. But their praise or blame has little independent critical value; they are like rusted weathercocks, and may serve at best to give us an imperfect hint of the way the wind blows.

Above the public and reviewers and apart from them was the smaller class of lovers of literature and authors by profession. These, in so far as they belonged to the older generation, tended naturally to adhere to the stately classical tradition and would have nothing to do with a literature which they regarded, in the circumstances not unreasonably, as ranting and extravagant. Of the younger generation not a few, stepping carefully in the well-worn track, shared this unfavourable opinion.

Alone a few young men of ardent literary intelligence or curiosity, instinct with a new vision and seeking new forms to contain and express it, discovered that a spirit akin to their own was stirring somewhere in the great rubbish-heap presented to English readers under the name of German literature. Among the writers who towards 1790 stand on or near the threshold of their career German literature counts as an educational factor, whether they study it at first hand or are satisfied to approach it through translations and the reports of the better-informed. By their means filters through, very slowly at first, some genuine information about German literature to the general public.

The indiscreet enthusiasm of the lower strata of the reading public for the mere sensationalism or sentimentality of German books was a hindrance to the more serious study of the literature. It cast a shade of discredit over the whole subject. Those who prided themselves on a finer literary taste might fear to be classed with a rabble destitute of literary pride. Even those who, like Coleridge or Scott, studied German literature at first hand, became, when the fresh glow of their ardour had faded, rather ashamed of it, and adopted, no doubt partly in self-defence, something of a patronising tone when referring to it. Those alone, who, like Taylor of Norwich or Crabb Robinson, undertook and persevered in an intensive study of the language and literature of Germany, abstained generally from this ridiculous and unseemly condescension.

After 1813 the destinies of German literature in England enter on a new phase. The blame attaching to it is gradually removed, and the way is prepared for Carlyle, who lays the massive pillars of the bridge that was to establish closer intellectual communication between the two countries. Our study concludes with the opening of this third stage, which may be placed in the early twenties of the nineteenth century.

CHAPTER II

Henry Mackenzie's Lecture

ON April 21, 1788, a paper on the German Drama was read before the Royal Society of Edinburgh by Henry Mackenzie, a member of the legal profession and a writer of some celebrity at that time. It was probably on this occasion that Schiller's name was first publicly mentioned in the British Isles, though within ten years it was to be almost as well known there as in Germany. The paper was afterwards (in 1790) published in the Transactions of the Society to which it was first communicated. By the novelty of its subject, and by its rather startling eulogy of Schiller's *Räuber*, it aroused widespread interest.

At this time it was scarcely realised in England that an intellectual and literary movement of importance had been in progress in Germany for some forty years. "It would, I imagine," says Leslie Stephen in his *Studies of a Biographer*, "be difficult to find a single direct reference to a German book in the whole English literature of the eighteenth century." Various causes were at work, however, to awaken the English mind from this indifference. Among these must be counted the close relations between the English court and Germany, the increasing political weight of Prussia during the eighteenth century, the use of German auxiliaries in the American war[1], and later the declaration of war against France (1793) which, troubling one source of intellectual supply, would favour the eagerness to discover and tap new ones.

From 1750 onwards a certain rather indiscriminate activity in translation from German is apparent. Before this time it

---

[1] F. Jeffrey, in the Edinburgh Review for January 1804, emphasises this cause of the improved knowledge of German literature: "During the American war, the intercourse with Britain was strengthened by many well-known causes. The German officers in our service communicated the knowledge of their books and language. Pamphlets, plays, novels, and other light pieces, were circulated in America, and found their way, after the peace, into England"; loc. cit. Jeffrey's Review of Lichtenberg's *Vermischte Schriften*.

had been confined almost entirely to scientific and theological works.

Of the greater names, Wieland is best represented, owing perhaps to his approximation in style and temper to classical and Romance ideals; seven of his works appeared in translation between 1764 and 1790. Klopstock's *Messias*, translated by Mrs Collyer and her husband, gave rise to some imitations, though it was on the whole unfavourably received[1]. Lessing was not well known; the *Fables* and *Nathan der Weise* were translated and an adaptation of *Minna von Barnhelm* (*The Disbanded Officer*) was produced at the Haymarket in 1786[2]. Goethe's *Werther*, though at the disadvantage of appearing at first in a retranslation from the French, scored a success on its appearance in 1779; and new editions of this translation appeared at intervals up to 1795[3].

Other translations of *Werther* appeared in 1786 (the first version from the German text) and in 1789. A dramatisation of the novel, by Frederick Reynolds, was performed at Bath in 1785, and subsequently at Covent Garden and in the provinces. Parodies, imitations and other productions inspired by the book were very numerous. J. M. Carré, in his *Bibliographie de Goethe en Angleterre*, pp. 25–29, has collected criticisms of *Werther* and testimonials to its notoriety from eighteenth-century periodicals and other sources. From these it is clear that while the public was raving and weeping about *Werther*, reviewers had already begun to protest against the sentimentality, immorality and general perniciousness of the popular favourite. Such reproaches, applied to German literature in general, tend to become stereo-

---

[1] Mackenzie, in his *Account of the German Theatre*, speaks of Klopstock as being "but little known in this country, though his genius is revered, even to idolatry, in his own"; the latter statement would have been truer if Mackenzie had put it in the past tense.

[2] The alleged translation of *Laokoon*, 1767, mentioned by Goedecke (*Grundriss*, IV[2], 144) apparently never existed; see J. L. Haney, *Americana Germanica*, vol. IV, no. 2, p. 13. Haney shows how the mistake probably arose. W. Todt (*Lessing in England*, p. 5) gives 1826 as the date of the first translation into English of *Laokoon*.

[3] See J. M. Carré, *Goethe en Angleterre*, chap. I, and *Bibliographie de Goethe en Angleterre*, chap. I. See also A. E. Turner's rectifications and additions to Carré's statements in Modern Language Review, vol. XVI, July–October 1921, pp. 364–370.

typed, recurring frequently, with slight variations, in the thirty years succeeding Mackenzie's lecture. As far as *Werther* is concerned, their censures were not apparently effective. Carré notices eighteen British editions of various new translations of the novel between 1790 and 1830[1].

Herder and Schiller were not among those translated before 1790. Of lesser writers Gessner was the most popular. Several of his works were translated, and *Der Tod Abels* scored a phenomenal success; it was translated more than once, and Mrs Collyer's translation numbered eighteen editions in 1782[2]. Gellert's *Leben der schwedischen Gräfin G.* was also considered worth more than one translation. Rabener's satires, Haller's *Usong*, Schönaich's *Hermann*, Bodmer's *Noah*, were likewise ingredients in the not very appetising or nourishing hotchpotch of German literature offered by the translators to the English public.

This scanty representation of German literature was as yet supplemented by no critical opinion based on a more general knowledge of the subject. William Taylor of Norwich, though, to use his own expression, he was "pervasively studying German literature" as early as 1782, did not begin his critical activities until much later. Interest in German literature at this time appears to be confined almost entirely to a public which gaped, perhaps unintelligently, at its sentimentalities; we may account it a sign of grace, of a certain freshness and spontaneity of feeling, that it appreciated *Werther* so warmly; a less favourable conclusion may be drawn from the eighteen editions of Mrs Collyer's *Death of Abel*.

There existed, however, before and after 1790, a propagandist group in England, whose activities in promoting interest in German literature may be mentioned here, more especially as it is seldom referred to in this connection, and has not, I think, been made the subject of particular study since the appearance of the articles of F. Althaus in 1873, and of K. H. Schaible's *Geschichte der Deutschen in England* in 1885[3].

[1] Carré, *Bibliographie de Goethe en Angleterre*, pp. 29–30.
[2] Haney, *German Literature in England before* 1790.
[3] See the Bibliographical Note to this chapter. The few notes that follow in the text are drawn chiefly from Althaus, Schaible, and my reading in the periodical literature of the time.

I refer to a small band of Germans living in England, who beguiled the tedium of their exile by teaching English to Germans and German to Englishmen, by composing and publishing Grammars of their native tongue for the use of English students, and by translating German works into, it is to be feared, not unexceptionable English, and English works into presumably correct German.

Such was the Rev. Dr G. F. Wendeborn, who came to England about 1767. He settled in London as pastor of a German church at Ludgate Hill[1]. For many years he was the London correspondent of a Hamburg newspaper, and he wrote descriptive books about England[2]. More to our purpose is his *Elements of German Grammar*, first published in 1774; a second edition appeared in 1790[3], a third in 1797. At the time when Wendeborn's *Elements* first appeared it had little competition to fear. A Grammar by James John Bachmaier, M.A., was published in 1751 and reached a third edition in 1771. According to Schaible, Wendeborn, in the second edition of his Grammar, speaks of other German Grammars as extant; Schaible was unable to trace them[4]. But the wave of enthusiasm for German literature, to which we may probably attribute the comparatively rapid sale of Wendeborn's second edition, attracted rivals into the field. In 1799 two German Grammars were published, one by W. Render, the other by George Crabb; in 1800 Crabb issued a second edition with much-needed improvements[5] and in the

[1] For some account of German churches in London in the seventeenth and eighteenth centuries, see Schaible, K. H., *Geschichte der Deutschen in England*, pp. 368 ff.

[2] The Monthly Review for 1788 (Appendix to vol. LXXVIII) reviews his *Zustand des Staats etc. in Grossbritannien*.

[3] The Monthly Review for June 1791 notices an *Introduction to German Grammar* by Wendeborn. This apparently is a different work from the *Elements*; cf. Schaible, *Geschichte*, p. 346.

[4] Schaible, *Geschichte*, p. 346. Previous to Bachmaier there are at least three German Grammars for English learners: Martin Aedler's *High Dutch Minerva à la Mode* (1680), one by Offelen in 1687, and John King's *English and High-German Grammar* (1706), (Schaible, *Geschichte*, p. 339).

[5] Crabb's first edition was full of errors; the Monthly Review commented upon them severely (August 1799) and took credit to itself for the improvements of the 2nd edition, which it pronounced (December 1800) to be "one of the best German Grammars now extant in the English language." Schaible (*Geschichte*, p. 347) instances Crabb's translation of German *Talk*

same year yet another Grammar appeared, by Georg Heinrich Noehden. Render and Noehden belong to our propagandist group.

Noehden came to England in 1793[1] and, collaborating with J. Stoddart, was among the early translators of Schiller. In 1793 appeared their *Fiesco, Don Carlos* in 1798. Schiller expressed approval of these translations[2]. Noehden's Grammar (1800) had a second edition in 1807, which was highly praised by the Monthly Review for May 1808. In 1807 he also published *Elements of German Grammar*[3]. Noehden afterwards, in 1818, became tutor to the Crown Princess of Saxe-Weimar; but he did not remain long in this post, if it is true that, as Althaus asserts, he was curator of the numismatic collection in the British Museum in 1820. He died in 1826[4].

Althaus does not know the date of the Rev. Dr Wilhelm Render's arrival in England; he places it between the 70's and 90's[5]. In 1798, in a translation from Kotzebue (*Count Benyowski*), Render designates himself "Teacher of the German Language in the University of Cambridge."[6] We have already noticed him among the translators of *Werther*; he also translated *Die Räuber*[7] and the Monthly Mirror of May 1800 notices his translation of *Der Geisterseher*. He was the author of a *Tour through Germany* (1801). Besides the Grammar published, as we mentioned, in 1799, he wrote a *Complete Analysis of the German Language* (1804), and his *Complete Pocket Dictionary* was reviewed in the Eclectic Review of April 1807. There is one small fact mentioned by Professor Carré and by Althaus[8] which

---

by English *Conversation*; and quotes the following remarkable statement of a rule for declension: "All feminine nouns of gods, angels, devils and women are declined in the following manner," etc.

[1] Althaus, *Beiträge zur Geschichte der deutschen Colonie in England*, p. 538.

[2] Rea, *Schiller's Dramas*, pp. 28 f. and p. 41.

[3] At least I understand this to be a separate book: see Monthly Review, May 1808.

[4] Althaus, *Beiträge*, p. 539, and Rea, *Schiller's Dramas*, p. 28, note 1.

[5] Althaus, *Beiträge*, p. 540.

[6] Monthly Review, July 1798.

[7] The third in Rea's list (1799). Rea pronounces it quite worthless (Rea, *Schiller's Dramas*, pp. 12, 145). See also L. A. Willoughby, *Die Räuber* (Milford, 1922), p. 68.

[8] Carré, *Goethe Bibliogr.* p. 30; Althaus, *Beiträge*, p. 540.

throws a somewhat odd light on the reverend gentleman's character. In the preface to his translation of *Werther* (1801), he expresses his wish to do justice to the talent of his friend, Baron Goethe. He tells us that he knew Werther personally, and studied at Giessen with a brother of Charlotte. In the Appendix to the translation, he reproduces (or at least produces) a conversation he had with Werther a few days before his death. These fictions were perhaps not without value as an advertising device, but they do not seem commendable in any other respect. According to Althaus (loc. cit.) F. Gotzberg, another translator of *Werther* (1802), similarly claimed acquaintance with Werther's family, and spoke of him as "one of the foremost literati of his country."

If Render may be taxed with overstepping the bounds of intellectual honesty, another member of our group, Rudolf Erich Raspe, transgressed even more palpably. His presence in Great Britain appears to have been due to the fact that he had abstracted valuables from a museum at Kassel, of which he was curator[1]. In spite of this ominous prelude to his English visit, he is perhaps more notable to us than any of those more respectable contemporaries among whom I have placed him. From his native Hanover he brought a collection of anecdotes relating to the Freiherr von Münchhausen, and these, with amplifications, he embodied in the narrative of that superlative liar, the Baron Munchausen[2]. Raspe translated from the German, Lessing's *Nathan* (1781) among other works[3].

The translation of German books and the compilation of German Grammars were occupations that met with some encouragement and perhaps suitable pecuniary reward in the last decade of the eighteenth century and the succeeding years. The same cannot be affirmed confidently of the efforts of those Germans who endeavoured by lectures or publications to convey the doctrines of Kant to the British understanding. The leaders of this forlorn hope were Nitsch, Wirgman and Willich.

---

[1] Schaible, *Geschichte*, pp. 392–393.
[2] *Baron Munchausen's Narrative of his marvellous travels and campaigns in Russia*, 1785; 7th edition, 1793 (*Cambridge Hist. of English Lit.* vol. x, p. 424). Bürger translated it freely into German in the year following its publication.
[3] Haney, *German Lit. in England*, and Schaible, *Geschichte*, pp. 392–393.

Professor F. A. Nitsch lectured on Kant in London in 1795 or 1796[1] and his *General and Introductory View of Professor Kant's Principles* was noticed in the Monthly Review of January 1797.

Thomas Wirgman also wrote an exposition of Kant's philosophy. He kept a goldsmith's shop, and Leslie Stephen supposes that his father kept the toy-shop in St James's Street, where Samuel Johnson bought silver buckles in 1778[2].

Wirgman was taken by his friend Richter, another Kantian, to hear Nitsch lecture. This, it appears, was a turning point in Wirgman's life. He became an enthusiastic Kantian, and wrote an essay on Kant in the *Encyclopaedia Londinensis*. It was also separately printed, and he sent a copy to Dugald Stewart for the purpose of converting him to Kantism; it need hardly be said that the intended effect did not follow. His "disinterested proselyte-making zeal" for Kant's doctrines struck Crabb Robinson as "a curious and interesting phenomenon. He worships his idol with pure affection, without sacrificing his domestic duties."[3] When Madame de Staël was in England, he tried to enlighten her on his favourite subject; but the lady, it is to be feared, had little time to spare for pure reason[4]. In 1812, there was a meeting between Coleridge and Wirgman, at which Godwin was apparently present[5].

Dr A. F. N. Willich had attended Kant's lectures[6]; and in 1798 he published *Elements of the Critical Philosophy*. In the European Magazine of January 1800 he took the Abbé Barruel to task for the mistaken views on Kant which he had expressed

---

[1] Or both. Leslie Stephen, *Studies of a Biographer*, vol. II, p. 51, gives 1795; the English Review for April 1796 informs its readers that "Mr Nitsch has opened a course of lectures on the Critic of Speculative Reason at No. 16, Panton Square, Haymarket."

[2] Stephen, *Studies of a Biographer*, vol. II, p. 49, note.

[3] H. C. Robinson, *Diary*, Feb. 17, 1818.

[4] Stephen, *Studies of a Biographer*, vol. II, p. 51.

[5] From the typewritten copy of Crabb Robinson's unpublished Diary: "June 1, 1812. (Godwin) mentioned the meeting between Coleridge and Wirgmann. He [Godwin presumably. F. W. S.] understands less of Kant the more he hears of it, and believes there is nothing in it." Coleridge subsequently spoke of Wirgman (or Wirgmann, as Crabb Robinson sometimes writes it) as knowing nothing about Kant, as being a mere formalist; from which it is safe to conclude that he and Coleridge disagreed on the subject (*Typed Diary*, August 13, 1812).

[6] Stephen, *Studies of a Biographer*, vol. II, p. 46.

in his *Histoire du Jacobinisme*. Willich was by no means ex-
clusively devoted to the cause of the Critical Philosophy, however. He had been physician to the Saxon Ambassador, Count
Brühl[1], and wrote *Lectures on Diet and Regimen*, and a *Domestic
Encyclopaedia*, which were reviewed in the English Magazine in
September 1799 and September 1802 respectively. He wrote a
Life of Kotzebue, published as an Appendix to Miss Plumptre's
translation from Kotzebue, *Lovers' Vows*[2]; and he translated
Hufeland's *Makrobiotik*. We shall meet him in the course of
our study in yet another capacity, as instructor to a German
class in Edinburgh in 1792[3].

No doubt many names and activities could be added to this
list, and a fuller plan of this campaign of "peaceful penetra-
tion" might yield curious information. Was not the *German
Museum* one of its set battles? We cannot help suspecting
that the contributions are to some considerable extent of German
origin[4]. The scanty notes given above may at least serve to
suggest that the part played by German residents in what
Leslie Stephen calls the importation of German was not quite
negligible. They have carried us, however, far beyond our
starting-point, Henry Mackenzie's lecture. At that time Wendeborn's Grammar was in its first edition; the seed of German
propaganda fell as yet, it may be supposed, on stony soil,
through which Mackenzie was now about to drive a notable
furrow.

Henry Mackenzie brought to his subject, with something of
the calm reason of maturity, the weight of an established reputation. He was forty-three years of age at the date of his
lecture. A member of the legal profession, he was attorney for
the Crown in Scotland at this or at a subsequent time. His

---

[1] idem, p. 47.

[2] Or probably rather *The Natural Son*. The play in question is, I take it,
Kotzebue's *Kind der Liebe*, appearing as *Lovers' Vows* in Mrs Inchbald's
adaptation, as *Lovers' Vows or The Child of Love* in Stephen Porter's translation, and as *The Natural Son* in Anne Plumptre's. The three versions belong
to 1798.

[3] For further details relative to the study of Kant in England at this
time as also respecting Willich, Nitsch and Wirgman, see Leslie Stephen,
Studies of a Biographer, vol. II: *The Importation of German*.

[4] See especially those signed P. W.

literary repute amounted almost to fame; in 1771 had appeared his *Man of Feeling*, a novel which attained widespread popularity, and the title of which was frequently used to designate its celebrated author. He wrote other novels, which served to keep his name before the public without, perhaps, adding materially to his reputation. His literary activities were not confined to fiction; he was the author of unsuccessful plays, edited short-lived periodicals, and contributed literary and political essays to periodical literature. It was, then, no literary tyro who rose to address the Royal Society of his native city, but one qualified by age and reputation to command an attentive and sympathetic hearing.

Henry Mackenzie was not acquainted with the German language at this time[1]. He mentions the principal, if not the only, sources of his knowledge of the German drama; these were the *Nouveau Théâtre allemand* of Friedel and de Bonneville (1782–85) and the translations (also French) of Junker and Liebault. The former contained an *Histoire abrégée du Théâtre allemand*. After pointing out[2] that Germany has only recently acquired the right to take her place among the literary nations, he bases a slight and superficial account of the progress of the German theatre since Gottsched on the information given by his French translators, and particularly on that prefixed to Friedel's collection[3]. Proceeding to describe his personal impressions of the modern German play he emphasises, reasonably enough, the predominance of situation over character; he notes, less reasonably perhaps, a contradiction between language and action: " ... By a combination not unfrequent among senti-

---

[1] So we conclude from his remark that "the language of Germany, however, has not yet attained, *as those who know it inform us*, that perfection and regularity necessary to stamp the highest value on the productions composed in it" (loc. cit. p. 155).

[2] The following notice of Mackenzie's paper is based upon Henry Mackenzie's *Account of the German Theatre* in the *Transactions of the Royal Society of Edinburgh*, vol. II, 1790, part II, pp. 152 ff.

[3] See Hans Schwarz, *Henry Mackenzie*, Inaugural-Dissertation, Winterthur, 1911, p. 129. Schwarz also points out in a note (loc. cit.) that this source had been previously drawn upon for an article entitled *Sketch of the Origin and Progress of Dramatic Poetry in Germany* (Edinburgh Magazine, 1876). He suggests that Mackenzie may have had his attention called to the German drama by this article.

mentalists, the language is highly virtuous, while the action is libertine and immoral. From the author of the *Sorrows of Werter*, this does not surprise...". He comments on the violence of the passions and terrors of the German stage, but on the whole prefers them to "the flat insipid representation of restrained passions and chastened manners" too frequently met with outside Germany. "Bold, forcible and rich" are the epithets he chooses to characterise the German drama as a whole.

He examines half-a-dozen plays of Lessing and Goethe, awarding them very tepid commendation. He finds a "want of comic humour" in *Minna von Barnhelm*; of *Emilia Galotti* he thought better on a second reading. *Götz von Berlichingen* he held to be over-rated in Germany, owing, he supposed, to its "national quality": "The simple manners, the fidelity, the valour and the generosity of a German knight, are pourtrayed in a variety of natural scenes." Trained in the classical tradition, Mackenzie overlooked the charm of this evocation of the past, which appealed so keenly to Scott; and he does little justice to the freshness and boldness of the colouring of Goethe's picture, which, it is true, may have been considerably blurred in the French reproduction. *Stella*, of course, strongly excited his moralising mood. After Lessing and Goethe he places Brandes as, in his opinion, "next entitled to notice"; but although he speaks of him as being "one of the ablest German dramatists" he gives very little space to him.

Perhaps the moderation with which he expresses his approval of the dramatists mentioned above is in part a rhetorical precaution; for after these *piano* passages we are all the more effectively roused by the *sforzando* vigour of the phrase with which he introduces *Die Räuber*: "But the most remarkable and the most strongly impressive of all the pieces contained in these volumes is...*Les Voleurs*, a tragedy by Mr Schiller, a young man, who, at the time of writing it, was only twenty-three...", and for once he gives rein to a generous and almost complete enthusiasm. His reserve is swept aside by over-whelming admiration for "this wonderful drama"; its characters and situations are "most interesting and impressive," its language "in the highest degree eloquent, impassioned and sublime." He favours his readers with a detailed account of the play, illustrated by extracts, and he devotes more than a quarter of his total space to this subject. "I have ventured this long and particular account of the tragedy in question, because it appears to me one of the most uncommon productions of untutored genius that modern times can boast." This flash of insight from the cautious Mackenzie saves the lecture from the imputation of uninspired mediocrity which it might otherwise deserve. He adds, it is true, a prudent *caveat* with regard to the danger of a play which "covers the natural deformity of criminal actions with the veil of high sentiment and virtuous feeling"; but this warning is scarcely more than a piquant discord in the paean of praise.

Mackenzie's position in the social and literary world of his time, the circumstances in which he gave his opinion to the public, together with the very decided, the almost impassioned tone in which he characterised the genius of Schiller, must be taken into consideration in estimating the probable effect of his lecture on the public mind. The paper "made much noise, and produced a powerful effect," Scott tells us, recalling the circumstances that led to his own pre-occupation with German literature[1]. It was printed in the *Transactions of the Royal Society of Edinburgh* (1790), and reprinted in the Edinburgh Magazine of 1790, and in the Sentimental and Masonic Magazine (Dublin, 1792)[2], in the latter case, however, without the author's name.

As a critical study of the German drama the value of the paper is not high. Mackenzie, as we saw, could not read the originals of the plays discussed; his critical faculty does not strike us as keen or powerful, and only his enthusiasm for *Die Räuber* seems to endow it with imaginative insight. But with all its defects, and with its still more lamentable lack of definite qualities save in the one instance, Mackenzie's paper might well stir public opinion simply by the novelty of its subject, by its revelation of a literary world whose existence had hitherto been scarcely

[1] Scott, *Essay on Imitations of the Ancient Ballad.*
[2] Rea, *Schiller's Dramas*, p. 7, note 1 and p. 10.

suspected, and whose remoteness and strangeness (not to mention the pecuniary value of its products) was soon to attract bolder spirits to attempt its exploration.

With his paper to the Royal Society of Edinburgh Henry Mackenzie had apparently shot his bolt in the matter of his public connection with German literature. We cannot be certain that any further sign of interest in the subject emanated from his pen, and as far as we are concerned he sinks back, after this single and somewhat momentous appearance, into honourable obscurity[1].

Some part, perhaps considerable, of Mackenzie's enthusiasm for *Die Räuber* should be attributed to the influences of the time. The Age of Reason in literature was drawing to a somewhat dreary close; towards 1789 revolution was in the air, revolution in politics, mind and manners; and what J. G. Robertson calls "the great revolutionary drama of German literature" made its appeal by no means exclusively to the literary judgment of men. The novelty of the subject, the unbridled expression of emotional crises, so stimulating after "the flat insipid representation of restrained passions and chastened manners" of which the Man of Feeling complains, the atmosphere of romantic horror which broods over the play, caught and held for a time the minds of the young and ardent generation which was to witness or produce the revolution in our own literature.

Thus Coleridge, at Cambridge, carelessly picks up *The Robbers* in a friend's room one stormy November evening of 1794, carries it away, and at midnight sits down to read it. Somewhat more than an hour later he throws the book down and taking pen and paper, seeks to relieve his overwrought feelings in a letter to his friend Southey.

I had read, chill and trembling, when I came to the part where the Moor fixes a pistol over the robbers who are asleep. I could read no more. My God, Southey, who is this Schiller, this con-

---

[1] He was probably the author of *Dramatic Pieces from the German*, 1792; these were C. H. von Ayrenhoff's *Postzug*, Goethe's *Geschwister* and Gessner's *Unterhaltungen eines Vaters mit seinen Kindern*. See Helen M. Richmond, *Mackenzie's Translations from the German*, Modern Language Review, vol. XVII, October 1922, p. 412.

vulser of the heart?...I tremble like an aspen leaf. Upon my soul, I write to you because I am frightened...Why have we ever called Milton sublime?

and so forth. And in the Sonnet "*To the Author of the 'Robbers'*"[1] he pours out his enthusiasm for the "Bard tremendous in sublimity" in a scarcely more chastened mood. In later days, as will appear and as might be expected, he saw reason to modify very considerably his opinion of *Die Räuber*[2].

Had we Wordsworth's impressions on first reading *The Robbers*, we should doubtless find them recorded in a more sober tone; but the play affected him definitely enough to leave its mark on his *Borderers* (composed 1795–96).

Peacock, in his *Memoirs of Shelley*, mentions *The Robbers*, with Goethe's *Faust* and four novels of Charles Brockden Brown, as being "of all the works with which he was familiar, those which took the deepest root in his (Shelley's) mind, and had the strongest influence in the formation of his character"; a remark worth noting in this context, but requiring, it may be thought, considerable deductions from its dogmatic absoluteness. That the drama was eagerly received by the public appears from the record of the translations. There were four translations within ten years, and the first of these, by Alexander Fraser Tytler (1792), reached a fourth edition in 1800[3].

[1] The Sonnet contains the lines:
> "Ah Bard tremendous in sublimity!
> Could I behold thee in thy loftier mood
> Wandering at eve with finely frenzied eye
> Beneath some vast old tempest-swinging wood!"

to which Lamb refers in an amusing, not too gently satirical letter written to Coleridge on the eve of his departure for Germany: "Finally, wishing Learned Sir, that you may see Schiller and swing in a wood (vide Poems) and sit upon a Tun, and eat fat hams of Westphalia, I remain, your friend and docile Pupil to instruct CHARLES LAMB." That the gentle Charles could be bitter on occasion, is sufficiently demonstrated by the *Theses Quaedam Theologicae* that accompany this letter. Coleridge had been, I think, altogether too seraphically doctoral and annoying on questions of theology about which he and Lamb differed. See E. V. Lucas, *The Life of Charles Lamb*, London, 1905, pp. 133–134.

[2] Coleridge, *Letters*, E. H. C., vol. I, pp. 96–97, and Coleridge, *Poetical Works*, vol. I, p. 72 and note, pp. 72–73.

[3] Rea, *Schiller's Dramas*. Margaret W. Cooke, Modern Language Review, vol. XI, no. 2, pp. 156–175. Willoughby, Modern Language Review, July–October 1921, *English Translations and Adaptations of Schiller's Robbers*.

Mackenzie's lecture is the starting-point of Schiller's fame in England. If it is hard to determine to what extent it was responsible for the sudden remarkable increase in the general interest in German literature in England during the ensuing decade, it is at least safe to affirm that he hit upon the psychological moment for his pronouncement, and he must be counted among those who did good service in helping to dispel the clouds of ignorance in which the subject of German literature was enveloped.

Periodical Literature 1788–1818 and Two Propagandists, William Taylor and Henry Crabb Robinson

THE survey of a representative selection of the periodical literature of the last decade of the eighteenth century and of the two succeeding decades will throw some light on fluctuations of the interest of the English public in German literature.

In the eighteenth century there was very little periodical criticism in the sense in which we now understand the term. It was not then the fashion for persons of any literary eminence to contribute reviews to the periodicals[1]. With few exceptions, reviewing was in the hands of hacks whose qualifications do not appear to extend much beyond the assumption of authority and a certain smartness and facility of style. The reviews, of German works at least, are for the most part expressions of opinion based neither on any particular knowledge of the subject nor on any well-defined standard of criticism, and stated in a conventional jargon.

With the new century matters begin to improve. The Edinburgh Review (1802) and its rival the Quarterly Review (1809) make their appearance. Now apparently for the first time the practice of affording contributors substantial remuneration was introduced, and to this must be ascribed in a great measure, no doubt, the improvement in the quality of the contributions[2]. It became worth the while of a Scott or a Southey to place their great knowledge and talents at the service of a Constable or a princely Murray. But the improvement is confined at first to a few of the leading periodicals, and before 1818 notable reviews of German literature might almost be counted on one's fingers, if we except the work of William Taylor of Norwich; although, during a part of this time at any rate, we find translations from German reviewed in considerable numbers.

[1] James Grant, *The Great Metropolis*, pp. 252–253.
[2] idem, pp. 253–254.

In April 1790, the Speculator, a short-lived paper appearing twice weekly, began a series of articles on German literature[1], whose author appears both intelligent and comparatively well-informed. He begins by commenting on the prejudiced neglect of German literature in England. "To attract some share of attention to a subject where curiosity is so laudable, and by giving an idea, faint as it may be, of the exertions of the Germans, in works of taste and imagination...will be attempted in a few sketches." The author probably knew German[2]. In the first number he gives a brief account of the rise and development of German literature, and in the following a comparison of French and German drama. He mentions, though only in passing, Leisewitz, Gerstenberg (whom he calls Garstenberg), and Klinger. Of Goethe his opinion is more favourable than Mackenzie's; he speaks of "the exquisitely feminine traits of his *Stella*," and of *Götz von Berlichingen* he says that "as it imitates the wildness of Shakespeare, (it) is animated with a portion of his spirit." The last numbers are devoted to Schiller, and to an analysis of *Kabale und Liebe*, with a clumsy translation of Act v. This series of articles is noteworthy as an early attempt to supply the public with information regarding German literature, and is conspicuous by its isolation in the periodical writing of the time. If we are to believe Nathan Drake, the editor of the Speculator, these articles contributed "in no small degree to turn the attention of the British literati" to German literature[3]. The Analytical Review for April 1791 noticed the Speculator's articles on German literature, and commended them highly, as did the Monthly Review for February 1792.

The next ten years witnessed an outpouring upon England of the dregs of German literature, and towards the end of that period Kotzebue's murky star had arisen. The Anti-Jacobin, a weekly paper founded by Canning and his friends in 1797 to

---

[1] Signed H. or S. To be attributed, according to Cushing's *Anonyms* (*A Dictionary of revealed Authorship*, London, 1890, Article *Speculator*), to Edward Ash, M.D., 1770–1829.

[2] He says of the prose of the German dramatists: "It neither neglects the elegance of structure nor the harmony of cadence."

[3] Nathan Drake, *Essays etc. illustrative of the Rambler, Adventurer and Idler*, 2 vols., London, 1810.

support the Government, attacked German literature for its subversive tendencies, and illustrated its short career—for it lasted less than eight months—by the rather celebrated parody *The Rovers*, which appeared in two of its numbers in June 1798. *The Rovers, or the Double Arrangement*, in spite of the reminiscence of *The Robbers* in the title, is directed rather against *Stella* and Kotzebue than against Schiller. The satire is amusing enough and on the whole good-natured, and it seems unreasonable of Niebuhr to have become so cross about it[1]. The opening scene is a direct parody of *Stella*, describing the meeting of Matilda and Cecilia—both pining for the faithless Casimere—at the Weimar Inn. Another theme is introduced when the Hostess of the Inn asks the Waiter (who proves to be a Knight Templar come down in the world) whether he has carried dinner to the prisoner in the vaults of the Abbey. Rogero, the said prisoner—victim of "the cruelty of a Minister—the perfidy of a Monk"—makes the hit of the play with a song which even now retains a comic savour, and may be known to the reader:

> Whene'er with haggard eyes I view
> This dungeon, that I'm rotting in,
> I think of those companions true
> Who studied with me at the U-
> Niversity of Gottingen,
> Niversity of Gottingen, etc.

Three Acts are given *in extenso*, namely I, II, and IV, Act III being replaced by the notice that it "so nearly resembles the concluding Act of 'Stella' that we forbear to lay it before our Readers."

In 1799 and 1800 the attack on the German drama was repeated in the Meteors, an even more ephemeral publication, in whose numbers for December 1799, and January, February 1800, appeared a play called *The Benevolent Cut-throat* ("*Not* by Kotzebue, but by Klotzboggenhagen"). The satire here is obvious and clumsy, but it afforded no doubt amusing reading to those who were satiated with Kotzebue.

Whatever the effect of these parodies may have been on the

---

[1] He appears to have missed the fun of it, and treats it as a deliberate international insult.

more literate public—a question we shall touch upon later—
the interest in German literature was still considered sufficiently
strong in 1800 to warrant the publication of a monthly paper
devoted chiefly to German matters. This was the German
Museum[1].

A venture of the same kind had been attempted some years
earlier. In November 1795, the Analytical Review published a
"Prospectus of the Plan of a concise Review of original German
books." Remarking that the German language was no longer
looked upon with indifference, it defined the chief aim of the
projected Review as being "to give the true characters of such
original German books, as may most likely interest the greater
part of English readers... who are desirous of being somewhat
better acquainted with the *present* state of German literature,
and who have already applied, or intend at some future period to
apply, to the study of the language itself." It was to be published
quarterly, "or oftener if it meet with approbation." The publishers were G. Mudie and Son, Edinburgh, and J. Johnson,
London. In February 1796, the Analytical Review[2] advertised
the first number of the *Concise Review of Original German Books*.
I have not seen a copy of it, nor do I know whether the publication was continued. It is scarcely probable that there was
sufficient serious interest in German literature at that time to
support such an enterprise.

The German Museum cast its net more widely. From the
Preface we learn that it aspires "to make the English reader
more intimately acquainted with the literary labours of Germany,
to portray the national character and manners of the country...
Each number will comprise an historical account of the rise and
progress of German Literature; biographical sketches of eminent
authors of Germany and the North of Europe, together with

---

[1] "The German Museum or Monthly Repository of the Literature of
Germany, the North, and the Continent in General. London. Printed for
C. Geisweiler and the Proprietors." Three volumes were published, from
January 1800 to June 1801. If, as I suggested above (p. 26), this was the
undertaking of German residents in England zealous for the honour of the
Fatherland, the enterprise might be explicable even on the supposition that
interest in German literature had already sunk very low. The chart (p. 45)
suggests, however, that in 1800 the decline was not yet strongly marked.

[2] Johnson was the publisher of the Analytical Review.

a critical account of their works"; extracts, selections from periodical publications, articles on works preparing for the press, discoveries and improvements, maps, engravings, new establishments and institutes, obituary notices, favourite German songs, set to music, with an English translation "adapted to the same" are further allurements dangled before the eyes of the public.

The composition of the paper was not without merit. It gave numerous translated extracts from reputable German writers, among them Klopstock, Leisewitz, Bürger, Hölty, Jean-Paul, Schiller, Goethe. The verse translations were faced by the original text, a very sensible plan. In June 1801, appeared the translation from C. F. D. Schubart's *Der Ewige Jude*, which unexpectedly links the German Museum with the higher walks of English literature by attracting the notice of the youthful Shelley in somewhat romantic circumstances (see below, p. 147). Various items of information about German life and literature were duly provided. In April 1800, Dr Willich falls foul of the Abbé Barruel on the subject of Kant[1]; and in the second volume an extremely compressed outline of the Kantian philosophy is given. The promised *Account of the Rise and Progress of Literature in Germany* was begun, and proved exceedingly dull and bad. Indeed, there hangs a cloud of dullness over the whole work. The style is constrained, and one at least of the contributors (he who signs P. W.) was clearly a foreigner. There was little attempt at literary criticism. Probably enough the German Museum was chiefly written by Germans who, though painstaking, were not specially qualified to deal with the literature of their country. Its existence terminated after eighteen months, having indeed coincided with a sharp decline of public interest in the subjects it dealt with[2]; and further enterprises of the kind were out of the question for many years to come[3].

[1] I have not had an opportunity to ascertain whether this is a mere reproduction of Willich's polemics in the European Magazine for January 1800 (see above, p. 25), or an unmasking of his batteries from a new vantage-point.

[2] Assuming, that is, that generally speaking the amount of space devoted to a subject in the periodicals is a gauge of the public interest in it. For a short discussion of the subject, see below, p. 47.

[3] For some information concerning the editorship of the German Museum,

Carlyle, reviewing in 1831 the *Historic Survey of German Poetry* of William Taylor of Norwich, prefaces his justly severe criticism by the remark: "Be it admitted without hesitation that Mr Taylor, in respect of general talent and acquirement, takes his place above all our expositors of German things."[1] It was his general talent and acquirement, unsupported though they were (Carlyle points it out with sufficient vigour, and the modern reader will confirm his verdict) by solid judgment, that made the work of William Taylor particularly valuable in the earlier days of English interest in German literature. In the years between 1788 and 1818[2] he is almost the only reviewer of German works who is at all extensively acquainted with German literature.

Taylor was born in 1765, and his acquaintance with German literature begins much earlier than that of any of the writers to be subsequently dealt with. With a view to preparing him for a business career, Taylor's father took steps to enable him to acquire a sound knowledge of the Continental languages. At the age of fourteen he was sent on a tour in the Netherlands, France, and Italy; and his letters home, written in the languages he is studying, seem to show that he had remarkable linguistic facility. He had scarcely returned from his first expedition when, in April 1781, he was sent to Germany, where he remained for about eighteen months, chiefly at Detmold. His instructor in German, writing to Mr Taylor at the conclusion of his residence at Detmold, reports that William "by applying with great assiduity to the reading of our best authors, has acquired an extensive and well-grounded knowledge of our language, which he thoroughly understands and speaks with great fluency."[3] After leaving Detmold in July 1782 he travelled about Germany for some months. A clerical friend in Detmold had provided him with introductions to persons of distinction, to Goethe among others; but it seems probable that he did not make use of this opportunity[4].

see H. G. Fiedler, *Goethe's Lyric Poems in English Translation*, Modern Language Review, vol. XVIII, Jan. 1923, pp. 51 ff.

[1] T. Carlyle, *Critical and Miscellaneous Essays*, Chapman and Hall, 4 vols., vol. II, p. 313.

[2] Taylor's reviewing activity begins about 1793.

[3] J. Robberds, *Memoir of William Taylor of Norwich*, vol. I, p. 30.

[4] cp. J. M. Carré, *Quelques Lettres Inédites de William Taylor, Coleridge*

It was not for several years after his return to England (at the age of seventeen, be it remembered) that Taylor's knowledge of German literature was to be put to any public use. It was, indeed, only gradually that he turned to literature as his principal occupation. Meanwhile he was reading German and instructing his friends in this and other languages.

From 1790 onwards he translated from German, and in 1793 begins his activity in periodical criticism which extends over the next thirty years.

Some account will be given later (see p. 65) of his translation of Bürger's *Lenore*, which was published in the Monthly Magazine for March 1796, but had been circulating in MS for some time previously. In 1791 he published for private circulation a translation of Lessing's *Nathan der Weise*, and in 1793 appeared his rendering of Goethe's *Iphigenie*[1]. Some shorter translations appeared in periodicals, and in the course of his reviewing he had occasion to translate numerous extracts from various authors. As a translator he was perhaps commendable rather for a certain boldness and vigour than for accuracy or delicacy. As a reviewer he had, with most serious defects, the merit of arresting the attention of his readers by a forceful dogmatism and an indulgence in eccentricities which, if taken in sufficiently small doses, is rather pleasant and stimulating; though the wilful oddity of his style has none of the force of Carlyle's. Sir James Mackintosh characterised it happily when he remarked: "I can still trace William Taylor by his Armenian dress, gliding through the crowd, in Annual Reviews, Monthly Magazines, Athenaeums, etc."[2]

His first critical ventures appeared in the Monthly Review, in which, between 1793 and 1799, he published 200 articles[3]. Towards the end of this period the management of the Monthly

---

et Carlyle à Henry Crabb Robinson sur la Littérature allemande, Extrait de la Revue Germanique de Janvier-Février 1912, p. 35. Robberds, on the other hand, inclines to think that Taylor had met Goethe (Robberds, *Memoir*, vol. 1, p. 32).

[1] The sale of the translation was very limited; not many more than 150 copies had been sold in 1804. And of his *Ellenore*, which he reprinted from the Monthly Magazine, 200 copies remained on his hands out of an edition of 300. See Taylor's Letter to Robert Southey, Robberds, *Memoir*, vol. 1, p. 485.

[2] idem, p. 62.   [3] idem, p. 126.

Review was taken over by G. E. Griffiths, son of the original editor, Dr R. Griffiths; and Taylor was subjected by the new management to such considerable annoyance that he severed his connection with the review[1]. He had already, in 1796, established a connection with the Monthly Magazine, which began to appear in that year; and his contributions to this paper continued till 1824. Between 1800 and 1810 he also contributed to the Critical Review, the Annual Review, and the Athenaeum. In 1810 he again began to write for the Monthly Review, and continued to do so till 1824[2]. Altogether he contributed about 1750 articles to the reviews between 1793 and 1824[3], a large proportion of which dealt with German writers. The vast body of critical work on German literature occasioned in this way formed the basis of his *Historic Survey of German Poetry* (1828–30). Carlyle's criticism of the *Historic Survey* may be recommended to those who would obtain a lively notion of its quality without the tedium of perusing it[4].

We need not concern ourselves here with the minutiae of Taylor's account of German writers. The *Survey* is rather chatty than historic. The numerous translations maintain a good level, and the book is not utterly dull; nor, in spite of the untimely intrusion of erudition[5], is it too pretentious. It is, however, badly constructed, and indeed is too obviously strung together from Taylor's collection of review articles. One may appreciate it best by resolving it into its component parts, by regarding it as a series of lively if wrong-headed essays on

[1] He had to complain particularly of outrageous alterations of text in the articles contributed by him, an editorial liberty which G. E. Griffiths justified on the curious ground that, as the articles were unsigned, the form in which they appeared was the concern only of the ostensible editor, "*his* property and *his* person solely being affected by its success or its failure." G. E. Griffiths to W. Taylor, Robberds, *Memoir*, vol. 1, p. 197.

[2] Robberds, *Memoir*, vol. 1, p. 126.

[3] Herzfeld, *William Taylor of Norwich*, p. 28.

[4] T. Carlyle, *Critical and Miscellaneous Essays*: "Taylor's Historic Survey of German Poetry."

[5] Southey expressed very frankly his opinion of Taylor's style in a letter to Taylor himself (February 14, 1803): "Now I will say what for a long while I have thought, that you have ruined your style by Germanisms, Latinisms and Greekisms, that you are sick of a surfeit of knowledge, that your learning breaks out like scabs and blotches on a beautiful face" (Robberds, *Memoir*, vol. 1, pp. 452 f.).

German writers. One can then realise what the value of the single articles must have been, as a means of rousing or sustaining interest in German literature among review readers. He has a trick of catching our attention, even though he cannot hold it long, by his very oddities of style—his "Armenian dress." As criticism his work has no longer much interest for us, and cannot at any time have been a very reliable guide to the public; but the copious and tolerable translations gave his readers some opportunity of criticising on their own account and might stimulate them to acquire a knowledge of the originals.

Bouterwek is, by Taylor's admission, his "instructor and guide," and Bouterwek's history stops at the beginning of the century. Carlyle is no doubt right in judging that Taylor is hopelessly behind the times in his point of view. We must remember that his direct contact with German literature, his immersion in it, so to speak, belongs to the early eighties of the preceding century; and Carlyle may be harsh, but he is not altogether unjustified in remarking: "'The fine literature of Germany' no doubt he has 'imported'; yet only with the eyes of 1780 does he read it." On more than one occasion in his correspondence with Southey[1] he deplores the decadence of German literature, and that at a time when the Romantic School was in the ascendant. It is not surprising that his history deals summarily with the Romantics. They are for him mere "shooting stars," "winged ephemerons of the atmosphere." Novalis,

[1] W. T. to R. S. December 23, 1798. An acquaintance has just returned from Germany. He tells Taylor, who ought to have known better than to endorse his remarks, that "all the new publications are trash, the poetry, translated—the novels, hocus-pocus tricks—metaphysics, the jargon of Kant —morals, the barbarism of French licentiousness—history, mere catalogues of old books. The sunset of German literature is come" (Robberds, *Memoir*, vol. I, pp. 236 f.). And again in 1800 (April 27, to Robert Southey): "Dr Reeve (not the pessimist who brought the previous ill-tidings, but clearly of a similar cast) is here, fresh from Germany...The Germans have buried all their genius: Wieland is deaf, blind and moped; Goethe alone remains. Good sense has not thriven; physical and metaphysical quacks have usurped the thrones of reputation. Dr Gall and Fichte are more talked of than Soemmering and Martens" (!) (ibid. vol. II, pp. 125 f.). But he had not waited for these travellers' tales to forebode the worst for Germany, for in an article of the Monthly Review on Wieland's works, at least probably by Taylor (vol. XVIII, Appendix, 1795, p. 523) occurs the remark: "His (Wieland's) career began with the dawn, and has perhaps extended to the sunset of German literature."

Tieck and Fouqué are "luminous insects"; I find no mention of H. von Kleist, Friedrich Schlegel or E. T. A. Hoffmann. He has flashes of felicitous characterisation, but they are rare. One may quote, as an example of these and of his peculiar style, a remark of his on Schiller's *Räuber* (vol. III, p. 173 of the *Survey*): "The diction harmonises marvellously with the convulsionary movement of the incidents: it stalks about for metaphors on giant limbs, and writhes with the agonies of passion and emotion."[1] A glaring instance of Taylor's lack of literary judgment is his unbounded and persistent admiration of Kotzebue; and were there no other reason to suspect his good taste, this unfortunate enthusiasm would provoke grave doubts in us. "The most of what Mr Taylor has written on Schiller, on Goethe, and the new Literature of Germany, a reader that loves him, as we honestly do, will consider unwritten, or written in a state of somnambulism," says Carlyle; and there appears no reason to reconsider the verdict. Carlyle took the trouble to make a little calculation of the errors of statement occurring in the three volumes. That is, he studied six pages of the book for the purpose, and discovered thirteen errors in them. "Now," he concludes, "if 6 gives 13, who sees not that 1455, the entire number of pages, will give 3152 and a fraction?"

But with all his errors of statement and errors of judgment, Taylor did good service in early days by keeping the subject of German literature before the minds of the review-reading public in a form that could scarcely fail to awaken interest. His knowledge of the German language and literature, though inaccurate, was considerable; the abundant facility with which he wrote, the surprising and sometimes forcible peculiarities of his temperament and style, his own real if rather superficial enthusiasm for his subject, his dogmatism, his lively though peculiar and limited intelligence, fitted him for the rôle of propagandist.

---

[1] The following remark on Schiller is interesting as criticism: "His characters are heroic, colossal, sublime in virtue and in vice, but they have no ease, no little traits of nature; they explain themselves, but they never betray themselves" (To Southey, October 14, 1805; Robberds, *Memoir*, vol. II, p. 100). Taylor is perhaps thinking more particularly of the *Braut von Messina* here, though, in the context, it appears to be of general application.

His usefulness must progressively decline after 1818, as the treatment of German literature is entrusted to writers of better quality, and the kind of information he possesses becomes more common. For the earlier period, it appears hardly an exaggeration to assert that without him scarcely a single intelligent remark on German literature would have been made public from one year's end to another.

For with few exceptions the quality of the information and comment on German literature at this early stage was inferior. The reviews of books are mostly brief, especially if we deduct the extracts given from the works reviewed, which, no doubt owing to their serviceableness as padding, ran to excessive length. Praise and blame have a tendency to assume stereotyped forms, but on the whole the blame finds livelier expression. The ever-recurring reproach is that of immorality; but extravagance, sentimentality and general absurdity are also imputed[1]. The periodicals, save in a few cases (e.g. the Monthly Review before 1800 *pro* and the Anti-Jacobin *contra*), do not take sides very definitely for or against German literature, praise and blame alternating according to the standpoint of the reviewer. The Monthly Review up to ca. 1802, seems very well disposed towards German literature, finding (probably under Taylor's guidance) even Kotzebue very much to its taste; it is rather severe, however, even at this time, towards German novels, and is actively opposed to Kant's philosophy. To be interested in German works belongs to the tradition of the Monthly Review, which noticed original German literature as early as 1759[2]. But towards 1802 its tone changes, and becomes undeniably antagonistic[3]; towards 1814, perhaps a little earlier, it swings round to a more liberal attitude. The former change was probably due to the change in the management which occurred

[1] cp. the list of translations 1795–1806, Appendix V. It will be seen that the reviewers had to deal with much obscure and presumably inferior material, and their blame, though not attached solely to the worst productions, was no doubt exacerbated in other cases by the constant friction with these.

[2] In this year it reviewed Gleim's *Scherzhafte Lieder*. In its 36th volume appeared the notice on Lessing's *Laokoon* already referred to; see above, p. 20, note 2.

[3] cp. M. R., December 1802, the review of Holcroft's translation of *Hermann und Dorothea*, with its elaborate sneering irony.

about this time, R. Griffiths retiring from the joint editorship
and leaving the Review in the hands of his son, G. E. Griffiths.
This change, as we have seen, brought about Taylor's secession
from the staff. And no doubt the renewal of his relations with
the Monthly Review in 1810 at once marks a change in its
temper and helped to render it favourable to German literature.

In 1802 the enthusiasm for German productions which had
mounted rapidly during the last decade of the eighteenth
century, had begun to decline in England, so far as we can judge
from the evidence afforded by the periodical literature of the
time. The following remarks from a review of W. Render's
Tour through Germany (Critical Review, December 1801) would
represent, I think, the average reviewer's opinion on the subject
of German literature at its date, though expressed with a very
unusual distinctness and sobriety.

> In history, poetry, and every branch of polite literature, they [the
> Germans] are only beginning their career...We are far from enter-
> taining the idea expressed by a celebrated French author, that it
> is impossible for a German to be a man of taste or wit; but we cannot
> expect in German literature a miracle which has happened in no
> other, that the *belles-lettres* should be cultivated with success at the
> very commencement of a literary progress. The German works which
> have faintly aspired to the name of genius have not yet been tried
> by the voice of time; and such are the remaining marks of barbarism
> and prolixity (the latter a most unclassical defect), that it will prob-
> ably be long before Germany shall produce a classical author,
> admitted like those of England, France, Spain, and Italy, into
> universal fame. In short, we admire the Germans merely as disciples,
> but cannot venerate them as masters; nor can candour abstain from
> a smile, when a German critic pronounces the dictates of his own
> imperfect taste upon the works of more enlightened nations.

The last thrust is probably directed at Render, to whom we
do not grudge it.

To illustrate the fluctuations of English opinion concerning
German literature, I have introduced here a diagram showing
the amount of attention bestowed upon German literature in
certain periodicals between 1786 and 1821.

The indications of the diagram must be taken as only
approximately representative, since in compiling the figures on

which each division of the diagram is based only three periodicals were used. The continuous line indicates the numbers of
articles dealing with German literature or literary men and
reviews of German books; the broken line the total number of
pages in the articles; as has been mentioned, a heavy deduction
must be made from the latter number if we consider only the
amount of actual critical and other commentary in the reviews,
on account of the large proportion of space taken up by quotation; but this probably does not affect the significance of the

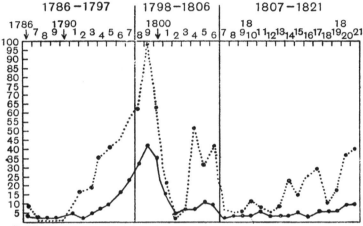

Full line gives the numbers of articles.
Dotted line gives the numbers of pages.

Diagram. Articles on German Literature in Periodicals between 1786 and 1821.

diagram, since editors would presumably regulate the amount
of space given to German literature by their estimate of its
importance to the public, and the reviewer would insert as many
extracts from the book reviewed as he conveniently might, in
order to save himself trouble. The diagram extends by a few
years beyond our limits on either side, in order to show the
movement of public opinion from the time it was first roused
to consciousness of the existence of German literature to the
time when (having in the interval swallowed its less wholesome
ingredients too voraciously, and suffered surfeit and disgust in

consequence) it began to renew its appetite, and to feed, this time, with better discretion and under better advice.

The figures for each division of the diagram being based on three periodicals only, the fluctuations are more sudden than would have been the case had a larger number of examples been analysed: for instance, the soaring of the dotted line from 1803 to 1804 is due chiefly to the fact that the editor of the Critical Review printed, for reasons of his own, two deplorable articles on Klopstock running to a total of thirty-two pages, written, as we may infer from the style, by a German, who combines immeasurable admiration for Klopstock with unfathomable stupidity and that spirit which Heine terms *pudeldeutsch*.

Periodicals were chosen that covered as much of the ground as possible. Unfortunately the change of editorship of the Monthly Review, and that at a critical moment—just when the fervour for things German was beginning to cool—rendered it of no evidential value in the second division, and similar cases occurred elsewhere. The arrangement finally adopted will appear from the following table:

1786–1797	1798–1806	1807–1821
Monthly Review	—	Monthly Review
Critical Review	Critical Review	—
European Magazine	—	European Magazine
—	British Critic	—
—	Monthly Magazine	Monthly Magazine

My object was to obtain three series homogeneous in themselves, each including one of the three critical moments, or moments of fluctuation, i.e. that of the first awakening of interest in German literature, that of its climax and fall, and that of its recovery. The changes of periodicals, corresponding to the divisions of the diagram, fall at moments of a less crucial nature. But it should be noticed that after such a change we are not working on the same basis as before it and that the differences from one side of the vertical line to the other may be attributed partly to the change in the material analysed. Had we kept the Monthly Review and the European Magazine in 1798 and 1799, for instance, our dotted line especially would have soared more sharply even than it does. The fall in the dotted line at 1807 does not however appear to be due altogether to the change of periodicals—at least the British Critic, if retained (which it could not profitably be on account of a supervening change of management), would have given similar results.

Keeping our diagram in view, we can establish from it some facts regarding fluctuations in the English opinion of German literature during the whole period, and comment upon them in the light of facts otherwise ascertainable.

We have already taken for granted that there is a close relation between the variations in the space allotted to a subject by the periodicals and the state of public opinion relative to that subject (cp. p. 37, note 2, and p. 45). This, I think, is a legitimate assumption, since the sales of a periodical must depend largely on its providing its readers with the kind of mental fare for which there is a present appetite[1]. But though the relation is necessarily close, it is not invariable. The periodicals, for instance, will generally lag a little behind public opinion where there is a change from increase to decrease of interest or vice versa; though once the periodicals have discovered that, e.g. the demand for a subject is increasing, they may increase the supply beyond what is required at a given moment, and thus in a sense outrun public opinion where a change of the *rate* of interest is concerned. These features of variability in the relation of periodical literature and public opinion do not prevent the former from representing a continual approximation to the latter; the degree of approximation varies, it is true, within certain limits; but if we are considering a period of several years, this variability will not affect our results very materially, though we shall do well to bear it in mind. The attitude of a periodical towards a given subject is perhaps not related quite so simply to public opinion; for the reviewer takes upon himself the function of guiding the blind monster. The Review has its traditions, and looks to the reviewer to conform to them upon

---

[1] And we must not overlook the fact that periodicals are, and at that time were to a much larger extent, I think, advertising media for the publishers. The number of reviews of German books would rise and fall with the number of publications, even if the reviewer could not commend these.

the whole. Authors and public, on the other hand, are busy destroying the old tradition and forming a new one; and here, in attitude, in tone, the periodicals may lag definitely in some cases behind public opinion. If they serve to restrain it, they will not hold it back altogether, and it may go its way unheeding the warning bark, as we saw where *Werther* was concerned, when the public showed itself more intelligent than its reviewers (see p. 20). Perhaps it is not too much to say that, during the period we are examining, English public opinion is undergoing a mild Romantic crisis, while periodical criticism has scarcely modified its classical ideals.

We may assume, I think, that no very important fluctuations would show on a diagram for periodicals previous to 1786. Previous to 1750 the lines would probably approximate to zero. From 1790 onwards, our chart indicates attention to German literature increasing fairly constantly, and becoming more and more intense from 1795 onwards. Between 1788 and 1795 few works of eminence, however, reached the English public from Germany. Tytler gave *The Robbers* in 1792, Taylor's *Iphigenia in Tauris* appeared in 1793, *Kabale und Liebe* was translated in 1795; otherwise I find only work of second-rate importance at best published in translation during these years. The years ensuing, up to 1799, show a continued increase in the popularity of German books. In 1796 the translators made two grand discoveries: Bürger's *Lenore* and Kotzebue. Five translations of *Lenore*[1], one of them in two separate editions, appeared in the course of the year. The astonishing popularity of Bürger's famous ballad was more creditable to the public than its eager reception of Kotzebue. In 1796 his *Indianer in England* and *Negersklaven* were translated, and in 1798 three translations of *Menschenhass und Reue* (*The Stranger*) appeared; the play was performed for the first time at Drury Lane on March 24, 1798[2]. The enthusiasm for Kotzebue and all his works reaches its maniacal climax in 1799, in which year I count twenty-seven

[1] By J. T. Stanley, H. J. Pye, W. R. Spencer, W. Taylor and W. Scott. Stanley's translation appeared in an *édition de luxe*, at 5s., besides in that issued at 2s. 6d.

[2] For very full information on the subject of Kotzebue's popularity, see Walter Sellier, *Kotzebue in England*, Inaug. Diss., Leipzig, 1903.

translations or adaptations from Kotzebue, and there may well have been more. Many of these are duplicates or multiplicates, for so precious was Kotzebue to the public, or so inadequate were the translations, that the previous existence of one or several versions was apparently but a slight obstacle to issuing another. In the next year the deluge has abated, and after this we find him only occasionally represented.

The worthier works which had reached the public during this time must have been robbed to a large extent of their due effect by the taste for Kotzebue. Between 1796 and 1801 all Schiller's extant plays were translated, as were Goethe's *Götz von Berlichingen, Stella, Clavigo, Die Geschwister* and *Iphigenie*. An occasional translation from Wieland (Sotheby's *Oberon* in 1798 being the most important of these), from Haller's poems, and an adaptation from Lessing's *Minna von Barnhelm* (*The School for Honour*) almost closes the list of notable literature from the German for these years.

The sharp decline noticeable on our chart after 1799, and particularly after 1800, has been attributed to the destructive effect of the Anti-Jacobin's *Rovers* on the prevailing taste for the German drama. But it is difficult to imagine that this and similar parodies can have solely or even chiefly determined so radical a change of attitude in the large public which the numbers of miscellaneous translations presuppose. It is more reasonable to regard the taste for German horrors and sentimentalities as having at last been glutted by the trash so liberally provided for it; the swiftness and duration of the reaction was due no doubt to the deleterious nature of the matter absorbed. Between 1800 and 1818 there are few new translations of major works of German literature. The most important are Coleridge's translation of *Wallenstein* (1800), Mellish's *Maria Stuart* and Holcroft's *Herman and Dorothea* (1801), and the translation, by J. Black, of A. W. Schlegel's *Lectures on Dramatic Art and Literature* (1815)[1].

The full recovery from this state of surfeit lies outside our chronological limits; but the chart indicates the beginning of

---

[1] For translations of Goethe's lyrics, see H. G. Fiedler, Modern Language Review, vol. XVIII, January 1923, pp. 51 ff.

it, and a continuation of the chart on a similar plan—which for want of leisure must be left to a successor—would show, I am convinced, an upward movement of the lines for some time to come, the tendency corresponding this time to an increasing knowledge and appreciation of the sounder elements in German literature. Before leaving the subject we must glance at the conditions which led to this revival of interest in German literature, and which provided it with a more solid basis than existed in the past.

An indirect cause of paramount importance has already been touched upon: the founding of the Edinburgh Review in 1802, of its rival the Quarterly in 1809, and the fashion established by these great reviews of enlisting the special knowledge and the riper intelligence of the day for critical comment on current literature. The hack-work of the older reviews still remained, no doubt; but channels now existed, and in increasing numbers, through which a Carlyle, a De Quincey, a Lockhart could profitably transmit to the public their informed and matured opinions about German literature.

As early as January 1804 the Edinburgh Review, in a criticism of G. C. Lichtenberg's *Vermischte Schriften*, dealt with German literature in a style of rational liberality which was new to the English reading public. Francis Jeffrey was the author of the article, and although he classes Schiller with Kotzebue and Iffland, he is alive in other respects to the injustice done by English opinion to the greater literature of Germany, and correctly estimates the ill-effects of the translators' choice of subjects:

For these fifteen years it has been a common and a reasonable opinion in that country (Germany), that profligate plays, forbidden to be acted in their most cultivated provinces, and novels inculcating suicide or adultery, constitute, in the opinion of the British nation, the most valuable part of German literature. Among ourselves it has sometimes been supposed to form the whole of it...We possess, indeed, very few translations of respectable German works; and the mischief that was reasonably apprehended from the contagion of those we have had the folly to receive, has been sufficient to induce many to reject, in the lump, the productions of that country.

In 1806 (April) Jeffrey reviewed Taylor's translation of *Nathan der Weise*, which he found not at all to his taste. Indeed, of the half-dozen reviews dealing with German literature appearing in the Edinburgh Review before 1818, all are somewhat hostile (and some vehemently so) with the exception of Sir James Mackintosh's review of Mme de Staël's *Germany* (October 1813).

The Quarterly Review has only three articles on German literature previously to 1820, and in these does not show itself as "savage and tartarly" as its rival. But the only one of these that has any importance is that reviewing de Staël's *Germany*.

This book was a second and more direct cause of the coming change of opinion in England respecting German literature. The work, it will be remembered, had had its adventures before reaching England with Mme de Staël. The edition of it published in France in 1810 had been destroyed by Napoleon's police, who discovered in it, or were directed to discover in it, a spirit intolerable to a properly constituted despotism. The manuscript fortunately escaped destruction, and after the intervening years of her exile in the northern parts of Europe Mme de Staël published it in 1813, a few months after her arrival in England. The English translation appeared in the same year. Crabb Robinson, who in Jena days had helped her to understand the philosophy of Kant, was again serviceable in arranging with Murray for the publication.

The book must have been a surprising revelation to those in England whose opinion of German literature had been formed only through the medium of the extant translations and of critical comment in the periodicals. The effect may have been mitigated somewhat by the fact that the author was a foreigner; yet her obvious partiality for England and her hostility towards Napoleon would induce the English public to be lenient towards this defect. *De l'Allemagne* is most attractively written, and its qualities of brilliancy, *verve*, assurance are not, as might have been feared, altogether lost in the very creditable English translation.

Part I, named *Of Germany and of the Manners of the Germans*, presented a lively picture of the German temperament and of the conditions of social life in Germany, such as had not been presented before to the English public. German life, especially that of intellectual circles, with its varieties in several German-speaking regions—Vienna, Saxony, Weimar, Berlin—is dealt with in a series of chapters which convey an impression of wide and intelligent observation. A great people, hitherto judged on the evidence of fragmentary and prejudiced glimpses, was now generously portrayed in its manners, habits of thought and social customs, German peculiarities of mind being sharply and luminously, if too antithetically, contrasted with those of the French. The second part of the book treats of literature. After a brief and insufficient, if always intelligent, sketch of the history of German literature, she proceeds to an individual study of the great modern writers. The criticism is not profound perhaps, but—at this stage a more valuable quality for propagandist pur-poses—it is stimulating. Part III gives a sketch of German philosophy which might at least serve as an introduction to its study.

On the whole this was a very noteworthy book, presenting German intellectual life in something like its true proportions. The greater luminaries are recognised as such, and the com-parative distance between them and the lesser is indicated. Goethe puzzled and annoyed her, one gathers, but in spite of a certain reluctance and pettishness she could not hide how much he impressed her. Her chapter on *Faust* shows clearly enough how slight was her understanding of it; but here as throughout she inspires a wish to make a closer acquaintance with her subject.

De Staël's book was reviewed at length and favourably in the weightier portion of the English press. And henceforth there existed in English a pronouncement on the importance of German literature by a writer of note, which relegated the slap-dash wholesale condemnations of it to the rubbish-heap[1].

A third cause of the better appreciation of German literature which marks the revival of interest in it was the lapse of time since it was last the object of sustained attention. In the twenty

[1] R. C. Whitford, *Madame de Staël's Literary Reputation in England*, may be consulted for particulars of sales, reviews, etc. (*University of Illinois, Studies in Language and Literature*, vol. IV, no. 1, February 1918).

years succeeding 1800 the staying-power of the German intellectual movement had manifested itself. Time, moreover, had helped to sift the grain from the chaff. The light of Goethe and Schiller, as could not but be patent to all who now studied the subject, was of a different origin and temperature from the flare of Kotzebue, which at one time dazzled equally, but had long since fallen to ashes.

* * *

The influence exercised by William Taylor of Norwich and the reviewers upon the general opinion of German literature had a counterpart in the activities of Henry Crabb Robinson. He published translations from German and articles on German literature, but his chief influence was personal. As the friend of Coleridge, Wordsworth, Lamb, Carlyle, as a welcome guest in literary and artistic circles, he brought his influence to bear immediately upon the intellect and imagination of England. The efficacy of his propaganda in favour of German literature, and particularly of its chief Goethe, though not an easily calculable factor, must be reckoned among those which contributed to the better understanding of the subject. If its quantity may be rated low, its quality is, in more than one respect, of a high order. In the first place, Robinson's knowledge of Germany and German literature is clearly in advance of that of any of his English contemporaries whose utterances on the subject are recorded in this earliest stage of German studies in England[1];

[1] Professor Carré is mistaken, I think, in calling Coleridge "le germaniste le plus compétent" of England in 1816 (Carré, *Goethe en Angleterre*, p. 92). Crabb Robinson, in knowledge of German literature and in the appreciation of its relative values as well as in his command of the language appears to me easily to surpass Coleridge, who was an indifferent German scholar, at any rate in 1800, when he translated *Wallenstein*; and he was then fresh from his visit to Germany (see p. 121). Robinson possessed German sufficiently well to have an article in German from his pen published, without corrections, in a German paper, the *Neue Berliner Monatsschrift* (see Sadler, *H. C. Robinson's Diary*, etc., 3rd edition, p. 85, and Karl Eitner, *Ein Engländer über deutsches Geistesleben*, who gives in part the text of Robinson's German article). The subject of the article was the opinion held in England respecting German works. Of Robinson's knowledge of German literature, Goethe, writing to Zelter, August 20, 1829, speaks in the following terms: "Zu gleicher Zeit war ein Engländer bei uns, der zu Anfang des Jahrhunderts in Jena studiert hatte und seit der Zeit der deutschen Literatur gefolgt war auf eine Weise, von der man sich gar keinen Begriff machen konnte. Er war so

even Carlyle fell short of him in respect of general knowledge and grasp of things German. In the second place, his influence was backed by his intelligent enthusiasm and by the weight and charm of his personality. A review casually read may leave us very cool towards the subject of its eulogy. But when clever, agreeable Mr Robinson, leaning towards us confidentially over the walnuts and the wine, quotes *Faust* with an authentic German accent, and, translating his quotation, illustrates it by an anecdote from his personal reminiscences of the celebrated author (whose name, we learn on his authority, is not, as we had supposed, to be pronounced like the archaic or poetical form of the third person singular indicative of the verb "to go")[1], we are moved to take a more sympathetic interest in German literature, brought close to us in this insinuating and even flattering manner.

Robinson was not a creative artist, not primarily an original thinker; he was, in perhaps the noblest sense of the word, a dilettante. Born in 1775, he became interested at an early date in German literature, and his taste for it was strengthened in 1798 by a meeting or meetings with W. Taylor of Norwich. At this time he had already thought of paying a visit to Germany, and this plan he carried out in 1800. "I understood it to be a country in which there was a rising literature," he wrote to his brother in 1803[2]. "...I had sipped the cream of English literature which had surfeited me without nourishing me." In Germany he came into contact with those who could put him on the track of discovery of the best in recent German literature. At Frankfurt in 1801 he got into touch with the Romantic School through the Servieres (Charlotte and Paulina), who introduced him to the Brentanos, with whom, and in particular with

recht in die *merita causae* initiert, dass ich ihm, wenn ich auch gewollt hätte, und wie man wohl gegen Fremde zu thun pflegt, keinen blauen phraseologischen Dunst vor die Augen bringen durfte." Quoted by Eitner, loc. cit. pp. 394–395.

[1] See Gillies, *Memoirs,* vol. II, p. 147. That this was not the Edinburgh pronunciation alone is made probable by the form of Goëthe, commonly used by reviewers throughout the period; cp. also Lamb's remark about H. C. Robinson, who was visiting Italy: "I fear he will find the air of Italy too classic. His station is in the Hartz forest, his soul is *Bego'ethed*" (Letter to Wordsworth, January 22, 1830).

[2] Letter, November 28, 1803. J. M. Carré, *Revue Germanique,* juillet–août 1912, p. 397.

Christian, he became friendly. He now began to study German poetry and philosophy systematically, passing all his spare time with the Servieres or the Brentanos. November 17 to 19, 1801, he spent at Weimar, in the course of an excursion with J. G. Seume from Grimma, where he stayed for a couple of months. During the three days at Weimar, he met Goethe, Schiller, Herder and Wieland. From 1802 to 1805 he studied at Jena, an experience that he accounted one of the happiest of his life. He attended lectures, "on experimental physics, on aesthetics, on speculative philosophy, and on physical anthropology," among other things, and threw himself with zest into the flood of new ideas and opinions which were so strange and stimulating to his English mind. The intensity of the intellectual life in Jena at that time could have been equalled probably nowhere else in Europe. "On all points, natural philosophy, religion, metaphysics, there seems to be a uniform opposition between German and English opinion," he wrote from Jena to his brother Thomas. "You say with truth I am growing a mystic. I rejoice to perceive it. Mystery is the poetry of philosophy,"[1] a maxim which reveals Robinson as versed in Romantic doctrine, or at least in Romantic phraseology. At Jena he made the acquaintance of Schelling, and of the Kantian Fries, whom he much frequented. He dined every day at an inn, with students of the better class, where the conversation, he assures us, was "in the best University tone." He began already to propagate his newly acquired information and ideas by writing articles on German literature, Kant, etc. for Collier's Monthly Register and by attempting to convert his brother to the Critical Philosophy[2]. From Jena to Weimar was but a step, and Crabb Robinson came into contact with Herder, Schiller and Goethe. Goethe received him kindly, and Robinson dined with him several times. When Mme de Staël visited Germany, she found in Robinson the one man who could make German philosophy comprehensible to her[3]. Robinson afterwards regretted that

---

[1] H. C. Robinson, *Diary*, vol. I, p. 134. No date given.
[2] idem, pp. 138–145.
[3] She is reported to have remarked to the Duke of Weimar, who called on her when Robinson was present: "J'ai voulu connaître la philosophie allemande, j'ai frappé à la porte de tout le monde, Robinson seul me l'a

he had not made more use of his opportunities of conversing with the great poets of Weimar. When he revisited Weimar in 1818 Goethe was at Carlsbad, and he did not see him again till 1829, on the occasion of his third visit, when Goethe received him with the utmost graciousness, regarding him, as Professor Carré suggests, as an apostle who had done and would do good service in bearing the gospel of Weimar to England[1].

In 1805 Robinson returned to England. Between 1805 and 1810 he was spending much of his time abroad, in Sweden and Spain, as foreign correspondent of *The Times*. From 1810 onwards he lived in England, leaving it only on occasional excursions to the Continent. On settling in England he read for the bar, became a barrister in 1813, was leader of the Norfolk circuit, and retired in 1828. Both during his residence abroad and after his return to England Robinson published essays on German literature and translations from German writers; other translations and essays remained unpublished[2]. But, as we have

ouverte" (Ellen Mayer, *Begegnungen eines Engländers mit Goethe*, Deutsche Rundschau, August 1899, Heft 11, p. 179). Further evidence to the same effect is given in H. C. Robinson's *Diary* (3rd edition, vol. 1, p. 218). In the entry for July 11, 1813, we read: "Called this morning on Madame de Staël at 3 George Street, Hanover Square. It is singular that, having in Germany assisted her as a student of philosophy, I should now render her service as a lawyer." In a note to this is given a portion of a letter from J. Lambert to Thomas Robinson: "Trinity College, Cambridge, April 10, 1814. I was lately in company where a gentleman asserted that it was now generally supposed that the metaphysical part of Madame de Staël's famous work on Germany was in fact all written by a Mr Robinson, who had resided some time in Gottenburg (?), and was much more competent to the work than Madame de S. herself. My question is, 'Is the said Mr Robinson your brother Henry Robinson?'" Sadler's note continues: "It was added that another gentleman (to whom this was communicated as a piece of *news*) replied very coolly, 'Is that all? Why, she has told me this a hundred times'." Obviously the rumour reported here had exceeded considerably the facts of the case.

[1] Carré, *Goethe en Angleterre*, p. 94, and *Revue Germanique*, juillet–août, pp. 406–407.

[2] For details about Robinson's essays and translations, published and unpublished, see J. M. Carré, *Un ami et défenseur de Goethe en Angleterre. Henry Crabb Robinson* (1775–1867) *avec de sdocuments inédits, Revue Germanique*, juillet–août 1912, pp. 386–392. It may appear singular that Robinson did not become one of the foremost expositors of German literature in the English periodicals; but at the moment (about 1806) when he might have begun his career as a writer for the reviews, demand for the information he was better qualified to give than any man in England was at a low ebb, as we have seen. The articles and translations published attracted little attention,

mentioned already, it was his personal influence in favour of German literature that counted most.

If we read Crabb Robinson's published Diary with a view to ascertain along what lines this influence was chiefly exercised, we receive the impression that the light of Goethe's genius shone so brightly to Robinson's eyes that it almost eclipsed all fainter luminaries[1]. He is, among Englishmen of note, the first to realise clearly the literary importance of Goethe; on the aesthetic side, indeed, he has perhaps a more intelligent appreciation of him than any English writer previous to 1830, with the single exception of Shelley. A few quotations from the Diary may serve to confirm this view[2].

and Robinson's activity may have been checked by discouragement. But an entry in his Diary suggests the possibility of another explanation. Robinson, it seems, regarded it as decidedly beneath his dignity to appear publicly as an author, at any rate as an author of translations. In the *Typed Diary* is the following entry for November 14, 1813: "Called on Shoberl...S. showed me the MS of his Catalogue of Living Authors. To my consternation he had inserted my name with *all* my translations. He allowed me to erase the list from his Work...As he is an Author by trade, and a very mechanical one too, I could not point out to him how degraded I should feel were it known that I had written such books!!!" This is interesting as an expression of Robinson's opinion, and also as implying that he had published in book-form other translations besides the *Amatonda* from the German of Anton Wall, the only one usually attributed to him. Robinson's failure to appear more openly as the champion of German literature in the periodicals may, therefore, be due rather to fastidious pride than to the modesty, the lack of ambition, to which Professor Carré ascribes it (*Goethe en Angleterre*, p. 97).

[1] There can be no doubt as to the supreme place held by Goethe in Robinson's scale of literary eminence. At the same time, the Diaries as edited by Sadler may be misleading as to the relative amount of attention bestowed on Goethe and on other writers by Robinson, since Sadler would probably select for publication references to German writers well known to the English public, and would give most space to those best known. The history of Robinson's opinions on German literature can be given only after an exhaustive study of Robinson's unpublished papers. At the time the notes for these remarks on Robinson were collected, the unpublished Diaries were not available, having been rendered inaccessible to possible German bombs, and incidentally to research-students. The three volumes of Crabb Robinson's Diary, Reminiscences, etc., published by Thomas Sadler are but a meagre extract, it appears, from the ninety odd MS volumes which are preserved. Professor Carré has, of course, drawn upon these sources. By the courtesy of the Librarian of Dr Williams' Library I was enabled to supplement the printed Diary by some additional typed copies of the original for the years 1811 to 1815, from which I have occasionally quoted, referring to it as *Typed Diary*.

[2] Especially if they are compared with the remarks on the same subjects by Scott, Coleridge, Shelley and Byron (v. the respective chapters).

In 1812 he was reading *Dichtung und Wahrheit*, and on January 21, 1813, the book calls forth the following remarks:

It is a book to make a man wish to live, if life were a thing he had not already experienced [a remark which, coming from H. C. R., need not be interpreted as pessimistic or cynical]. There is in Goethe such a zest of living. The pleasures of sense and thought, of imagination and the affections, appear to have been all possessed by him in a more exuberant degree than in (by?) any man who has ever renewed his life by writing it.

On hearing a false rumour of Goethe's death (H. C. Robinson, *Diary* etc., vol. II, pp. 512–513), he wrote:

He had done his work; but though not the extinction, yet, to us, the eclipse of the mightiest intellect that has shone on the earth for centuries (so, at least, I felt) could not be beheld without pain. It has been my rare good fortune to have seen a large proportion of the greatest minds of our age, in the fields of poetry and speculative philosophy, such as Wordsworth, Coleridge, Schiller, Tieck, but none that I have ever known came near him.

And many years later, in 1858, he wrote: "Compared with Goethe, the memory of Schiller, Wieland, Herder, Tieck, the Schlegels and Schelling has become faint" (H. C. Robinson, *Diary* etc., vol. III, p. 464).

On reading *Faust, Erster Teil* (which, surprisingly, he did not do till November 1811) he betrays some agitation along with his delight. Robinson, we have seen above (p. 56, note 2) was not above social prejudices; and although his foreign experience must have accustomed him to theological and ethical speculations of a bolder type than those current in England at the beginning of the nineteenth century, yet in these matters also he shared some prejudices with his English contemporaries; though in Robinson these appear as honest and respectable scruples. From the *Typed Diary*, November 10, 1812:

On my walk to Camberwell [Robinson in later years seldom walked alone without taking a book with him] read Goethe's new *Faust*; a most astonishing performance on which I have no leisure now to speak. It is a most pregnant, and equally delightful and disgusting performance. A masterpiece of genius before which I bow with humility, and the beauties of which are so ravishing that I am ashamed and afraid to allow myself to feel offended by its moral and aesthetic deformities.

Nov. 11...Read *Faust* with delight on my walk.

Nov. 23. The day was fine, and on my walk finished that wonderful poem *Faust*. The Scene in the Brocken, the Walpurgis Nacht is very wonderful, but that, as well as the whole poem, leaves much to wonder at, as well as to admire. However a cold thinker in the closet may tolerate a speculation concerning the Supreme Being, which even supposes the possibility of his Nonentity, yet a poem addressed to the people, which treats of the deepest subjects in a style that supposes the utmost indifference to the result of the speculation...cannot well be justified...The poetic worth of the new scenes, more especially of Margaretha in person, is transcendent Goethe here as elsewhere maintains his character as the inimitable and incomparable poet.

Here again, then, we have the expression of that sense, almost universal among Englishmen, even of the most liberal culture, of that day, that Goethe's speculative daring and licence of description were at times of a dangerous tendency.

The idea emerges again in a letter of Robinson's to Wordsworth of July 1832 (H. C. Robinson, *Diary* etc., vol. III, p. 10):

Thinking of old age, and writing to you, I am, by a natural association of ideas, reminded of the great poet lately dead in Germany. As one of his great admirers, I wished but for one quality in addition to his marvellous powers—that he had as uniformly directed those powers on behalf of the best interests of mankind, as you have done....

With these misgivings in his mind, he turned with relief to that one of Goethe's longer works where speculation has perhaps least part, to the large, serene, noble simplicity of *Hermann und Dorothea*:

March 10, 1833. I went on reading *Hermann und Dorothea*, which I have just finished (we must of course take this to refer to a re-perusal of the work). I hold it to be one of the most delightful of all Goethe's works. Not one of his philosophical works, which the exclusives exclusively admire, but one of the most perfectly moral as well as beautiful. It realises every requisite of a work of genius. I shed tears over it repeatedly, but they were more tears of tenderness at the perfect beauty of the characters and sentiments. Incident there is none.

While admiring Schiller he placed him, as it were, at the foot of Goethe's pedestal. Speaking of the correspondence between Schiller and Goethe, in 1829 (*Diary* etc., vol. II, p. 429), he remarked:

A delightful effect is produced by the affectionate reverence of Schiller towards Goethe; and infinitely below Goethe as Schiller must be deemed in intellect and poetical power, yet as a man he engrosses our affection. Goethe seems too great to be an object of love, even to one so great as Schiller...Schiller was raised by Goethe, and Goethe was sustained by Schiller; without Schiller, Goethe might have mournfully quoted Pope's couplet:

> "Condemned in business, as in life, to trudge
> Without a second, and without a judge."

...Goethe was able to read himself in Schiller, and understood himself from the reflection.

Tieck he considered, after Goethe's death, to be "incomparably the greatest living poet in Germany" (*Diary* etc., vol. III, p. 10).

There is much evidence in his Diary that Robinson was by no means disposed to keep his knowledge and opinions of German literature to himself; that he delighted to impart to others—even to Lamb, violently recalcitrant to German literature—the treasures to which he held the key; and although the range of his propagandist activity was limited, it was highly important, lying as it did about the very focus of the English intellectual world.

CHAPTER IV

Sir Walter Scott

THE interest of A. F. Tytler in German literature, resulting in 1792 in his translation of *Die Räuber*, may have contributed to arouse a similar interest in his young friend Walter Scott. At any rate, he seems to have encouraged an enterprise in which Scott and a group of friends combined in order to further their knowledge of the language and literature of Germany, attractive at that time by their very strangeness and inaccessibility[1].

It was before Christmas, 1792, the year in which he was called to the bar, that Scott with half-a-dozen congenial spirits formed a German class under the direction of Dr Willich, whose range of interests extended, as we have seen, from the universals of Kant's doctrines to the particulars of household management (see above, Chapter II). In his *Essay on Imitations of the Ancient Ballad*, Scott gives a cheerful account of the German class, which was carried on during the winters 1792–93 and 1793–94[2]. The neophytes did not approach their initiation into the German mysteries in any marked spirit of reverence, but rather with a desire to relieve the tedium of the early stages by as much incidental amusement as possible. Dr Willich, we infer, may have found the high spirits of his charges rather overwhelming. They were eager enough to learn, but not always agreed with their teacher as to the best means of attaining that end. He selected Gessner's *Tod Abels* as a suitably easy work for the beginners to essay their forces upon. They, however, "with one consent voted Abel an insufferable bore," and wished

[1] Lockhart, *Memoirs*, vol. I, pp. 174 ff. Willoughby (Modern Language Review, July–October 1921, p. 297) must I think be mistaken in asserting that A. F. Tytler was a member of the German class. That the class was composed of beginners appears almost certain from Scott's description of it, and it was formed towards the end of 1792: what should Tytler, who published his translation of *Die Räuber* in 1792, be doing "dans cette galère"? That he is not mentioned by Scott or Lockhart in this connection is further evidence to the same effect, if such be required.

[2] Lockhart, *Memoirs*, p. 191.

to begin at once with Goethe and Schiller and others whose
names had come to them with all the attraction of novelty
through Mackenzie's lecture. Willich predicted, says Gillies[1],
that "Mr Scott would never succeed, as he attempted to come
at once to the superstructure without laying a stable foundation." Indeed, as Scott tells us, being averse to the tedium of
learning grammatical rules, he fought his way to the knowledge
of German by his acquaintance with the Scottish and Anglo-
Saxon dialects, a method that no doubt accounts for the sometimes amusing inaccuracies of the *Götz* translation. "At
length," Scott concludes, "in the midst of much laughing and
little study, most of us acquired some knowledge, more or less
extensive, of the German language, and selected for ourselves,
some in the philosophy of Kant, some in the more animated
works of the German dramatists, specimens more to our taste
than the *Death of Abel*."

John Macfarlan of Kirkton, the Kantist of the party, does not
seem to have made much of his line of study[2], though we find
him at work on the transcendental philosophy in 1796, and
perhaps intending to write on the subject; for Miss Cranstoune,
in a letter to Scott from Montrose, tells him that "Erskine is in
London, my dear Thomson at Daily; Macfarlan hatching Kant."[3]
Both Thomas Thomson and William Erskine, to whom she
may be supposed to refer here, were members of the German
class; and Lockhart mentions the value to Scott of Erskine's
moderating influence in the matter of imitation of German
thought and style[4]. Neither Thomson nor Erskine appear to
have followed up their German studies to any discernible effect,

---

[1] Gillies, *Recollections*, p. 265.

[2] Stephen, *Studies of a Biographer*, vol. II, p. 46.

[3] The letter is undated in Lockhart. We can approximately date it by the
remark occurring in it: "Taylor's translation of your ballad is published."
Taylor's translation of *Lenore*, to which this of course refers, was first published in the Monthly Magazine of March 1796.

[4] Lockhart, *Memoirs*, vol. I, pp. 176–177. "I conceive there is no doubt
that his companionship was, even in those days, highly serviceable to Scott
as a student of the German drama and romance...He appears to have run
at first no trivial hazard of adopting the extravagances, both of thought and
language, which he found blended in their works with such a captivating
display of genius." Possibly Lockhart over-rated Scott's danger of becoming
unduly Romantic.

though they are described by Lockhart[1] as turning zealously to the popular literature of Germany. Erskine was promoted to the Bench as Lord Kinneder; Thomson devoted his energies to legal and antiquarian research; both remained among Scott's intimate friends[2].

The Edinburgh German class has a twofold interest historically: as a symptom of awakening interest in German literature in the minds of the rising generation, and as the basis of Scott's dealing with German literature. Considering Scott's early enthusiasm for the latter and the extent of his reading in the language, the limited amount of demonstrable German influence in his work is a matter of surprise. It is true that Brandl, and many commentators after him, have attributed such influence rather lavishly; but a close examination of many of the cases instanced leads, I think, to the conclusion that these writers have alleged influence unduly. Some of the instances will be discussed in detail later.

After making all necessary deductions from the exaggerated claims just referred to we shall, it is true, have occasion to note in Scott's writings the indubitable borrowing of elements in certain situations and characters from German originals. But it is noteworthy that where his borrowing has been most flagrant, as in the case of the White Lady of Avenel or of Fenella in *Peveril of the Peak*, he has, by his treatment of the elements borrowed, entirely changed the character that belonged to the originals; what he has borrowed is little more than some details of the material form in which the spirit of Undine or of Mignon is incarnate. Nor can it be said of Scott, at any rate in the instances just mentioned, that in transforming these materials he lent them an additional grace and finish. He is rather like the barbarian who steals images from the temples of Greece and hacks them into a likeness of his own crude conceptions. Such

[1] Lockhart, *Memoirs*, vol. I, p. 175.
[2] Haney (*Americana Germanica*, vol. IV) in his excellent review of *German Literature in England before* 1790, makes too much perhaps of the scope and importance of the German class when he speaks of "The organization of the Edinburgh coterie which undertook the study of German during the last decade of the century." In these terms we hardly recognise our waggish law-students.

a procedure would not be quoted to prove the influence of classical culture upon the barbarian, though it would be evidence that he had been brought into contact with it, and such contact might not be devoid of effects upon his general outlook and conduct. Without wishing to imply that the relative cultural inferiority of the barbarian to classical civilisation is to be transferred by analogy to Scott's situation with regard to German literature, I think that in the latter case also the chief influence must not be sought in what he has borrowed and adapted to his use; it may rather be deduced from the main lines of Scott's German reading. We notice that the vast majority of books in his German collection, numbering over 300 volumes, are of antiquarian and folk-lore interest (see Appendix 1, *Scott's German Books*). The intellectual and literary revival in Germany at the end of the eighteenth and beginning of the nineteenth century had little meaning for him save in so far as it supplied him with materials for the study of customs and manners of past ages, or with models for their treatment in fiction.

This was, it appears to me, the essential, almost the sole point of Scott's contact with German literature where influence made itself seriously felt. Nor is this surprising; for if it be admitted that, as was claimed in the Preface, the way for influence must be prepared by previous tendencies in the consciousness influenced, we shall be inclined, in applying this principle to Scott, to consider that German literature and thought could scarcely affect him in any other way. Apart from his enthusiasm for Bürger's *Lenore*—and that at an early date, before his characteristics as a man and a writer were fully determined—there is little to show that his intellectual and imaginative trend ran in any sense parallel to the lines of philosophic and aesthetic inquiry of Schiller and Goethe or to that conception of consciousness as the mere daylit fringe of the total personality which is implicit in Romanticism. Scott, in his attitude to life, belongs much rather to the eighteenth century than to the Romantic Revival. His use of Romantic machinery rather confirms than invalidates this view; for when he departs from the rationalistic conception he does so with a self-conscious effort and a clumsy effect as remarkable as the ease with which he moves on the superficies of the rational world; to plunge beneath the surface, a spontaneous action with the German Romantics, is for him an operation requiring a diving-bell or other apparatus which takes him indeed to a certain depth but cuts him off, as a condition of his safe descent and return, from all contact with the life that has its being in the insecure and twilit regions.

Let us see how far the ascertainable facts of Scott's dealings with German literature confirm this opinion.

We have seen how Scott first plunged into the study of the German language, with more audacity and enthusiasm perhaps than skill and perseverance. By 1794 he had attained, it may be supposed, at least a certain facility in reading the language. It was in the course of this year, or early in the year following[1], that Scott made his spirited translation of Bürger's ballad *Lenore*. *Lenore*, which was first printed in 1773 in the *Göttinger Musenalmanach* for 1774, did not begin its career of popularity in England for many years. To William Taylor of Norwich belongs the credit of its discovery and of its earliest known translation (in some respects an adaptation); this was not published till 1796, in the Monthly Review of March. Taylor, however, by his own account[2], had written the translation in 1790. We may safely assume that before long it was known and admired in the Norwich circle; in 1794 Mrs Barbauld carried a copy with her on her visit to the Athens of the North[3]. We have already seen that in the year 1796 appeared four other translations of Bürger's ballad (see above, p. 48). A sixth translation,

---

[1] For a discussion of the date of the *Lenore*-reading, see Appendix II.

[2] Robberds, *Memoir*, vol. 1, p. 91.

[3] There are other good reasons for supposing that Taylor's *Lenore* translation was known and discussed previously to 1796. Robberds tells us that William Taylor's earliest productions were either privately printed or circulated in MS among his friends. The Monthly Review (July 1796, p. 322) speaks of Bürger's *Lenore* as having been "known in this country at least some years," which knowledge, in the absence of any other known source, we may fairly attribute to Taylor's version; and the Monthly Review adds: "We recollect that Dr Aikin, in his poems published in 1791, has taken the hint of a tale from this very piece, which he mentions to have come to his knowledge by means of the translation of a friend, since published, as we understand, in a new magazine." The reference to Taylor and to the Monthly Magazine, which began to appear in 1796, is clear.

said to be the most faithful, by the Rev. J. Beresford, appeared in 1800. Brandl[1] gives a list of parodies and hostile comments on the poem. In the years between 1796 and 1800 the clatter of Lenore's demon-horse sounded furiously through Britain.

To return to Scott's contribution to the popularity of *Lenore*. In 1794 Mrs Barbauld visited Edinburgh. Anna Letitia Barbauld, author of educational works, and a person of some celebrity in her time, was the sister of that Dr Aikin who heard of *Lenore* from William Taylor, and borrowed a theme from the poem (see note 3, p. 65). At a party at Dugald Stewart's house, she produced a copy of Taylor's *Ellenore* (the rendering of Bürger's ballad), and read it to the assembled company, who were "electrified"; Scott was not present[2]. A friend of Scott's, Mr Cranstoun, Stewart's brother-in-law, or his sister Miss Cranstoun, gave Scott an account of the reading, and recited the lines:

> Tramp! tramp! along the land they rode,
> Splash! splash! along the sea!

which, recurring in several stanzas of the poem, and being striking in themselves, had been remembered by his informant. Scott was fired by this account of Taylor's version with a strong wish to see the original; but it proved no easy matter to obtain it. At last his relative and friend, Mrs Scott of Harden, a lady of German descent, procured for him a copy of Bürger's works from Hamburg. After reading the ballad in German he lost no time in setting about a translation. "I well recollect that I began my task after supper, and finished it about daybreak next morning."[3] A few copies of the poem were privately printed[4]. His translation having met with a pleasing reception among his friends, he translated Bürger's *Wilde Jäger*, and "balladized one or two other poems of Bürger" according to his own account[5];

---

[1] In Schmidt, *Charakteristiken*, Berlin, 1886, pp. 246–247.

[2] By his own testimony, vide *Imitations of the Ancient Ballad* (*Minstrelsy*, vol. IV, p. 38), and the Introduction to *The Chase and William and Helen* (2nd edition, Edinburgh, 1807). Carré is therefore mistaken in asserting the contrary (see *Goethe en Angleterre*, p. 37, note).

[3] Scott, *Imitations*, p. 39.

[4] According to Captain Basil Hall, they were printed by Scott's friends as a surprise for the author (Hall, *Schloss Hainfeld*, p. 332).

[5] Scott, *Imitations*, p. 40.

but so far as I know, only the two just mentioned have been preserved. In 1796 he published the two ballads anonymously, under the title: *The Chase and William and Helen*; a second edition, this time with the author's name, appeared in 1807. From both Scott and Lockhart we learn that this first venture in publicity met with no striking success outside his circle of friends, partly at least on account of the numerous other translations of *Lenore* with which it had to compete, a handicap which Scott himself points out[1].

The Monthly Review, noticing the book at some length in its issue of May 1797, considers Scott and Taylor perhaps the most meritorious translators of Bürger. In spite of the comparative failure of the translation, it is probably of some importance in the history of Scott's development as a writer. He had tasted, in however slight a measure, of literary fame, and having done not ill, he felt the inclination and the power to prove that he could do better. Although some years were to pass before he found his way to any considerable quantity of original production, translation continued to afford him the satisfaction of literary effort, and his pen acquired facility in the exercise.

It was difficult at this time (about 1796) to procure books from the Continent; but his friend Mrs Scott obtained for him copies of the works of Goethe, Schiller and other German writers. George Constable contributed Adelung's German Dictionary. And apparently it was about this time[2] that his opportunities for extending his acquaintance with German literature were suddenly increased by his introduction to James Skene, a young man who, according to Lockhart, had just returned from

[1] idem and Lockhart, *Memoirs*, vol. I, p. 222. Gillies (*Memoirs*, p. 227) seems to be under the impression that Scott's translation of *Lenore* was the earliest and that it met with considerable success.

[2] In 1796 or 1797. Skene, in his *Memories of Sir Walter Scott*, gives 1794 as the date of his return from Germany; Lockhart (*Memoirs*, vol. I, p. 224) places it about the beginning of 1797. Scott, in the Introduction to Canto IV of *Marmion*, which is addressed to Skene, and was written about November 1807 (Lockhart, *Memoirs*, vol. I, p. 472), speaks of their having known each other well for eleven years. Skene wrote more than thirty years after the event, and there are inaccuracies in his account which incline us to accept his statements with reserve. 1796 would seem a likely date; with their common interest in German literature it seems improbable that their acquaintance should have remained for long a merely casual one.

Germany, where he had been living for some years in order to complete his education. Scott, hearing that he had brought back with him a collection of German books, was eager to make his acquaintance, and persuaded a mutual friend to introduce him, "The objects of his research," says Skene[1], "were there before him in a goodly range of German volumes, comprehending works of most of the German authors then in repute; they soon fixed his attention, and became the subject of our conversation...". Skene, according to Lockhart, had a thorough knowledge of the German language, and was of great assistance to Scott in his studies.

Thus armed, he became a "bold and daring reader, nay, even translator, of various dramatic pieces."[2] Of these longer unpublished translations we have certain record in three cases only: Jakob Maier's *Fust von Stromberg*, Babo's *Otto von Wittelsbach* and Iffland's *Mündel*, all to be placed in the years 1796–97[3] (v. Appendix III, Scott's unpublished Translations). Having exercised his "prentice hand" in this way, he undertook a task of greater importance, the translation of *Götz von Berlichingen*. He was engaged on this translation in 1798 or earlier, since M. G. Lewis was negotiating with the bookseller Bell for its publication in January 1799. It was published in the following February[4].

Erskine had introduced Scott to Matthew Gregory Lewis, who not only thus obligingly acted as a literary agent to Scott, but also enlisted him as a collaborator in his projected collection of translations and imitations of the more nerve-racking productions of Germany, which was subsequently to appear under the title *Tales of Wonder*. Lewis does not belong to Scott's group of friends, but to the literary, or semi-literary, semi-

---

[1] *The Skene Papers*, p. 3.

[2] Scott, *Imitations*, p. 42.

[3] For the dates I have followed the *Catalogue of the Library of Abbotsford*, p. 104, which agrees with the probabilities. For the rectification of titles and authors of the German originals (see Appendix III) my authority is A. R. Hohlfeld, *Studien zur vergleichenden Literaturgeschichte*, 1903, p. 500.

[4] Lockhart, *Memoirs*, vol. I, p. 256, and Scott, *Imitations*, pp. 27 ff. Apparently Lewis had not troubled to ascertain Scott's Christian name, as the author appears on the title-page as *William* Scott. See also Robberds, *Memoir*, vol. II, pp. 533 ff.

fashionable circles of London. But his rather pestilent activity in connection with German literature coincides with Scott's period of closest German study, and his momentary relations with Scott may serve as a pretext to say here as much as need be said of him.

Lewis is the typical representative of the love of crude sensationalism which characterises the first outburst of enthusiasm for German literature in England. Completing his education in Germany, where he met Goethe, he was irresistibly drawn towards the inferior productions of German literature, some of which he set about translating or adapting. His first and most notorious literary effort was the novel *The Monk* (1795), which rivalled the *Schauerromane* in its accumulation of extravagance and horror. The immense popularity of the novel taught "Monk" Lewis, as he was henceforth very generally called, how nearly the public taste coincided with his own, and he continued for the next fifteen years to gratify it abundantly. Besides collections such as the *Tales of Wonder*, *Tales of Terror* (1801), *Feudal Tyrants* (1807), *Romantic Tales* (1808), he produced several translations or adaptations of Kotzebue's plays, a novel and melodrama after Zschokke's *Abällino*, and other specimens of original or borrowed *diablerie*, to use the not unapt if bastard term current at that time. In adapting *Kabale und Liebe* under the title *The Minister* he showed better taste. Lewis, in pandering to the desire for German sensationalism or German sentimentality in its debased forms, contributed no doubt to bring about the disrepute which attached so long to German literature in England. We shall meet him again, however, in a more honourable rôle, entertaining Byron and Shelley with an account of *Faust* and extempore translations from it. Scott, it may be noted[1], speaks rather favourably of Lewis's imitations of German ballads, such as his Lenore-imitation, *Alonzo and Imogen*, which occurs in *The Monk*. But the modern reader will agree rather with Coleridge's verdict: "New metres, such as have been attempted of late in e.g. 'Alonzo and Imogen,' and others borrowed from the German...(produce)...an effect not unlike that of galloping over a paved road in a German stage-wagon

[1] Lockhart, *Memoirs*, vol. I, p. 256, and Scott, *Imitations*, pp. 27 ff.

without springs."[1] Lewis appears to have been an amiable creature in his social relations, and was philanthropically interested in the condition of the slaves on his West Indian property, which he visited twice in order to secure humane treatment for the negroes.

Scott, replying in 1827 to a friendly letter from Goethe, in which the latter touched on his translation of *Götz von Berlichingen*, cited it as an instance of his "good taste and consummate assurance," in that he had overlooked "that it is necessary not only to be delighted with a work of genius, but to be well acquainted with the language in which it is written, before we attempt to communicate its beauty to others." This modesty is not misplaced. Scott's errors of translation in his *Götz* are sufficient to convince us that his method of learning German, if it had enabled him to grasp with ease the sense of a German text, had not given him that accurate knowledge of the tongue desirable in a translator[2].

In the same year (1799) another translation of *Götz* was given to the English public, that of Rose d'Aguilar. Neither the latter translation nor that of Scott met with any success.

But no doubt the public reception of Scott's translation was of less importance in the history of literature than the effect of the enterprise on the author. The general view that *Götz von Berlichingen* helped to determine the character of Scott's subsequent literary work is confirmed, it appears to me, by the similarity of manner of Scott's evocation of the past and that of Goethe in *Götz*[3]. The attempt to draw aside the veil of years

[1] Coleridge, *Biographia*, vol. II, p. 28.

[2] For some errors in Scott's translation, and for arbitrary changes made by him in the text, to suit his own taste or that of his readers, see Brandl, *Goethe-Jahrbuch*, Dritter Band (1882), pp. 63 ff. The translation of *Götz von Berlichingen* as printed in the Bell edition has been revised by another hand.

[3] Gillies displays critical acumen unusual in him when estimating the effect of the translation on Scott: "There is every reason to believe that the *Goetz of Berlichingen* had more influence in disposing his mind for the course which he afterwards pursued than any other production, either foreign or domestic, which fell in his way...Here, at least, was a real and well-known historical hero of the olden time—a man whose character was so far from being fabulous, that he has left his own very curious autobiography—and without the slightest departure from the realities of life, brought out in a manner till then unprecedented in modern art." Gillies, *Recollections*, Fraser's Magazine, 1835, pp. 265–266.

and show us a past epoch in something of the detail of its customs, manners and speech was a novel undertaking at the time *Götz* was written. The antiquarian details, which contributed to the interest and convincingness of Goethe's drama, are much more incidental there, as elsewhere in his work, than in Scott's romances in verse and prose. The realisation of the literary effects to be derived from such local, or chronological colour, combined with his antiquarian leanings, induced Scott to seize upon and develop this characteristic, which became in his work of predominating importance.

Apart from this general influence, much has been said of direct adaptation by Scott of themes and characters from *Götz von Berlichingen*. To begin with those imitations which cannot be regarded as accidental, the Vehmgericht motive (*Götz*, Act v) recurs in the *House of Aspen* (written probably 1800) and in *Anne of Geierstein* (1829). Scott's interest in this romantic tribunal is shown further by the presence in his library of at least four works on the subject[1]. The scene in *Ivanhoe* (II, chapter VI) where Rebecca describes to the wounded hero the progress of the attack on the castle of Front-de-Boeuf reminds us of the scene in *Götz* (Act III) where a man-at-arms performs a like service for Selbitz. The resemblance, as pointed out by Abramczyk, who makes a detailed comparison of the original and the imitation[2], is very close and extends to verbal similarities. We may note the resemblance to another German original, emphasised by the quotation from Schiller's *Maid of Orleans* at the head of the chapter in which the scene occurs:

> Ascend the watch-tower yonder, valiant soldier;
> Look on the field, and say how goes the battle.

Since the appearance of Professor Brandl's essay on *Die Aufnahme von Goethes Jugendwerke in England*[3], it has been

---

[1] C. P. Kopp, *Über die Verfassung der heimlichen Gerichte in Westphalen*, 8vo, Göttingen, 1794. Paul Wigand, *Das Femgericht Westphalens*, etc., 8vo, Hamm, 1825. Dr Ludwig Tross, *Sammlung merkwürdiger Urkunden für die Geschichte des Femgerichts*, 8vo, Hamm, 1826. Loève-Veimars, *Précis de l'histoire des Tribunaux secrets, dans le Nord de l'Allemagne*, etc., Paris, 1824.

[2] Abramczyk, *Über die Quellen zu Walter Scott's Roman: Ivanhoe*. Inaugural-Dissertation, Halle a. S., 1903, pp. 113–114.

[3] *Goethe-Jahrbuch*, Dritter Band, 1882.

customary to attribute to *Götz* considerable influence of detail on the *Lay of the Last Minstrel* (1805) and *Marmion* (1808)[1]. Of the *Lay of the Last Minstrel* Brandl says:

Trotz des engen Anschlusses an alte Traditionen und historische Details, welche die zahlreichen Anmerkungen dokumentieren sollen, zeigen die Grundzüge der Fabel und der Charactere unverkennbare Ähnlichkeit mit dem *Götz*. Das ganze dreht sich um die Belagerung eines Schlosses durch Übermacht. Ritter Deloraine, der Hauptvertheidiger, hat zwar nicht die gemüthvollen Seiten des Götz, aber er hat sich ebenso Gewaltthätigkeit und Selbsthilfe zu Schulden kommen lassen, und ebenso muss er trotz seiner Streitlust thatenlos unter Frauenpflege liegen, während draussen die Feinde die Mauern umschliessen. Die übrigen Vertheidiger sind tapfere Freiheitskämpfer und wollen von Übergabe anfangs nichts wissen. An ihrer Spitze steht die Schlossbesitzerin, an Unerschrockenheit und weiblicher Hoheit ein Abbild der Elisabeth. Ihr Sohn, der einziger Knabe im Epos, erinnert an den Knappen Georg; denn trotz seiner Jugend beschäftigt er sich am liebsten mit Speeren und Rossen, so dass ihm ergraute Soldaten grossen Kriegsruhm prophezeien. Aber, trotz aller Kühnheit muss sich die Besatzung allmählich zu einem Vertrage bequemen, welcher allerdings nicht, wie im *Götz*, auf Urfehde hinausläuft, sondern auf ein Turnier. Kaum ist er geschlossen, so erscheint ungeahnter Ersatz; vielleicht ein Anklang an die zeitgemässe Hilfsleistung des treuen Sickingen. — Neben diesen kriegerischen Ereignissen spielt auch eine Liebesepisode: das sanfte Schlossfräulein ist in einen Feind des Hauses verliebt und erklärt sich, gleich der Maria im Goethe'schen Drama, in einer zärtlichen Scene bereit ihm die Hand zu reichen, um dadurch die Zwietracht der Familien in Freundschaft zu verwandeln. Allein da sich hier der Liebende nicht flatterhaft, sondern ritterlich ehrenhaft bewährt, also kein Contrast zwischen einem biederen Götz und einem wortbrüchigen Weislingen zu zeichnen war, steht diese Episode in keinem inneren Zusammenhange und verräth sich dadurch um so gewisser als geborgt. So hat Scott den allgemein menschlichen Rahmen für seine glänzenden romantischen Detailschilderungen in wesentlichen dem *Götz* entlehnt, und selbst die Compositionsweise erinnert an den letzteren; denn die Handlung entwickelt sich nicht in ruhigem epischem Fluss, sondern ruckweise, in sceneartigen Situationsbildern.

I have quoted the above passage *in extenso* because it appears

---

[1] As, for instance, J. M. Carré, in *Goethe en Angleterre* (pp. 40 ff.), who in the main follows Brandl.

to me that, in spite of the weight lent to it by Brandl's name, many of its statements will not bear scrutiny without losing the evidential value which they may seem, in his presentation, to possess. Scott, as we know, and as is apparent from the Notes to the *Lay*, was steeped at this time in the history and tradition of the Border; and the siege of Branksome is an incident of a type of such common occurrence in the history of this region that the choice of it by Scott was not necessarily influenced by *Götz*; at most one can say that a recollection of the siege in *Götz* may have been a factor in his choice. The outlawry of Götz and of Deloraine, taken in connection with the sieges of Branksome and of Jaxthausen by the forces of law and order, may indeed be regarded as a probable reminiscence of the situation in *Götz*. But this is at most one *Grundzug* of the poem; the Gilpin Horner incidents and the *gramarye* theme are of more importance. The Lady of Branksome has little in common with Elizabeth; can we imagine the latter dabbling in black magic? Yet this, and a certain masculine courage which was a marked attribute of the historical original of Scott's Lady of Branksome, are her leading characteristics in the poem (see Scott's Note IX to the *Lay*). Margaret's relation to Cranstoun has, I think, no close analogy to that of Maria to Weislingen; that a maid should love one who is of the opposite faction to that of her friends and relatives is a theme as old as Romeo and Juliet, or Troilus and Cressida. George, the half-grown hero of *Götz*, would not be flattered by the resemblance imagined between him and the high-spirited urchin of six or seven years of age, who capers round the hall at Branksome with a broken spear for a charger. Of course Scott may have remembered George in tracing the likeness of the heir of Branksome, but I submit that there is nothing whatever to show that he did so. With regard to the manner of composition, in short scenes and incidents, Scott in his preface seems to attribute it to the imitation of the ancient metrical romance; Professor Brandl's supposition that it is imitated from the episodic manner of *Götz* is therefore superfluous[1].

[1] From the Preface to the *Lay*: "As the description of scenery and manners was more the object of the author than a combined and regular narrative,

The influence of *Götz* on *Marmion* is even more problematical. In the fifth stanza of Canto First we have a description of Marmion which makes it extremely improbable that his character or behaviour will coincide, in more than the most fortuitous and fleeting manner with those of Weislingen; and this proves to be the case. To say that he is Weislingen, "nur energischer und grossartiger," as does Brandl (loc. cit., p. 69), is an assertion that appears to me erroneous. Can one trait in Marmion's character be cited which places him, with Weislingen, in a special category of humanity? He is faithless to his love; but this is not a characteristic so uncommon as to require a particular explanation; and the relation of Marmion to women is as different as possible from that of Weislingen. Of Marmion Scott says:

> If e'er he loved (Weislingen!) 'twas her alone
> Who died within that vault of stone.
> *Marmion*, Canto v, xxviii.

His relation to Constance and Clare is quite unlike that of Weislingen to Maria and Adelheid; he woos Clare for her lands (Canto v, xxviii); Constance, whom "he loved alone," he had betrayed from ambition. A woman who has reason to hate him ministers to him in his last moments, as Maria ministers to Weislingen; this may not be an accidental resemblance; but it is not a very striking one, the other circumstances of his death being so totally different; and at any rate it is a resemblance limited to one feature of one incident in a poem full of incidents. To say that Marmion dies "halb in Weislingens, halb in Götzens Art," appears to me a very forced interpretation of the death-scene[1]. The resemblance between the scene where Eustace and

the plan of the Ancient Metrical Romance was adopted, which allows greater latitude in this respect than would be consistent with the dignity of a regular Poem."

[1] Professor Brandl maintains his contention as follows: "Schliesslich wird Marmion verwundet und muss sterben, halb in Weislingens, halb in Götzens Art. Einerseits nämlich taucht in ihm der quälende Gedanke an seine verlassene Geliebte auf, er glaubt sie zu sehen wie Weislingen den Geist Marias [Weislingen takes Maria for the ghost of Maria; Marmion, seeing Clare as he lies wounded, is uncertain for a moment, in his stunned condition, whether it is Constance or Clare that he sees; a very different matter]; alle haben ihn verlassen, nur seine zweite Geliebte, die schwer beleidigte Clare, ist in den letzten Augenblicken bei ihm [Clare, as we have seen, was not a Geliebte

Blount watch the battle and that in the third Act of *Götz* where Selbitz asks for news of the fight and of Götz, also cited by Professor Brandl (loc. cit., p.69) is too general, perhaps, for us to conclude with confidence that there has been imitation[1].

Scott was possibly influenced by reminiscences of *Götz* in some of the broad outlines of the *Lay of the Last Minstrel*, and a few resemblances of detail between *Götz* and the *Lay* and *Marmion* may not be accidental: more than this cannot, I think, be profitably affirmed on the subject.

After publishing his translation of *Götz von Berlichingen* Scott did not venture immediately on original production in the fullest sense of the term; he composed, probably in the following year (1800), a drama, *The House of Aspen*, which he styles, in his Advertisement to the piece (written in 1829), a rifacimento of Veit Weber's[2] *Heilige Vehme*, and in a letter of 1811[3], "a sort of a half-mad German tragedy." This work remained for the present in MS. It was not published till 1829, when it appeared in Heath's *Keepsake*. *The House of Aspen*, as Petri points out, marks the transition from translation to original production[4]. The period of his more intensive pre-occupation

---

at all for Marmion, but courted solely for her wealth], sie klärt ihn über die Folgen seiner Untreue auf, sie bittet er, für ihn zu beten [where, in the midst of his cursing frenzy, does he ask Clare to pray for him?]. Andererseits ist auch der unerschütterte Kampfesmuth des Götz in ihm, und schon ausathmend reckt er sich noch einmal auf [no, he only waves his broken sword above his head] und ruft 'Victory, victory!' Man sieht, wie sich die Nachklänge des Goethe'schen Dramas in Scott's Gedächtnis verwirrten und verdunkelten" [which seems to imply that there are a number of themes from Götz appearing, recognisable though blurred, in *Marmion*: I think that I have shown above that Professor Brandl does not prove this. I have passed over one or two further instances adduced by Professor Brandl, not, I think, more conclusive than those discussed (see Brandl, *Goethe-Jahrbuch*, Dritter Band, 1882, pp. 68–70).]

[1] Lockhart however almost certainly refers to this scene (as appears from the context) when he remarks (*Memoirs*, vol. I, p. 259): "But who does not recognise in Goethe's drama the true original of the death-scene of Marmion, and the storm in Ivanhoe?" The latter was conceded above; the former I am inclined to regard as a plausible guess.

[2] Scott invariably calls him Beit Weber—a relic of his slovenly method of learning German, which apparently led him to confuse German *v* and *b*.

[3] To Lady Abercorn, May 17, 1811. *Familiar Letters of Sir Walter Scott*, Edinburgh, 1894, p. 217.

[4] Dr A. Petri, *Über Walter Scott's Dramen* (1. Teil), *Jahresbericht über die Herzogliche Realschule zu Schmölln S.A.*, Schmölln, 1910.

with German literature may now be considered as drawing to an end; at any rate, the evidence that he is busied with it is scanty henceforth. Before examining it, we will deal briefly here with minor translations, including a few published subsequently to 1800.

Frederic and Alice, together with another poem by Scott, *The Fire-King*, was published in Lewis's *Tales of Wonder* (1801). Scott tells us in a note to the former poem[1], that it is "imitated rather than translated from a fragment introduced in Goethe's *Claudina von Villa Bella*," that is, from *Der Untreue Knabe*[2]. *The Fire-King*, though placed by Scott's editors among the poems from the German, has not, I believe, been shown to derive from any German source[3]. Scott's account of its composition does not suggest that there was any German original in his mind when he wrote the ballad:

Lewis, who was very fond of his idea of four elementary kings, had prevailed on me to supply a Fire King. After being repeatedly urged to the task, I sat down one day after dinner, and wrote the "Fire King," as it was published in the *Tales of Wonder*...Dr Leyden, now no more, and another gentleman who still survives, were sitting at my side while I wrote; nor did my occupation prevent the circulation of the bottle[4].

The Erl-King, which also belongs to this period (between 1796 and 1800[5]), is a translation that has met with considerable

[1] Scott, *Poetic Works*, p. 653.
[2] Brandl, *Aufnahme*, p. 49, sees Lenore-influence in the line "starts the steed and snuffs the air," and in the ghostly chorus. I would concede the latter much rather than the former. The horse in *William and Helen* is itself ghostly, and does not snort from fear. Resemblances of this kind have no evidential value whatever, as far as I can see, though Brandl and others frequently adduce them. Such instances might be multiplied, but henceforth I will discuss only those that appear to have some importance.
[3] Hohlfeld (*Scott als Übersetzer*, p. 503) says: "Vielleicht gelingt es, eine deutsche Vorlage nachzuweisen." He is unacquainted with (or very properly ignores) Roesel's extraordinary assertion that *The Fire-King* is a *Verschmelzung* of *Lenore* and *Der Untreue Knabe* (Roesel, Ludwig Karl, *Beziehungen*, p. 50).
[4] Scott, *Imitations*, Appendix.
[5] It probably belongs to the summer or autumn of 1797. It is included with the direction: "To be read by a candle particularly long in the snuff," in a letter to Miss Rutherford, Ashestiel, no date, placed by Lockhart among letters of October 1797. Scott mentions in the letter that Lewis has already made a translation of the poem (Lockhart, *Memoirs*, vol. I, pp. 239–240).

favour from German critics (see Weddigen, *Geschichte der Einwirkungen* etc., p. 16, and Roesel, *Beziehungen*, p. 36). But compared with the original it is weak and mawkish, and it is disfigured by awkward rhythms and obvious sacrifices to rhyme. In the *Rhein-Wein Lied* ("What makes the trooper's frozen courage muster?") from *The House of Aspen*, Scott has imitated the metre, and two lines of the eighth stanza of the *Rheinweinlied* of Matthias Claudius. Scott was Quartermaster of the Royal Edinburgh Light Horse, and in 1799 wrote a *War-Song* for this troop; it was in the metre and was set to the music of C. F. D. Schubart's *Abschiedslied der nach Afrika ziehenden Soldaten*, which had been recited in his presence by James Skene[1]. The *Noble Moringer* appeared in the Edinburgh Annual Register for 1817[2]. It is a free translation of *Der edele Möringer* from the *Sammlung Deutscher Volkslieder* of Büsching and von der Hagen (Berlin, 1807). Scott gives the reference in his notes to the poem. *The Battle of Sempach* belongs to 1818. Scott, in a note, says that it is a literal translation of an original which appears in *Des Knaben Wunderhorn*[3].

With regard to another translation, which belongs to an earlier period, that of Goethe's *Klaggesang von der edlen Frauen des Asan Aga*, mentioned by Brandl[4] as having been included among the poems in the *Apology for Tales of Terror* (1799), I have had some difficulty in finding reliable references to it. It is not included in Logie Robertson's edition of Scott's Poetical Works (London, 1913), although the statement appears in the preface that "this Edition of the Poetical Works of Sir Walter Scott is believed to contain every known poem and fragment of verse that he wrote." Lockhart[5] has the following reference to it: "...he also versified at the same time [as the translations from Maier and Iffland, see p. 68] some lyrical fragments of Goethe, as, for example, the Morlachian Ballad, 'What yonder glimmers so white on the mountain,' and the

---

[1] Lockhart, *Memoirs*, vol. I, p. 296, and *Skene Papers*, p. 14.
[2] *Cambridge Hist. of English Lit.* vol. XII, p. 373.
[3] Hohlfeld (*Scott als Übersetzer*, p. 505) calls it a very exact translation. For details about Scott's error in attributing the German original to a nonexistent Albert Tschudi, see Hohlfeld, loc. cit. pp. 504–505.
[4] *Goethe's Jugendwerke*, p. 50.   [5] *Memoirs*, vol. I, p. 215.

song from *Claudina von Villa Bella.*" The latter has already been referred to. The Morlachian Ballad is evidently the *Klaggesang*, which has the indication following its title: "Aus dem Morlakischen," and the first four lines of which read as follows:

> Was ist Weisses dort am grünen Walde?
> Ist es Schnee wohl, oder sind es Schwäne?
> Wär' es Schnee, er wäre weggeschmolzen;
> Wären's Schwäne, wären weggeflogen.

In the *Scott Exhibition* (1871) *Catalogue* (W. Stirling-Maxwell) 1872, there is a reference to this translation. In the list of Original Manuscripts lent to the Exhibition, appears the notice on p. 123, under the date 1798:

283. The Lamentation of the Faithful Wife of the Asan Aga, from the Morlachian language. The Original Manuscript, 4to. Lent by Messers A. & C. Black. [The MS has since been presented to Mr D. Laing.] In twenty-seven stanzas, beginning—
> "What yonder glimmers so white on the mountain,
> Glimmers so white where yon sycamores grow?
> Is it wild swans round Vaga's fair fountain?
> Or is it a wreath of the wintry snow?"

This spirited translation from the German Ballad by Goethe has probably never been printed. The handwriting is about 1798, and the translation was well known to some of Scott's early friends...

The specimen given suggests that the translation was a free one. That the poem was included in the *Apology for Tales of Terror* (1799) we may perhaps infer from the fact that Ballantyne, who printed the dozen or so copies of the *Apology*, had expressed himself as being particularly charmed with the "Morlachian fragment after Goethe."[1] I do not find the *Apology for Tales of Terror* either in the Catalogue of the British Museum or in that of the Advocates' Library of Edinburgh[2].

---

[1] Lockhart, *Memoirs*, vol. I, p. 275.

[2] Lockhart (*Memoirs*, vol. I, p. 275): "I believe exactly twelve copies of William and Helen, The Fire-King, The Chase, and a few more of those pieces, were thrown off accordingly [by Ballantyne] with the title (alluding to the long delay of Lewis's collection) of Apology for Tales of Terror, 1799." (*Cambridge Hist. of English Lit.* vol. XII, p. 373): "*Apology for Tales of Terror,* Kelso, 1799. (Only about twelve copies printed. Includes his Bürger translations, and a few other ballads afterwards included in M. G. Lewis's *Tales of Wonder*, 1801)."

Scott's activity as a translator from German appears to have ceased almost entirely, as might be expected, from the moment when he found it possible to draw directly from his own stock of information and imagination for the purposes of literary production. But that he did not suffer what knowledge of German he possessed to lapse entirely, we may infer from the translations in 1817 and 1818, and from the dates of publication of many of the German books in the Library at Abbotsford, more than half of which are subsequent to 1800. It is fairly clear that his interest in German literature, especially where its themes approximated to his antiquarian interests, never entirely ceased, and that Gillies, who notes that "he always spoke with animation and pleasure of his early German studies"[1] is wrong in doubting "Whether his reading in the language extended much beyond those volumes which he translated before the year 1800."[2] His use of themes borrowed from German sources continues at intervals until close upon the end of his life.

In the Prefaces to the 1830 edition of his works Scott did not fail to acknowledge in some instances his indebtedness to German literature for situations and characters occurring in his writings.

These and some further instances which have been alleged may be briefly discussed here in chronological order. First may be mentioned the influence of the Harper's song in *Wilhelm Meister* on the opening scene of the Lay, instanced by Coleridge (see p. 132).

In *Old Mortality* (1816) occurs a detail of influence from Tieck to which Coleridge, and he alone so far as I know, calls attention. In a letter to Allsop, of April 8, 1820, he remarks: "I perceive from that passage in the *Old Mortality*, where Morton is discovered by Old Alice in consequence of calling his dog Elphin, that Walter Scott has been reading Tieck's Phantasies [sic; a mistake of the editor of the letters for *Phantasus?*] (a collection of faery or witch tales) from which both the incident and the name is borrowed."[3]

---

[1] Gillies, *Memoirs*, p. 265.   [2] Gillies, *Recollections*, p. 502.

[3] A. Turnbull, *Biographia Epistolaria*, London, 1911, p. 187. This refers doubtless to the incident in *Der blonde Eckbert*, where Walther, after listening to Berta's strange story of her life with the old woman, the bird and the dog,

In *Ivanhoe* (1819), vol. II, chap. VI, there is a reminiscence of *Götz von Berlichingen*, as well as of Schiller's *Jungfrau von Orleans*; this has been discussed above (see p. 71).

In *The Monastery* (1820) the White Lady is an unskilful adaptation of Fouqué's Undine. Scott in his Introduction remarks:

The ingenious Compte (sic) de la Motte Fouqué composed, in German, one of the most successful productions of his fertile brain, where a beautiful and even afflicting effect is produced by the introduction of a water-nymph, who loses the privilege of immortality[1] by consenting to become accessible to human feelings, and uniting her lot with that of a mortal who treats her with ingratitude. In imitation of an example so successful, the White Lady of Avenel was introduced into the following sheets.

"Introduced" seems correctly to describe the manner, singularly lacking spontaneity, in which the supernatural element is treated by Scott in *The Monastery*. In a note to vol. II, p. 324 (Border Edition of the Waverley Novels, London, 1893), Scott mentions that the "contrivance of provoking the irritable vanity of Sir Piercie Shafton, by presenting him with a bodkin, indicative of his descent from a tailor, is borrowed from a German romance by the celebrated Tieck, called Das Peter Manchen (sic; doubtless *Das Petermännchen* is intended) i.e. The Dwarf Peter"; Scott gives an outline of the story, with which I am not acquainted[2].

We discover, I think, a further detail of treatment borrowed

---

says on wishing her good-night: "...Ich kann mir Euch recht vorstellen, mit dem seltsamen Vogel, und wie Ihr den kleinen Strohmi füttert." Berta had not mentioned the dog's name, and Walther thus appears to be possessed, in some unaccountable way, with knowledge of Berta's past life. *Der blonde Eckbert* is one of the seven tales in the first volume of *Phantasus* (1812). The name of the dog here is Strohmi; but another of the tales in the collection is *Die Elfen*; perhaps Coleridge refers to this, and means that the incident is borrowed from *Der blonde Eckbert*, the name of the dog in *Old Mortality* from the title of this other story.

[1] This is an error, I think. Undine, when describing her race to Hildebrand, does not claim immortality for them; on the contrary, she alludes expressly to their death; and she wins a soul by wedding Hildebrand.

[2] Gillies, *Recollections*, Fraser's, 1835, p. 265: "I have heard him [Scott] speak with peculiar interest of the *Petermännchen*, a production of *diablerie*, which his own genius had probably invested with interest which no other reader could have discovered in it."

from *Undine*, if we compare Father Eustace's repeated impres
sion that a white figure haunts his path, and his subsequent
tracing of the fancy to some imperfectly-seen natural object,
and the similar experience of Undine's foster-father while
tending his nets: "Ja, als er die Augen nach dem Walde aufhob,
kam es ihm ganz eigentlich vor, als sehe er durch das Laubgitter
den nickenden Mann [Kühleborn, Undine's Uncle] hervor
kommen...". "...Der weisse, nickende Mann ward nämlich
urplötzlich zu einem ihm längst wohl bekannten Bächlein, das
schäumend aus dem Forste hervorrann, und sich in den Landsee
ergoss" [*Undine*, Erstes Kapitel]. In this instance Scott has,
I think, reproduced the effect suggested by the passage quoted
with skill and delicacy.

In *Kenilworth* (1821), chap. VII, is a scene which comparison
shows clearly to have been borrowed from Goethe's *Egmont*;
that, namely, in which Amy Robsart admires the Earl in his
magnificent court-dress, as does Klärchen the similar display
by her lover in *Egmont*, Act III. It has been affirmed by several
writers[1] that Scott was indebted to the astrological episodes in
Wallenstein for the astrological scene in *Kenilworth*, chap. XVIII.
Wolf claims that the figure of Seni in *Wallenstein* has contributed
to the formation of Leicester's Alasco. But in the absence of
any specific resemblances (and I do not find that any are adduced)
the suggestion does not appear worth much. Seni and Alasco
are different in character and situation: Alasco a charlatan, Seni
sincere; the relation of Alasco to Leicester by no means identical with that of Seni to Wallenstein. With regard to the
astrological theme in general, it could scarcely be missed by a
writer of historical romances. Scott has used astrological terms
and ideas in *Guy Mannering*. Although it is not impossible that
the scenes in *Wallenstein* called his attention to the literary
effects to be drawn from the subject of astrology, in the absence
of specific resemblances this can be no more than an idle
speculation.

In the Introduction to *Peveril of the Peak* (1825), Scott
remarks:

[1] Martin Wolf, *Walter Scott's Kenilworth*, 1903, p. 47. T. Rea, *Schiller's
Dramas*, p. 73. A. Brandl, *Coleridge*, p. 280.

The character of Fenella, which, from its peculiarity, made a favourable impression on the public, was far from being original. The fine sketch of Mignon, in Wilhelm Meister's Lehrjahre, a celebrated work from the pen of Goethe, gave the idea of such a being. But the copy will be found greatly different from my great prototype; nor can I be accused of borrowing anything, save the general ideas, from an author, the honour of his country, and an example to the authors of other kingdoms, to whom all must be proud to owe an obligation.

This is a handsome acknowledgment of his debt. It must be admitted that he made no remarkably successful use of the materials borrowed. Roesel[1] raises the question of the influence of Mignon on another character of Scott's, that of Annot Lyle in the *Legend of Montrose*. This is perhaps an extreme example of the lengths to which unfounded attribution of influence can be carried. Annot Lyle is eighteen; her features have "a playful yet simple expression" (Waverley Novels, Centenary Edition, vol. VI, chap. VI, p. 200); she seems "the gayest and happiest of maidens," "communicating to others the cheerfulness that filled her own mind." She is as different in temperament, then, as possible, from the *farouche* and variable Mignon. The only points of resemblance that I have discovered between her and Mignon are surely not peculiar to these two: her birth is shrouded in mystery, and she sings. The mystery of her birth, when revealed, has no striking analogy to that of Mignon.

In the *Doom of Devergoil* (1817–18: published 1830), Scott, according to Petri[2], used a theme borrowed from the story of Musaeus, *Stumme Liebe*, and acknowledges having done so in his preface.

We return to the exterior evidence of Scott's interest in German literature.

Towards 1807 he seems to have been reading German fiction, since in a letter to George Ellis, of February 23, 1808, he mentions that some time previously he had written him "a swinging epistle of and concerning German Romances, with

[1] *Beziehungen*, p. 78.
[2] Dr A. Petri, *Über Walter Scott's Dramen* (1. Teil), *Jahresbericht über die Herzogliche Realschule zu Schmölln S.A.*, Schmölln, 1910, p. 14.

some discoveries not of my own discovering."[1] Possibly his interest lapsed after this for a while. For some years to come I find small indication of it. The next reference by Scott to German literature that I have noted is in a letter to Lady Abercorn (*Familiar Letters of Sir Walter Scott*, vol. I, pp. 217–218) of May 17, 1811. In answer to some inquiry about an unpublished work of his (*The House of Aspen*) he says: "I do not know anything of a play of mine, my dear friend, unless it be a sort of a half-mad German tragedy which I wrote many years ago, when my taste was very green, and when, like the rest of the world, I was taken in by the bombast of Schiller." The year 1811 was in the midst of the period of discredit which befell German literature in England after its early triumphs. When Carlyle and others had helped to create a more reasonable public opinion, Scott allowed himself to revert to his earliest impression. In the Advertisement to *The House of Aspen* (dated April 1, 1829) he speaks of the days when "the magnificent works of Goethe and Schiller were for the first time made known to the British public, and received, as many now alive must remember, with universal enthusiasm." We can hardly doubt that it was the efforts of the later critics of German literature, and most directly no doubt those of his son-in-law Lockhart, that induced Scott to revise so thoroughly his opinion of Schiller.

In the Diary kept by him during his voyage to the Shetland Isles, from July to September 1814, a production where any preoccupations of the kind might be expected to leave traces, no reference to German literature is, *sauf erreur*, to be found[2].

In May 1818, Scott, meeting his future biographer F. G.

---

[1] Unfortunately I have not been able to find the letter here referred to. It might throw light on the state of Scott's opinion of German literature at this time, and give us a clearer idea of the direction and extent of his German reading.

[2] Lockhart (*Memoirs*, vol. II, p. 320) thinks that Scott was the author of the rhymed versions from the Niebelungenlied in Weber's *Illustrations of Northern Antiquities*, published in 1814. It seems probable that Scott's interest in German literature revived shortly after this time; not only have we the translations of 1817–18, and the German theme in the *Doom of Devergoil*, but R. P. Gillies suggests that his own first notions of the "inexhaustible mine of the richest ore" hidden in the German language, which induced him in 1816 to begin his "gropings in the dark after foreign literature," were obtained from Sir Walter Scott (Gillies, *Memoirs*, p. 217).

Lockhart, who had recently returned from a visit to Germany, talked with him about that country and its recent literature. He referred to Goethe as "his old master." In October of that year Lockhart was on a visit to Abbotsford. Scott borrowed his copy of *Faust*, "I believe in a more complete shape than he had before seen that masterpiece."[1] Scott was moved to admiration by the work, though he made some observations of an unfavourable nature on the *Prolog im Himmel* and the conclusion[2].

It may be supposed that Lockhart, who had but lately returned from Germany, and was afterwards to be counted among the defenders of Goethe in England[3], would stimulate Scott's interest in German literature. I can produce, however, little evidence to this effect beyond the fact that in *Ivanhoe*, *The Monastery*, *Kenilworth* and *Peveril of the Peak*, which belong to 1819, 1820, 1821 and 1823 respectively, there occur themes borrowed from German literature; whereas none are found, so far as I know, in the works published between 1810 and 1819.

[1] This clearly means *Faust, Erster Teil*, 1808, and suggests that Scott had previously read *Faust, Ein Fragment*, 1790, in which form alone the work appears in his library (v. Appendix I).

[2] Lockhart's account (*Memoirs*, vol. III, p. 222) of the effect of the *Faust*-reading is as follows: "When we met at breakfast, a couple of hours after [that is, after he had borrowed Lockhart's copy] he was full of the poem—dwelt with enthusiasm on the airy beauty of its lyrics, the terrible pathos of the scene before the *Mater Dolorosa*, and the deep skill shown in the various subtle shadings of character between Mephistopheles and poor Margaret. He remarked, however, of the Introduction (which I suspect was new to him) that blood would out—that consummate artist as he was, Goethe was a German, and that nobody but a German would ever have provoked a comparison with the book of Job, 'the grandest poem that ever was written.' He added that he suspected the end of the story had been left *in obscuro*, from despair to match the closing scene of our own Marlowe's Doctor Faustus." May it not be pertinent to inquire whether, if a German could provoke comparison with the "grandest poem ever written," he might not attempt to rival Marlowe? Either Lockhart's account or Scott's logic would seem at fault here.

[3] Lockhart was among those to whom Carlyle offered one of the four medals sent to him by Goethe in 1828 for distribution among the "Wohlwollenden." Carlyle, writing to Scott (April 13, 1828), to whom two further medals had been specially sent by Goethe through Carlyle, thus expresses himself on the subject of Lockhart: "Perhaps Mr Lockhart, whose merits in respect of German Literature, and just appreciation of this its patriarch and guide, are no secret, will do me the honour to accept of one" (*Journal of Sir Walter Scott*, New Edition, Edinburgh, 1891, p. 901). No study of Lockhart's relation to German literature has yet been made, so far as I know, though it would seem that he played a not unimportant part in the period of reviving interest subsequent to 1818.

In 1819 he waxes very enthusiastic about Fouqué's *Undine*, and even thinks of dramatising it, as we gather from a letter to Daniel Terry of November 10[1].

In 1827 he wrote a long paper on E. T. A. Hoffmann, containing a not very liberal estimate of his genius. He notes at this time in his Diary (May 5, 1827), while he is "working away upon those wild affairs of Hoffmann," that he thinks he has forgotten his German very much, which suggests that for some time before this he had allowed his interest in German literature to lapse. In this same year he was flattered by the reception of a letter from Goethe "which I must have read to me," he remarks in his Diary of February 20, 1827; "for though I know German, I have forgot their written hand." Goethe he now thinks "a wonderful fellow—the Ariosto at once, and almost the Voltaire of Germany[2]. Who could have told me thirty years ago I should correspond and be on something like an equal footing with the author of the Goetz?"

In 1828, writing to a young man of the name of Gordon, to whom he had shown helpful kindness, he gives him some advice on translating *Die Fahrten Thiodolfs des Isländers*, by Fouqué, a copy of which he sends him.

Finally, in 1831, in his Diary, he speaks of reading "stupid German novels in hopes a thought will strike me when I am half occupied with other things." He had hoped to see Goethe on his return journey from Malta, but Goethe's life closed before his wish could be fulfilled, and Scott had barely reached his home a few months later when he too died.

Regarding as a whole Scott's relation to German literature, we can hardly consider it to have been such that its influence upon him, in any full and general sense, can be named wide or

---

[1] Lockhart, *Memoirs*, vol. III, p. 331. In a letter to Terry of January 1823, he gives the names of some German writers whose works would be suitable for translation: Musaeus, Fouqué, and, as he invariably calls him, *Beit* Weber. He suggests that a translator should use his discretion in treating passages containing "affectation of deep metaphysical reflexion and protracted description and discussion."

[2] An echo, I suppose, of Madame de Staël's remark on Wieland: "In his prose writings he bears some resemblance to Voltaire, and in his poetry to Ariosto." *Germany*, by the Baroness Staël Holstein. Translated from the French. 3 vols. London, 1813, pp. 235–236. As applied to Goethe, the remark does not seem apt.

deep. The decisive moment of the influence is that of his translation of *Götz*, which, as Gillies remarks[1], was "a spark to kindle the train." After the period (ca. 1792–1800) of somewhat intensive pre-occupation with certain of its productions, and those, to judge by the works selected by him for translation, not representative of its noblest development, he becomes, as far as we can judge, a desultory reader in German literature. His knowledge of the language was at no time scholarly. Of German literature as a whole he can hardly be said to have known anything. It is probably fairly clear from the evidence given above that his German reading was not directed at any time towards the acquiring of a sound knowledge of the literature, but was guided merely by some curiosity about that part of it that was becoming celebrated among his countrymen, and by a more personal attraction and sympathy for works which chimed with his own antiquarian and folk-lore interests. Even here it is perhaps rather the subject-matter than the manner of treatment which interests him. German literature exploited the Middle Ages earlier and with more determination than did English literature, and in so far as it dealt with the concrete detail of medieval life and custom, might be profitably investigated for information. But the particular use made of the Middle Ages by the Romantics in Germany, as of a world sufficiently remote from latter-day pre-occupations to serve as a background for the play of the deeper forces of mind and of nature, was completely alien to Scott's inclinations. It is true that he admired *Undine*; it would be difficult for an informed literary taste to refrain from doing so; but we see what the theme borrowed from this tender masterpiece becomes at his hands in *The Monastery*: a grotesque and clumsy decorative effect.

Save in his early phase of enthusiasm he hardly appears to have troubled at any time to form an independent judgment even of such portions of German literature as were well known to him. His estimate of their value seems to fluctuate with the tides of general opinion, though in one instance, not mentioned above, he forestalled it: this was in his appreciation of Coleridge's translation of *Wallenstein*, from which he frequently quoted in his chapter-headings.

[1] Gillies, *Recollections*, p. 263.

The remarkable change in his estimate of Schiller has already been noticed (p. 83), and I suggested that here he had simply adopted the view of better informed and more enthusiastic contemporaries. Nor do we find him expressing any opinion of Goethe that shows much independence of appreciation. Brandl[1] goes too far in suggesting that Scott's feelings for Goethe were characterised by a constant admiration and gratitude. Bernays[2] points out that he never attempted to grasp Goethe's work as a whole, and had no notion of the significance of *Faust*. Although we find him occasionally expressing admiration for Goethe, the testimony of Edward Cheney, who talked with Scott at Rome in 1832, about Goethe among other matters, shows that it was not whole-hearted, at any rate at that time.

He spoke of Goethe with regret; he had been in correspondence with him before his death, and had purposed visiting him at Weimar in returning to England...He did not seem to be, however, a great admirer of some of Goethe's works. Much of his popularity, he observed, was owing to pieces which, in his latter moments, he might have wished recalled. He spoke with much feeling. I answered that he must derive great consolation in the reflection that his own popularity was owing to no such cause[3].

The personal relation of Scott to German literature being, as I have shown above, in the main uncritical and confined chiefly to a narrow range of specialised interests, we shall not look to find him effective in spreading the knowledge of German literature in England, at least after 1800, when his main activity as a translator reaches its term. The published writings of his in which German literature is commented upon (as the Prefaces

[1] Brandl, *Goethe's Jugendwerke*, p. 70.
[2] Michael Bernays, *Schriften zur Kritik und Litteraturgeschichte*, vol. 1, pp. 90 ff.
[3] Lockhart, *Memoirs*, vol. v, pp. 414–415. Scott's answer, as reported by Mr Cheney, was: "It *is* a comfort to me to think that I have tried to unsettle no man's faith, to corrupt no man's principle, and that I have written nothing which on my death-bed I should wish blotted." A similar source of consolation is open, no doubt, to many writers: for instance, to the anonymous authors of Bradshaw's Railway Guide. But the assertion of one's own sense of blamelessness, harmless in itself, becomes ungracious when used to point the contrast between oneself and a brother-author less fortunate in this respect. Perhaps we may venture to hope that Cheney has reported Scott incorrectly.

to the 1830 edition of his works, the Essays on *E. T. A. Hoffmann* and on *Ballad Poetry*) are subsequent to 1826, when the topic of German literature was already becoming familiar to the English public. The extent to which he imparted interest in German literature to those with whom he was in a personal relation cannot be very accurately gauged in the present state of our information. We should expect it to be considerable before 1800 at any rate, and probably for some years after that. It seems probable that R. P. Gillies was originally attracted to German literature by hearing Scott talk about it.

To sum up, Scott's connection with German literature strikes us as rather incidental. He obtained from it guidance in the direction of his great talents as a writer, and returned to it for further hints, and for information along certain lines. But save in this narrow field of his interests, it had little meaning for him, and he appears to have had no intelligent appreciation of its greatest productions.

CHAPTER V

Samuel Taylor Coleridge (1772–1834)

"THERE is no doubt," says Henry Crabb Robinson, writing to Mrs Clarkson on November 29, 1811[1], "that Coleridge's mind is much more German than English." He adds that a German friend of his "has pointed out striking analogies between Coleridge and German authors Coleridge has never seen." The remark is true of Coleridge chiefly on his speculative side, the Coleridge of the *Table Talk* and of the *Lectures*. This aspect of Coleridge's relation to Germany belongs to the history of the influence of German philosophy on English thought, a subject closely related and complementary to the present study, but exceeding its limits[2]. With regard to the purely literary kinship and influence, matters stand somewhat differently, as will appear if we trace the history of Coleridge's relation to German literature.

Samuel Taylor Coleridge was born on October 21, 1772, at Ottery St Mary, in Devonshire. In 1782 he was placed at Christ's Hospital, where he already manifested studious and dreamy propensities, and that curiosity of the strange problems of mind and existence which he shares with the German Romantics. At the age of fifteen he is said to have turned from the study of medical science to the mysticism of Plotinus. In a letter to Thelwall, November 19, 1796, he defines in a few words the dominating characteristics of his intellectual temperament: "Metaphysics and poetry and 'facts of the mind' (i.e. accounts of all strange phantasms that ever possessed your philosophy dreamers, from Theuth the Egyptian to Taylor the English pagan) are my darling studies." Such had been the bent of his intellect from boyhood, and in later years it remained essentially unchanged.

[1] H. C. Robinson, *Diary*, vol. I, p. 352.
[2] See A. Brandl, *Coleridge und die englische Romantik*, 1886, and C. H. Herford, *The Age of Wordsworth*, London, 1909. For a recent and very interesting study of the subject see A. C. Dunstan, *The German Influence on Coleridge*, Modern Language Review, vol. XVII, July 1922, and vol. XVIII, April 1923.

It was at Cambridge, where in 1791 he came into residence at Jesus College, that he received his first recorded impression of German literature on reading Schiller's *Robbers*. This happened in 1794[1], and Coleridge, as we have seen (p. 30), experienced remarkable sensations on the occasion. *The Sonnet to the Author of the Robbers* was first published in 1796, but was written, we may suppose probably enough, while he was still in the flush of his excitement. In May 1796 it is by means of a translation of Schiller's works that he proposes to defray the expenses of a journey to Jena, where his fancy at the moment was to "study chemistry and anatomy." The scheme is characteristic of Coleridge, in the fine breadth of its conception, and also in that it was not carried out[2]. In a letter of May 6, 1796, to Thomas Poole[3], he sketches it as follows: he is learning German, and in about six weeks he will, he says, "be able to read that language with tolerable fluency." He is to make a proposal to Robinson, the London bookseller, to translate all the works of Schiller for the purpose mentioned above. He will bring back from Germany the works of Semler and Michaelis, besides those "of Kant, the great German metaphysician." On his return he proposes to open a school "for eight young men at £105 each, proposing to perfect them" in the study of man, which subject he subdivides into the study of Man as an Animal, Man as an Intellectual Being, and Man as a Religious Being.

Coleridge had been studying German for some time before this, for on April 1 of the same year, writing to Flower, editor of the Cambridge Intelligencer[4], he says that he has had thoughts of translating, with a refutation, Reimarus' *Fragmente eines Ungenannten*, published by Lessing, whom Coleridge regards

---

[1] Professor Brandl is mistaken in placing it at the beginning of 1795 (*Coleridge*, p. 125) if the date of Coleridge's letter to Southey (quoted on p. 30) is correctly given by his editor, E. H. Coleridge (see *Letters of S. T. Coleridge*, edited by E. H. Coleridge, 2 vols., London, 1895, vol. 1, p. 96). Besides, Coleridge left Cambridge in December 1794, and in his note to the Sonnet, speaks of taking *The Robbers* away with him on leaving a college-friend's room.

[2] J. Cottle, *Early Recollections*, vol. 1, p. 148: "I remember him (Coleridge) once to have read to me, from his pocket-book, a list of eighteen different works which he had resolved to write, not one of which he ever effected."

[3] Coleridge, *Letters*, Turnbull, p. 78.

[4] idem, p. 68.

as the author. They unite, he says, "the wit of Voltaire with the subtlety of Hume and the profound erudition of *our* Lardner." Of the Schiller translation we shall hear no more, but his interest in Lessing increases in the next few years, though the projects inspired by it never reach maturity.

We may thus probably place his earliest study of German in the first quarter of 1796. The desire to visit Germany remained steadfast, and was to be realised in 1798. Meanwhile Coleridge was, in his peculiar fashion, entering on the business of life. His principle appears to have been to obey the impulse of whatever mood chanced to be dominant, at least in so far as it was not unreconcilable with his religious and moral convictions. A first escapade, which broke the monotony of his academic career, had no serious consequences—he enlisted as a trooper in the 15th Dragoons, and was bought out by his brother. Returning to Cambridge for a while, he left it without a degree at the end of 1794.

It was in 1794, shortly following upon Coleridge's return to Cambridge after his brief appearance as Silas Tomkyn Comberback the Light Dragoon, that he made Southey's acquaintance at Oxford, and a close intellectual intimacy seems to have resulted from their meeting. Together they developed the Pantisocracy scheme for colonising the banks of the Susquehanna. In 1795, Coleridge married Sara Fricker; Southey, her sister Edith. Southey, however, proceeded immediately to Portugal, and as this step involved the abandonment of the Pantisocracy scheme, a coolness arose on the subject between the brothers-in-law. There was a reconciliation, prefaced by a quotation from Fiesco (see p. 99), on Southey's return to England in 1796; but they saw little of each other till 1803, when the Southeys settled at Greta Hall, Keswick, and the two poets and their families became for some years near neighbours. We may briefly discuss here the relations of Southey to German literature.

In earlier years Southey duly read those translations from German which by their freshness and revolutionary strangeness attracted the young men of his day who had a leaning towards literature and progressive thought. He read *Werther* at school by his own account, leaving Westminster with his head full of it[1]. *The Robbers* he must have read in 1792, for he wrote to his friend Bedford on November 20 of that year: "But, as the play says, beware of the beast that has three legs," meaning, as he proceeds to explain, the gallows[2] (cp. *Die Räuber*, Act 1, Sc. 2. Roller: "Nimm dich in Acht vor dem dreibeinigten Thiere"). His project of writing *The Banditti*, mentioned in a letter to Bedford, was, as Rea points out, probably suggested by Schiller's drama. In the same letter he asks whether Bedford has read *Cabal and Love*[3], the last act of which he finds "dreadfully affecting" in spite of a style of translation "for which the translator deserves hanging."[4] Fiesco he also knew at this time (cp. p. 99).

But Southey was a reader of omnivorous curiosity, and no especial interest in German literature need be assumed to account for this acquaintance with the best-known translations; nor, on the strength of such evidence, can Margraf's remark[5] be commended: "Southey hatte schon frühzeitig begonnen, sich mit der deutschen Litteratur vertraut zu machen." Southey's relation to German literature throughout is of the slightest; only for a short time is there an appearance of a deeper interest in it taking possession of him, and very little came of this interest apparently. He read Taylor's *Ellenore* and *The Lass of Fair Wone* (Bürger's *Des Pfarrers Tochter von Taubenhain*, Monthly Magazine, April 1796) and of the latter remarked that he knew "no commendation equal to its merit. The man who wrote that should have been ashamed of Lenora[6]. Who is this

---

[1] Southey, *Life*, vol. IV, p. 186, Letter to C. Townshend, June 5, 1816. Zeiger (*Deutsche Einflüsse*, p. 45) notes a strain of Wertherian sensibility in him from a letter of 1809, and calls attention to the course of reading in Epictetus which he undertook at eighteen to counteract such tendencies.

[2] Southey, *Life*, vol. I, p. 168.

[3] Rea, *Schiller's Dramas*, p. 21.

[4] Southey, *Life*, vol. I, p. 286, July 31, 1796.   [5] *Einfluss*, p. 36.

[6] In April 1799 he spoke more favourably of *Lenore*. To W. Taylor, April 15, 1799, he writes (Robberds, *Memoir*, vol. I, p. 274): "Excepting the two ballads which you translated his (Bürger's) other productions that have been Englished are of no great excellence. The 'Lenore' indeed is enough; it cannot be surpassed, and will not probably be equalled; yet the 'Parson's Daughter' (The Lass of the Fair Wone) struck me as the finer poem: the story of 'Lenore' once conceived, the execution was not difficult for a man of genius; but the excellence of the other ballad arises wholly from

Taylor?" The question was presently to be answered to his satisfaction. He made Taylor's acquaintance in 1798 through George Burnett, one of the Pantisocracy brotherhood, and passed some days at Norwich as his guest. As a consequence, he was infected (temporarily and without notable results) with Taylor's enthusiasm for German literature. Taylor's account of German eclogues stimulated Southey to revive an earlier plan of writing English ones, and he sent Taylor *The Old Mansion House* as a specimen soon after their meeting. He knew nothing of German eclogues, by his own account, save what he learnt in conversation with William Taylor, with the exception of one of Gessner's which he had seen "in a Devon and Cornwall collection of poems," and forgotten again completely[1]. Taylor gave him an account of the Musenalmanache which were published by German literary men, and Southey determined to edit a similar work, in order, partly, to publish in a more permanent form works of his which had appeared in the newspapers. He intended to call it an Almanack, "as the title will be recognised on the continent, and I hope to equal the continental collections." (To William Taylor, December 30, 1798 and February 24, 1799.) Such was the origin of Southey's *Annual Anthology*, published by his friend, the Bristol publisher, Cottle.

In February 1799, he wrote to Taylor, "You have made me hunger and thirst after German poetry."[2] But already on April 15 of the same year he remarks to Taylor[3]:

Thanks to the number of translations, I no longer hunger and thirst for the language, as I did some time since. Prose plays, I apprehend, suffer little from translation. [He appears to forget his laudable opinion, quoted above, that a translator may deserve hanging!] It is only Klopstock that I long to read[4], and Bodmer's

the mode of narration; and though such a tale might have occurred to a thousand poets, it is a thousand to one that none of them had found out the best way of translating it."

[1] Robert Southey to W. Taylor, July 24, 1798. Given in Robberds, *Memoir*.

[2] From Margraf, *Einfluss*, p. 36. As Margraf points out, p. 37, his reference to Kotzebue in a letter to Wynn (April 5, 1799) as an "unsurpassed and unsurpassable genius," must be attributed to Taylor's influence.

[3] Robberds, *Memoir*, vol. I, p. 275.

[4] Later, though perhaps without having read anything of Klopstock's in German, he expressed very faint esteem of Klopstock as a poet. To Neville

"Noah," on account of the subject, but the book is not get-at-able, or I should ere this have poked my way through it with a dictionary.

A schoolfellow had called his attention years before to the "Noachide" which had been translated in 1767[1], but the translation had never fallen in his way[2]. Taylor sent him the original, and with the help of patience and curiosity, together with a grammar and dictionary, which latter gave him only "a very dark-lanthorn sort of glimmer," he hoped to make his way through the book[3]. Taylor suggested to Southey that he should attempt a poem on the subject of the Flood, and he half-entertained the notion, but subsequently gave it up again.

On Coleridge's return from Germany, he planned with Southey a poem in hexameters on the subject of Mahomet; the idea may probably have been suggested to Coleridge by a perusal of Klopstock's *Messias*. Each of the collaborators wrote nothing beyond a fragment of the projected poem[4]. He was much interested in Coleridge's *Wallenstein*-translation. He preferred *Wallenstein* to Schiller's other plays, finding in the hero "that greatness and littleness united, which stamp the portrait."[5]

For the later years of his life I find very scanty record of interest in German literature. In 1815 he began giving German lessons to his little son Herbert; and expected to acquire the language in the process of teaching him; but after the child's death, though regretting his want of knowledge of the language, he felt at first that he would never have the heart to resume his studies[6]. In 1817 he worked through a German account of

White, October 10, 1809 (*Life*, vol. III, p. 258): "In Germany his day of reputation is already passing away. There is no other country where the principle of criticism is so well understood. But one loves Klopstock as well as if he had been really the poet that his admirers believe him to be...". At the date of this letter Coleridge and Southey had been near neighbours at Keswick for about five years, and it is not uninteresting to compare Southey's remarks with Coleridge's on the same subject (quoted on p.   ). But the latter sentiment, if it mean anything at all, is certainly not expressive of Coleridge's sentiments towards "Klubstick"!

[1] Haney, *German Literature in England before 1790*.
[2] Robberds, *Memoir*, vol. I, p. 280.   [3] ibidem.
[4] Robberds, *Memoir*, vol. I, p. 294, and Southey, *Life*, vol. II, p. 48.
[5] Southey, *Life*, vol. II, p. 40.
[6] To Neville White, February 16, 1815. To C. H. Townshend, June 5, 1816. Southey, *Life*, vol. IV, pp. 103, 187.

Masséna's campaign in Portugal, his knowledge of the subject helping him to make out the meaning[1]. There is perhaps evidence of some progress in his notice of May 6, 1824 (Letter to G. C. Bedford)[2] that he is reading "the Nibelungen in the original old German, and the modern German version, the one helping me to understand the other." And he was teaching a little boy German, as well as Dutch, Greek and Latin, in 1829. In Crabb Robinson's Diary, June 30, 1833, appears the notice: "Spent an agreeable evening with Southey. We read German."[3] This might imply much or little; and our other sources of information favour the latter interpretation.

Southey was charmed by *Undine* "surely the most graceful fiction of modern times." The only record I have found of his feeling about Goethe marks it as characteristic of the contemporary English attitude towards him. Robinson quotes, in 1829, a former remark of Southey's on the subject: "How many sympathies, how many dispathies, do I feel with Goethe!"[4]

A detailed account of Southey's merely incidental relation to German literature would not have been worth while, perhaps, had not Margraf[5] and Zeiger[6], and especially the latter, cited him among prominent instances of German influence on English letters, and conveyed, I think, a false impression of the extent of Southey's pre-occupation with German literature. With regard to the former we need not examine his treatment of the question in detail. But without erring notably from the facts, he has presented them (as usual, without giving sufficient references) in such a way as to create the impression of a much closer and more direct relation of Southey to German literature than is, I think, justifiable. Zeiger, whose preliminary account of the moments of Southey's contact with German literature is more careful and precise, loses all measure when he comes to the question of influence. Wat Tyler (1794) he believes to

---

[1] idem, p. 275.   [2] idem, vol. V, p. 177.
[3] H. C. Robinson, *Diary*, vol. III, p. 29.
[4] idem, vol. II, p. 439.
[5] E. Margraf, *Einfluss der deutschen Litteratur auf die englische*, etc. Inaug. Diss. Leipzig, 1901.
[6] T. Zeiger, *Beiträge zur Geschichte des Einflusses der neueren deutschen Litteratur auf die englische*. Inaug. Diss. Leipzig, Berlin, 1901.

have been influenced by *Götz von Berlichingen*[1]; the difficulty created by the fact that *Götz* was not translated into English till 1799 he eludes by suggesting that Southey had read the French translation in Friedel and De Bonneville's *Nouveau Théâtre allemand* (1785). In view of the fact that there is no scrap of evidence in support of this theory very striking resemblances would be required to induce us to accept it. Zeiger quotes parallel passages from *Götz* and *Wat Tyler*; but beyond vague resemblances of sentiment and situation, of no conclusive value, he has little to show. Zeiger next proceeds to find a trace of *Lenore*-style in the Ballad, *Lord William*, but his quotation from the poem does not seriously support his contention, and his subsequent comment is merely absurd. We have seen the somewhat tenuous relation of Southey's eclogues to poems of a similar type in German. Needless to say, Zeiger makes the most of it. With better foundation, Zeiger points out a relation between Southey's *Thalaba* and Wieland's *Oberon* in Sotheby's translation. Taylor wrote to Southey in January 1799, mentioning *Oberon* in connection with *Thalaba*, and Southey had read the poem by February 24, 1799[2]. It must be admitted that Zeiger makes out a good case for *Oberon*-influence on certain scenes of *Thalaba*, especially in the "Einsiedler" scenes, in the description of the traveller's first view of Bagdad, and in the Paradise of Sin. We may notice here in passing Southey's indebtedness to Niebuhr and other German descriptive writers for picturesque and other details of his epics, as acknowledged by him in his notes.

With regard to Southey's attempt to write hexameters, Zeiger says: "Er versuchte nämlich in Anschluss an Taylors Übersetzungen aus dem Deutschen englische Verse in Hexametern zu schreiben..." and again "er suchte nach deutschem Vorbild den Hexameter zu beleben." The former of these

---

[1] Zeiger, *Beiträge*, pp. 45 ff. The denial of Götz, when cited before the court at Weinsberg, that he is a rebel, and John Ball's similar denial in similar circumstances, is the only instance of definite likeness adduced by Zeiger; and we may well regard such an isolated instance as a coincidence. Or if there must be influence, why not from *Henry VIII*, Act III, Sc. 2: "*Surrey.* Thou art a proud traitor, priest. *Wolsey.* Proud Lord, thou liest."

[2] Zeiger, *Beiträge*, pp. 52–53.

remarks is not altogether in accordance with the facts, I think. He writes to Taylor on September 1, 1799: "Coleridge and I mean to march an army of hexameters into the country....We have chosen the story of Mohammed."[1] Thus it would seem to be rather Coleridge than Taylor who provided the stimulus for this abortive undertaking. And the idea of writing hexameters may have been in Southey's mind for some time previously; for in a letter to G. C. Bedford, October 1795, he exclaims: "Bedford, I have beheld that very identical tiger. There's a grand hexameter for you!"[2]

Southey's relation to German literature is, then, a very slight one; none of the great works of German literature appear to have made a lasting impression upon him, with the possible exception of *Werther* (see p. 92, note 1). Of direct influence, and that through translations only, we can point to a few scenes in *Thalaba*, and the renewal of his idea of writing eclogues.

To return to Coleridge, whom we left starting out into the world to fashion a career for himself. Southey and Pantisocracy now held his fancy spell-bound; and he married Sarah Fricker chiefly, one may think, for the sake of ensuring the expansion of the projected colony on the banks of the Susquehanna, where the Pantisocratic state was to be founded. But Southey, who had married Sarah's sister, soon attained a sobriety of outlook that caused him to judge the scheme unfavourably, and a coolness consequently arose between the brothers-in-law, though it does not appear that even Coleridge's ardour for the plan had retained all its warmth. Southey went to Portugal, and Coleridge lived on expedients of an unpromising kind—lectures, advances from the Bristol publisher Cottle, the editorship of the short-lived *Watchman*. He appears almost from the first to have been singularly indifferent to the attachments of married life, and long before the virtual separation from Sarah in 1811, his movements seem to be undertaken with a fairly complete disregard of the matrimonial tie. Lamb and Charles Lloyd are at first the successors of Southey in his enthusiastic friendship, but with a visit to Racedown and the Wordsworths in 1797 begins a deeper and more important influence in his life. Wordsworth

---

[1] Robberds, *Memoir*, vol. I, p. 294.   [2] Southey, *Life*, p. 249.

had a power of philosophic insight which, though the best and deepest of it was transmuted into the poetic synthesis, enabled him to come nearer an understanding of the problems that occupied Coleridge's seething brain than any other of his friends. There followed the close companionship at Nether Stowey and Alfoxden, the communion of two great poets in a world they were young enough or detached enough to treat as the mere argument and background of their speculations. It was with Wordsworth and his sister Dorothy that Coleridge, provided with funds by the liberality of the Wedgwoods, set out in September 1798 for Germany, the land of metaphysical promise.

By this time he had made some progress in the study of German, though it is not clear or probable that he had worked at the language systematically, nor that he was acquainted with much of its literature, either in the original or in translation.

I will add here the evidence I have been able to collect of his German reading prior to the German visit. Extracts from letters to Flower and Poole have been quoted showing that in the early part of 1796 Coleridge had begun the study of German. By December 1796 we have an opportunity of gauging his progress by a translation from Voss's *Luise*, of which he gives some thirty lines in a letter to Thelwall[1]. He is still at the stage where knowledge is supplemented by lively guesses. The passage translated is from the *Erste Idylle* (II. 379–416), in which the pastor of Grünau expresses his *aufgeklärte* theological views. Coleridge's worst "howler" in the version will serve to indicate the limits of his knowledge of German at this time; he translates "Mendelssohn! Der hätte den Göttlichen nimmer gekreuzigt!" by "Mendelssohn, who teaches that the divine one was never crucified."[2] In December 1797, as we learn from a letter to the Bristol publisher Joseph Cottle[3], he is translating Wieland's *Oberon*: "It is a difficult language, and

---

[1] *Letters*, E. H. C. vol. I, p. 203.

[2] Coleridge later (in 1802) entertained the idea of translating Voss's Idylls and in 1814 mentioned his *Luise* to Murray in terms of high praise (see p. 138).

[3] Undated in Cottle (*Recollections*, vol. I, p. 287), but given as December 2, 1797, in Turnbull's *Biographia Epistolaris*.

I can translate at least as fast as I can construe," (to me a some-what cryptic remark; but at any rate it does not seem to indicate great proficiency). In the same letter he speaks of daily study of German. Brandl[1] says that he translated from Klopstock in 1797, but this I think is unlikely[2]. I cannot trace any further reading in German during the period in question. Translations of German works read by him are traceable in greater numbers. He read *The Robbers* in 1794 (see p. 90), and in 1795 *Cabal and Love*, according to Haney, who refers us to *Conciones ad Populum* (1795) and Coleridge's condemnation therein of British recruiting methods[3]. We may infer that both Coleridge and Southey had read *Fiesco*; for the end of their quarrel over Pantisocracy was brought about by Southey, on his return from Portugal, sending to Coleridge a slip of paper on which was written the quotation: "Fiesco! Fiesco! thou leavest a void in my bosom, which the human race, thrice told, will never fill up." We may assume with Brandl that he followed Lamb's recommendation to read Taylor's *Ellenore* in 1796 (see p. 101). Emile Legouis, in *La Jeunesse de Wordsworth*, says that at the time of the visit to the Valley of Stones, in the summer of 1797, Coleridge was enthusiastic about the ballad; but I do not know on what evidence he makes the assertion. *The Wanderings of Cain* (1798) was an imitation of the *Death of Abel*[4]. He had read Schiller's *Geisterseher* by 1797, as is shown by his adaptation in *Osorio* of a theme from the tale (see p. 127).

At this early date Coleridge had already written no small proportion of that part of his work which places him in the first rank of English poets. *The Ancient Mariner* appeared in the *Lyrical Ballads* in 1798, and in 1797 he wrote the first part of *Christabel* and *Kubla Khan*. But although Southey called *The Ancient Mariner* an "attempt at German sublimity," no German influence has been convincingly shown to exist either in this poem

[1] A. Brandl, *Coleridge*, p. 240.

[2] cp. Satyrane's Third Letter, *Biographia Literaria*, 1817, vol. II, p. 240: "(Wordsworth) told him (Klopstock) that I intended to translate a few of his odes as specimens of German lyrics...", and Klopstock's remarks on his translators, quoted on p. 112.

[3] J. L. Haney, *The German Influence on S. T. Coleridge*, p. 4, Philadelphia, 1902.

[4] Coleridge, *Poetical Works*, vol. I, pp. 286–287.

or in any of the pieces just named. The influence of *Die Räuber* on *Osorio*, which also belongs to the writings previous to the German visit, will be discussed later. German influence on *The Ancient Mariner* and other early poems has been alleged by Brandl, on very insufficient grounds in my opinion.

I called attention in the Preface (pp. vi ff.) to the necessity of limiting the attribution of influence to those cases where there is a strong presumption in favour of it. That this warning is necessary will be exemplified by the following examination of six instances of alleged *Lenore*-influence. In order to state the case fully I have been obliged to adopt the tedious method of quoting in full the relevant passages, from the authors who attribute influence (Brandl and Margraf) and from the alleged imitation and original. The question appears to me to be of sufficient importance to justify a rather minute examination, for it affects the existence of comparative literature as a serious study. The examples given here are extreme, but in this one branch of comparative literature I could collect from other writers dozens, perhaps hundreds, of almost equally baseless allegations of German influence on English writers. I cannot conceive that a method of investigation which accepts all resemblances or analogies as evidence of influence can do anything but falsify our notions of the actual processes which characterise the development and interrelation of literatures, or of individual writers. We may feel confident that the development and interrelation are not accidental, that by patient and intelligent study of the facts the phenomena will show an orderly grouping; but we must collect our facts and verify them before we study them, and we are not stating verifiable facts at all, but arbitrary fancies, when we attribute influence on the ground of resemblance that may as likely as not be accidental—*a fortiori*, where the resemblance may be regarded as more probably accidental than not, or can reasonably be denied altogether.

I. ODE TO THE DEPARTING YEAR
published December 31, 1796[1]

A. Brandl, *S. T. Coleridge und die Englische Romantik*, p. 182:

Eine Höllenhexe tritt wieder auf, der Tod erschlägt sie, strafende Geister umtanzen bei Nacht und Nebel ihr Grab: gespenstisches Beiwerk aus Bürgers "Lenore," welche kürzlich mehrfach übersetzt und Coleridge von Lamb noch ausdrücklich empfohlen worden war; aber das mythische Urgeschöpf hat sich zugleich zu der Czarin Katharina verkörpert, weil diese die entsetzliche Erstürmung von Ismail veranlasst hatte.

This must refer to the third division of the *Ode to the Departing Year*. I append, to facilitate comparison, the Epode in question, and those passages in Taylor's *Lenora* (Monthly Magazine, 1796) which relate to spirits. The numbers in brackets refer to the stanzas of *Lenora*.

A

The passages in Bürger's *Lenore* (Taylor's Translation) in which spirits or ghosts are referred to:

(*a*) Hurrah! the dead can ride apace.... (40, 49, 55, 57.)

(*b*) The burial-party [presumably evil spirits] follow Lenora and the ghostly knight "ore feeld and flood." (46.)

(*c*) "Look up, look up, an airy crew
In roundel daunces reele:
The moone is bryghte, and blue the nyghte,
Mayst dimly see them wheele.

(*d*) "Come to, come to, ye gostlie crew,
Come to, and follow mee,
And daunce for us the wedding daunce
When we in bed shall be."

(*e*) And brush, brush, brush, the ghostlie crew
Come wheeling ore their heads,
All rustling like the wither'd leaves
That wyde the wirlwind spreads. (50, 51, 52.)

(*f*) And hollow howlings hung in aire,
And shrekes from vaults arose.... (64.)

---

[1] Coleridge, *Poetical Works*, vol. I, p. 160.

(g) But onwarde to the judgement seat,
Thro' myste and moonlighte dreare,
The gostlie crewe their flyghte pursewe,
And hollowe inn her eare.... (65.)

B

COLERIDGE'S "ODE TO THE DEPARTING YEAR," III[1]

38. I mark'd Ambition in his war-array!
I heard the mailed Monarch's troublous cry—
40. "Ah! wherefore does the Northern Conqueress stay?
Groans not her chariot on its onward way?"
Fly, mailed Monarch, fly!
Stunned by Death's twice mortal mace,
No more on Murder's lurid face
The insatiate Hag shall gloat with drunken eye!
Manes of the unnumber'd slain!
Ye that gasped on Warsaw's plain!
Ye that erst at Ismail's tower,
When human ruin choked the streams,
50. Fell in Conquest's glutted hour,
Mid women's shrieks and infants' screams!
Spirits of the uncoffin'd slain,
Sudden blasts of triumph swelling,
Oft, at night, in misty train,
Rush around her narrow dwelling!
The exterminating Fiend is fled—
(Foul her life, and dark her doom)
Mighty armies of the dead
Dance, like death-fires, round her tomb!
60. Then with prophetic song relate,
Each some Tyrant-Murderer's fate!

The following points should be noted:
The dancing ghosts of B 59 might be suggested by A (d) 3.
They are noisy (B 53) like those of A (f).
They have a misty appearance (B 54), which is also suggested of those in *Lenora* A (c) 4.
The last likeness is perhaps too common an attribute of ghosts to be taken reasonably into account. The dancing and yelling of the ghosts in both poems constitutes a resemblance.

---

[1] First Epode, ll. 38–61.

Yet to affirm that this *gespenstisches Beiwerk* is borrowed from Bürger's *Lenore* (or rather from Taylor's version in the Monthly Magazine, which, as Professor Brandl assumes, probably correctly, Coleridge read on Lamb's recommendation, see Brandl, *Coleridge*, p. 213) seems to me to be hardly warranted by the similarity. It is, of course, possible, and in view of Coleridge's probable reading of *Lenora* in the year in which the *Ode to the Departing Year* was written, some reminiscence of the ballad is not unlikely here; but the probability is not high enough to justify anything approaching a positive assertion on the subject.

THE BALLAD OF THE DARK LADIE

Brandl (*Coleridge*, pp. 229–230):

Auf die einleitende Geschichte von der herzlosen Dame folgt dann die eigentliche Erzählung und handelt von einem ebenso herzlosen Liebhaber. Er hat ein Fräulein ins Elend gestürzt. Er kommt, um die Sehnsuchtskranke zur Hochzeit zu holen. In der Dunkelheit, bei Sternenschein, will er sie in sein Heim führen. Ihr aber graut vor der Dunkelheit, sie möchte die Feier am hellen Tage und mit heiteren Gespielinnen begehen—wohl ein vergeblicher Wunsch. Hier bricht das Fragment ab, vermuthlich weil sich Coleridge bewusst wurde, wie nahe der Vorwurf an die "Lenore" streifte.

As Professor Brandl summarises the fragment, the suggestion is that the knight is of a ghostly nature, that his proposal to lead the lady to his castle when the darkness has fallen introduces a theme like that of the ghostly bridal in *Lenore*. This interpretation appears to me to be inadmissible. The fragment reads as follows[1]:

THE BALLAD OF THE DARK LADIE

A FRAGMENT

Beneath yon birch with silver bark,
And boughs so pendulous and fair,
The brook falls scatter'd down the rock:
    And all is mossy there!

And there upon the moss she sits,
The Dark Ladie in silent pain;
The heavy tear is in her eye,
    And drops and swells again.

[1] Coleridge, *Poetical Works*, vol. I, pp. 293 ff.

Three times she sends her little page
Up the castled mountain's breast,
If he might find the Knight that wears
    The Griffin for his crest.

The sun was sloping down the sky,
And she had linger'd there all day,
Counting moments, dreaming fears—
    Oh wherefore can he stay?

She hears a rustling o'er the brook,
She sees far off a swinging bough!
"'Tis He! 'Tis my betrothed Knight!
    Lord Falkland, it is Thou!"

She springs, she clasps him round the neck,
She sobs a thousand hopes and fears,
Her kisses glowing on his cheeks
    She quenches with her tears.

.   .   .   .

"My friends with rude ungentle words
They scoff and bid me fly to thee!
O give me shelter in thy breast!
    O shield and shelter me!

"My Henry, I have given thee much,
I gave what I can ne'er recall,
I gave my heart, I gave my peace,
    O Heaven! I gave thee all!"

The Knight made answer to the Maid,
While to his heart he held her hand,
"Nine castles hath my noble sire,
    None statelier in the land.

"The fairest one shall be my love's,
The fairest castle of the nine!
Wait only till the stars peep out,
    The fairest shall be thine:

"Wait only till the hand of eve
Hath wholly closed yon western bars,
And through the dark we two will steal
    Beneath the twinkling stars!"—

"The dark? the dark? No! not the dark?
The twinkling stars? How, Henry? How?
O God! 'twas in the eye of noon
    He pledged his sacred vow!

"And in the eye of noon my love
Shall lead me from my mother's door,
Sweet boys and girls all clothed in white
    Strewing flowers before:
"But first the nodding minstrels go
With music meet for lordly bowers,
The children next in snow-white vests,
    Strewing buds and flowers!
"And then my love and I shall pace,
My jet-black hair in pearly braids,
Between our comely bachelors
    And blushing bridal maids."

.   .   .   .

From this fragment we can infer that the Knight had promised to marry the Dark Lady, and almost certainly that he no longer intends to do so; his proposal to lead her to his castle after nightfall suggests merely that he wishes to keep their relation secret. From her address to him we can probably infer that she is his mistress already; from his reply, that he does not intend to remove the stain upon her honour. This interpretation of the fragment is confirmed by the poem called *Introduction to the Tale of the Dark Ladie*, as published in the *Morning Post*, December 21, 1799[1]. This poem is substantially the same as that called *Love* in the *Lyrical Ballads* and later collections of his poems; but contained, with some other minor differences, three additional verses at the end, which were to serve as a transition to *The Ballad of the Dark Ladie*. In the last verse he · sings to his Genevieve:

I promis'd thee a sister tale
Of Man's perfidious cruelty:
Come, then, and hear what cruel wrong
Befel the Dark Ladie.

Among the additional verses at the beginning of the poem are the following:

3

And now a Tale of Love and Woe,
A woeful Tale of Love I sing:
Hark, gentle Maidens, hark! it sighs
And trembles on the string.

[1] Coleridge, *Poetical Works*, vol. II, pp. 1052 ff.

4

But most, my own dear Genevieve!
It sighs and trembles most for thee!
O come and hear the cruel wrongs
Befel the dark Ladie!

The tale told in the *Introduction to the Tale of the Dark Ladie* is of a knight, driven mad by the disdain of his beloved, who rescues her from an attack by a lawless band, and dies, nursed by the repentant lady. The "sister tale," then, will be presumably of a woman whose faithful love is ill-requited, of a "cruel wrong" done to a woman. If these inferences are correct —and I do not think they can be disputed—there is not the remotest analogy between *Lenore* and *The Ballad of the Dark Ladie*. Margraf, *Einfluss*, p. 22, amplifies Professor Brandl's error in the following terms:

Auch das im Jahre 1799 in der "Morning Post" erschienene [an error, according to E. H. Coleridge, who says that the *Ballad* was first published in 1834 (see Coleridge, *Poetical Works*, vol. 1, p. 293); the error is probably repeated from Brandl, *Coleridge*, p. 229] und im Jahre 1834 zum erstenmal unter seinen Gedichten mit abgedruckte Fragment "The Ballad of the Dark Ladie" zeigt inhaltlich ein der "Lenore" nahe verwandtes Motiv. Auch hier weht uns ein Hauch wie aus einer Totengruft entgegen (!). Denn nach dem ganzen Eindruck der vorhandenen Strophen lässt sich wohl mit Recht vermuten, dass der Ritter, nach dem sich die dunkle Dame in Sehnsucht verzehrt, gestorben ist und durch ihr verzweiflungsvolles Klagen gezwungen dem Grabe entsteigt, um sie in der Geisterstunde, in sternenloser Nacht (!) zur Hochzeit auf sein Schloss zu führen.

THE ANCIENT MARINER

Brandl, *Coleridge*, p. 213:

In der Legende [of Paulinus, see Brandl, loc. cit. p. 211] lief das Fahrzeug auf den Strand: Coleridge liess es am Ziel versinken, wie das Ross nach der Hetzjagd in der "Lenore," wobei hervorzuheben ist, dass dieser Geisterritt bereits in der von Coleridge benützten Uebersetzung von W. Taylor (*Lamb*, 5 Juli 1796) auf das Meer ausgedehnt war.

THE RIME OF THE ANCIENT MARINER

The boat came closer to the ship,
But I nor spake nor stirred;
The boat came close beneath the ship,
And straight a sound was heard.

Under the water it rumbled on,
Still louder and more dread:
It reached the ship, it split the bay;
The ship went down like lead.

Stunned by that loud and dreadful sound,
Which sky and ocean smote,
Like one that hath been seven days drowned
My body lay afloat;
But swift as dreams, myself I found
Within the Pilot's boat.

TAYLOR'S "LENORA" (63)

And lo! his steede did thin to smoke,
And charnel fires outbreathe;
And pal'd, and bleach'd, then vanish'd quite
The mayde from underneathe.

And hollow howlings hung in aire,
And shrekes from vaults arose.

The reader may be safely left to draw his own conclusions from a comparison of the above passages. Margraf (*Einfluss*, p. 22) says:

Und wie in Bürgers Ballade das Geisterross nach dem unheimlichen Ritt auf dem Kirchhof in die Tiefe sinkt, so versinkt in der grausigen Erzählung des "Ancient Mariner" das Schiff nach der langen Geisterjagd in den Wellen.

KUBLA KHAN

Brandl, *Coleridge*, p. 194:

Die ganze sonst so friedliche Gegend nahm ein wildes, heiliges, verzaubertes Aussehen an, "als wäre sie bei halbem Mond durchjagt vom Weib, das nach dem Spukgeliebten jammert": Lenore!

This refers to the well-known lines:

But oh! that deep romantic chasm which slanted
Down the green hill athwart a cedarn cover!
A savage place! As holy and enchanted
As e'er beneath a waning moon was haunted
By woman wailing for her demon-lover!

Durchjagt is of course a mistranslation of *haunted*, and *Spukge-liebter* does not accurately render demon-lover. The mistranslation wrenches the meaning a little nearer to a resemblance with the *Lenore*-theme. In the original we shall hardly discover it, unless we are determined to do so. J. L. Haney (*Influence*, p. 8) remarks:

> If we must accept the line:
> > "By woman wailing for her demon-lover"
> as a direct influence of *Lenore*, to what source shall we turn for the similar idea
> > "And mingle foul embrace with fiends of Hell"
> expressed in the Sonnet on Mrs Siddons, which was written by Coleridge and Lamb two years before any English version of *Lenore* was printed.... The plea for *Lenore* influence on the 1797–98 poems seems far-fetched; the motive of the maiden and her ghostly lover was present in English balladry long before the time of Bürger and was familiar to every reader of Percy's *Reliques*.

The passage from the Sonnet to Mrs Siddons is:

> ...Those hags, who at the witching time
> Of murky Midnight ride the air sublime,
> And mingle foul embrace with fiends of Hell!

The idea thus expressed is considerably closer to the demon-lover of *Kubla Khan* than is the ghostly lover of Lenore; it would be unsafe to attribute the idea to either source (Bürger or Percy's *Reliques*), because there is no clear verbal similarity, and the general idea—of love between natural and supernatural beings—is found in most mythologies and in the traditions about witches; nor are we justified, on the present evidence, in looking elsewhere for the source of Coleridge's unique and unforgettable differentiation of it.

Margraf (*Einfluss*, p. 21), also sees *Lenore*-influence in the line from *Kubla Khan*.

LEWTI

OR THE CIRCASSIAN LOVE-CHAUNT

Brandl, *Coleridge*, p. 202:

Düster folgt ihm ihr (the beloved's) Gesicht durch die Mondnacht, wie das Weib in "Kubla Khan," das dem Dämon jammernd nachzieht; wie ein blasses, immer blasseres und ferneres Wölkchen, bis es dem Leichentuch der schönen Dame gleicht, die aus Liebe starb (Lenore).

One must suppose the bracketed word "Lenore" to imply that the lady who died of love is a reminiscence of Lenore. I cannot see any connection. I append the lines from *Lewti* referred to by Professor Brandl, adding only that the poem in its entirety, dealing with a lover's vain attempt to forget his unkind mistress, couched as it is in a rather precious and lusciously sentimental style, does not appear to me to be at all well described by Professor Brandl; it can hardly be described as *düster*, and the reference to the *woman wailing* of *Kubla Khan*, is not apt. He has also misunderstood the sense, I think: the face of Lewti's beloved does not follow him like the cloud; the "treacherous image" is in his own mind, is Lewti's image. The cloud reminds him of his own pale cheek; the moonlight shining on a rock reminds him of Lewti's forehead.

> I saw a vapour in the sky,
> Thin, and white, and very high;
> I ne'er beheld so thin a cloud:
>   Perhaps the breezes that can fly
>   Now below and now above,
> Have snatched aloft the lawny shroud
>   Of Lady fair—that died for love.
> For maids, as well as youths, have perished
> From fruitless love too fondly cherished.
> Nay, treacherous image! leave my mind—
> For Lewti never will be kind.
>
> *Lewti* (ll. 42–52)

CHRISTABEL

Brandl, *Coleridge*, p. 224:

Ihre Vorgeschichte (of Geraldine) schöpfte er grossentheils aus Bürgers "Lenore" in Taylors Uebersetzung: die Dame ist, wenigstens ihrer Erzählung nach, auf einem windschnellen Ross entführt und halbtodt vor Furcht hier abgesetzt orden; statt des schwarzen Leichenzuges, der Lenoren auf ihrem Ritt durch die Mondnacht aufstiess, will sie "den Schatten der Nacht" gekreuzt haben; noch zittert das verdorrte Blatt neben ihr wie aus Herzensangst.

Here is Geraldine's narrative:

> My sire is of noble line,
> And my name is Geraldine:
> Five warriors seized me yestermorn,
> Me, even me, a maid forlorn:
> They choked my cries with force and fright,
> And tied me on a palfrey white.
> The palfrey was as fleet as wind,
> And they rode furiously behind.
> They spurred amain, their steeds were white:
> And once we crossed the shade of night.
> As sure as Heaven shall rescue me,
> I have no thought what men they be;
> Nor do I know how long it is
> (For I have lain entranced I wis)
> Since one, the tallest of the five,
> Took me from the palfrey's back,
> A weary woman, scarce alive.
> Some muttered words his comrades spoke:
> He placed me underneath this oak;
> He swore they would return with haste;
> Whither they went I cannot tell—
> I thought I heard, some minutes past,
> Sounds as of a castle bell.
> Stretch forth thy hand (thus ended she)
> And help a wretched maid to flee.
>
> *Christabel*, Part 1, ll. 79–103.

Professor Brandl has surely misunderstood the line:

> And once we crossed the shade of night,

which I suppose to mean that they rode throughout one whole night. Some versions of the poem have:

> And twice we crossed the shade of night[1].

Professor Brandl's interpretation of it, as a meeting with something analogous to the burial-procession in *Lenore*, is unacceptable.

Margraf, *Einfluss*, p. 22, alludes to the same incident in the following words:

Von einem gespensterhaften Ritt auf windschnellem Ross erzählt auch der weibliche Vampyr Geraldine in dem romantischen Märchen

---

[1] Coleridge, *Poetical Works*, vol. 1, p. 219.

"Christabel," wobei sie den "Schatten der Nacht" gekreuzt haben will, während Lenoren ein schwarzer Leichenzug auf ihrem Ritt begegnet.

Where is the ghostly element in Geraldine's story of brutal abduction?

The alleged influence thus vanishes altogether on examination of four out of the six instances; the argument against it is strong in the case of the line from *Kubla Khan*; in the *Ode to the Departing Year* there is, perhaps, a slight probability in favour of it. All the cases are treated by Professor Brandl, and four of them by Margraf, as instances of unquestionable, or at least of highly probable influence, as may be inferred from the quotations given from these authors.

* * *

As we have seen, Coleridge and the Wordsworths left England on their way to Germany in September 1798. The first striking incident recorded of the German visit, was the meeting between Wordsworth and Coleridge and Klopstock. The friends had arrived in Hamburg apparently with a high opinion of Klopstock; but a nearer acquaintance with the poet seems to have damped their enthusiasm. Coleridge's first unfavourable impression of his personal appearance[1] was confirmed by the disappointing character of his conversation. This was carried on, it is true, under considerable difficulties. Klopstock knew next to no English; Coleridge was apparently quite unable to speak, or at any rate to understand, German at this time; which need not surprise us, in view of the apparently limited extent of his studies, and the fact that he was probably entirely self-taught; nor, it seems, was he acquainted with French sufficiently for the purpose of carrying on a conversation in the language, or even of understanding it when spoken[2]. Wordsworth, who knew no German worth mentioning, conversed with Klopstock in French. Coleridge, then, save for an occasional outburst in

---

[1] "...No comprehension in the forehead, no weight over the eyebrows, no expression of peculiarity, moral or intellectual, in the eyes, no massiveness in the general countenance." Satyrane's Third Letter.

[2] Though in a letter to Cottle, of December 1797, he speaks of studying French daily and of having attained a "very considerable proficiency" in it. But Coleridge was habitually sanguine about his achievements.

Latin (which, owing to the difference between the English and German fashions of pronouncing the tongue, may not have furthered matters appreciably) was largely dependent on Wordsworth's services as interpreter. Moreover, the Bard proved, in Coleridge's opinion, singularly ignorant of the past literature of Germany[1]. The general impression we obtain of the interview is one of constrained dullness; "the liveliest thing which he (Klopstock) produced in the whole conversation," Coleridge informs us, was a remark in English to Coleridge, expressive of his dissatisfaction with previous English translators of his works: "I wish you would render into English some select passages of the *Messiah*, and *revenge* me of your countrymen" (Satyrane's Third Letter).

Coleridge probably only met Klopstock once, but Wordsworth saw him several times, and Dorothy had at least a glimpse of him. On one occasion when Coleridge was not present Wordsworth and Klopstock discussed Wieland's *Oberon*, which the former had read in translation. He criticised adversely the sensual interest of the theme. On another occasion he asked Klopstock what he thought of Kant; Klopstock seemed "pleased to hear that as yet Kant's doctrine had not met with many admirers in England." It is rather singular, in view of the impression made on Coleridge, that the Wordsworths were struck by Klopstock's animation. William remarks in some surprise that Klopstock "expresses himself with the liveliness of a girl of seventeen. This is striking to an Englishman, and rendered him an interesting object...".[2] He found nothing

---

[1] Professor Karl Breul points out the improbability that Coleridge understood Klopstock on this subject. A misunderstanding might easily arise in the circumstances, especially as Coleridge at this point was conversing directly with Klopstock: "...I enquired in Latin concerning the History of German Poetry and the elder German Poets. To my great astonishment he confessed, that he knew very little on the subject. He had indeed occasionally read one or two of their older writers, but not so as to enable him to speak of their merits...the subject had not particularly excited his curiosity" (*Biographia Literaria*, vol. II, p. 239). Klopstock had first-hand knowledge of Old High German literature, and of that of other older Teutonic dialects; though his study in these subjects appears to have been of a desultory nature. "Sein unmethodischer Dilettantismus hinderte ihn nicht, reiche Kenntnisse über unser Altertum anzusammeln und auch den einen oder andern Fund in der Germanistik zu machen" (F. Muncker, *F. G. Klopstock*, Zweite Auflage, Berlin, 1900, pp. 385 ff.).

[2] W. Knight, *Life of Wordsworth*, vol. I, p. 172.

remarkable in Klopstock, however, beyond this peculiarity and the thickness of his legs, which it seems were swollen by illness. Dorothy, with more sentiment "could not look upon him, the benefactor of his country, the father of German poetry, without emotion."

At Hamburg, the friends parted, Coleridge settling for a time at Ratzeburg, the Wordsworths moving to Goslar in the Harz. This separation and the respective choices of residence appear to be a departure from their original programme for the German visit; for they had proposed to pass two years in Germany in order to learn German and acquire "a tolerable stock of information in natural science." For this purpose they were to settle in a village near a University. Neither Ratzeburg, some eighty miles east of Hamburg, nor Goslar, about that distance from Göttingen, seemed to advance the project materially. Coleridge afterwards moved to Göttingen, but the Wordsworths remained at Goslar almost all the time they stayed in Germany, which, however, proved a shorter period than they had expected. The visit, indeed, does not appear to have answered the purposes for which it was undertaken, as far as the Wordsworths are concerned. Their visit coincided with an exceptionally cold winter, and Wordsworth had a particularly cold room. Then there was "no society at Goslar," wrote Dorothy; the shy, reserved couple talked to the people of the house they stayed in, and apparently to no one else. William was very industrious, and they read German; but with singularly little result, to all appearance. They went on improving, however, if not so expeditiously as they might have done, Dorothy informs a correspondent. They fled when the warmer weather came, and after spending a week or two with Coleridge in Göttingen, in April 1799, returned to England. It had been, no doubt, a harrowing experience:

> I travelled among unknown men,
> In lands beyond the sea;
> Nor, England! did I know till then
> What love I bore to thee.
> 'Tis past, that melancholy dream!
> Nor will I quit thy shore
> A second time....

Nevertheless, he brought back from the alien land half-a-dozen of the most exquisite of his lyrics, and the joyful opening of the *Prelude*; and that, after all, was worth the misery, and was better than learning German. As late as 1802, Dorothy was trying, if a little languidly, to "keep up" her German[1].

A few words may be said here of the influence of German literature upon Wordsworth. Crabb Robinson[2] notices a "German bent" in Wordsworth's mind, and doubtless we may find in the general tenour of his philosophy, in his conception of the ultimate reality of existence as "the eternal deep haunted forever by the eternal mind," and of Nature as the infinitely various symbol of the omnipresent mind, a metaphysical tendency which we shall meet at that time more frequently in Germany than in England. But there is reason to believe that the "German bent" of his mind was original rather than acquired, that it was so native and so determined in its idiosyncrasy that it shunned rather than sought encouragement from without. The relation of Wordsworth to German literature appears to have been of the most superficial description. As we have seen, the opportunity of learning German was neglected. There is no evidence of much German reading on Wordsworth's part, either then or subsequently, and his opinions of German authors, when expressed, show neither liking for them nor understanding of them[3]. Goethe he disliked, recognising in the personages of his *Iphigenie* "none of the dignified simplicity, none of the health and vigour" of Homer's heroes and heroines. He accused him, if he is correctly reported[4], of an "inhuman sensuality," of "wantonly outraging the sympathies of humanity." We may certainly regard Wordsworth as one who viewed German literature from an immense distance, from the very heart of his insularity, with a prejudice which rendered him incapable of perceiving in it much that was akin to his own spirit. The influence appears to be slight, and limited to ex-

[1] W. Knight, *Life of Wordsworth*, vol. I, pp. 198 ff.
[2] H. C. Robinson, *Diary*, vol I, p. 482.
[3] cp. The Bishop of Lincoln's *Reminiscences of Wordsworth*, in Knight's *Life of W.*, vol. II, p. 324; also reports of his conversation on the subject by Mrs Fletcher and by Caroline Fox, idem, vol. III, pp. 417 f., 465 f.
[4] W. Knight, *Life of Wordsworth*, 1889, vol. II, pp. 324–325.

ternals, at any rate after the early impressionable years. For Wordsworth no doubt was subjected like most of his intelligent contemporaries to the spell of fascination of Schiller's *Robbers*, and it lent some traits to his *Borderers*, though they are of a general character—Marmaduke as a noble-minded outlaw is akin by position to Karl Moor; and as Rea points out after Zeiger, there is probably a reminiscence of Franz Moor and of Spiegelberg in Oswald[1]. Besides the fairly definite influence traceable in these particulars, there is an indefinite quality or savour about the whole play which in its insipidity suggests Schiller diluted almost past recognition.

Many more details of influence have been attributed to Schiller's drama in this case. Thomas Rea, in his book on *Schiller's Dramas and Poems in England*, has followed the old bad tradition of fixing upon every scrap of resemblance and interpreting it as due to influence. It is not worth while analysing the cases in which he discovers influence in the present instance. We may quote one example as typical of the worst of his method: "The sunset scene towards the end of *The Excursion* (Canto VI)[2] reminds one strongly of the scene at the Danube. *The glory of the setting sun calls forth solemn thoughts in Wordsworth, just as it does in Karl Moor.*" The italics are mine. Is it necessary to comment to the effect that the setting sun might probably have called forth solemn thoughts in Wordsworth even if he had never read *The Robbers*?

In a few cases Wordsworth has acknowledged obligations to German writers. The stanza of the ballad *Ellen Irwin* he imitated from *Lenore*[3], using "a construction of stanza quite new in our language," he says, "except that the first and third lines do not, in my stanzas, rhyme." In a note to *The Seven Sisters*, he mentions that the story is borrowed from Friederike Brun[4]. Zeiger[5]

---

[1] cp. Rea, *Schiller's Dramas*, etc., pp. 18 ff.

[2] "The Excursion, Canto VI." Rea must really mean *Excursion*, Book IX, I think.

[3] For Wordsworth's opinion of *Lenore*, see Robberds, *Memoir*, vol. I, p. 319.

[4] For a comparison of *The Seven Sisters* and *Die Sieben Hügel* of F. Brun, see Zeiger, *Beiträge*, pp. 29–30.

[5] *Beiträge*, p. 32.

points out a resemblance between the beginning of *Hart Leap Well* and Strophe 26 of Bürger's *Der Wilde Jäger*. Some ideas in the Sonnet beginning "I grieved for Buonaparte" are generally and I think correctly referred to the conversation between the Piccolominis and Questenberg, in Coleridge's *Wallenstein* (Act I, Scene 4) as their origin; the date of the Sonnet (1802) strengthens the probability that the resemblances are not accidental. Less certain appears to me to be the connection between Max's remarks *(Piccolomini*, III, 4) on Mythology and the lines in the Fourth Book of *The Excursion* beginning *Once more to the distant ages of the world*. Zeiger[1] apparently accepts the opinion of R. P. Gillies on this point; he supposes further that Schiller's *Götter Griechenlands* may have influenced the same passage, and this appears to me very much more probable; the resemblances here are noticeable. The passage from *Die Piccolomini* just mentioned may, however, be reasonably regarded as the origin[2] of some lines of the 1816 Ode beginning: "When the soft hand of sleep had closed the latch...".

The above-mentioned instances are all, or nearly all, that can, in my opinion, be safely attributed to German influence. They amount to very little—some outlines and a faint reflection of the spirit of *Die Räuber*, a disquisition or two on the mythopoeic faculty after Schiller, a metrical scheme from Bürger, a tale from Friederike Brun: the literature of Germany, in supplying the theme or the manner in these few cases, has not necessarily penetrated beyond the poet's superficial consciousness; and there is nothing to show that it ever did so.

We left Coleridge at Ratzeburg, where he was making a serious attempt to master the language. By October 20, he is writing poetry in German, which, he tells his wife with a certain *naïveté*[3], "has excited no small wonder here for its purity and harmony." He soon began serious reading in German, and while in Ratzeburg collected materials for a history of the German peasant, and incorporated them in a series of letters to his patron Josiah Wedgwood. He derived his information

---

[1] *Beiträge*, pp. 39–40.
[2] Those beginning: "And Ye, Pierian Sisters, sprung from Jove...".
[3] Coleridge, *Letters*, E. H. C., vol. I, p. 263.

"not so much from books as from oral communications from the Amtmann here."[1] By January 1799 he reads "German as English, that is without any mental translation." In the letter to Poole in which he gives this information, he mentions his design of writing a Life of Lessing, which he is going to prepare at Göttingen[2]: "I have already written a little life from three different biographies." This plan of writing a Life of Lessing, interwoven with a sketch of the rise and progress of German literature, was longer lived than many of his schemes, though it ultimately shared the fate that befell most of them, and lapsed into nothingness. He made serious preparatory studies for this one, and even progressed some way perhaps in its execution. Writing to the Wedgwoods on May 21, 1799, from Göttingen[3] he says that he has collected materials for a history of the "Belles Lettres" of Germany before the time of Lessing, and has made "very large collections" for a Life of Lessing. Writing to Thomas Wedgwood in January 1800 from London[4] he expresses the intention of taking up work on the Life of Lessing in the ensuing April. In July of the same year he is working at the Introduction to the Life of Lessing, which, with his usual optimism, he trusts "will be in the press before Christmas, that is, the 'Introduction,' which will be published first." The last we hear of it from Coleridge is, I think, in a letter to Davy, October 9, 1800[5]. "The works which I gird myself up to attack as soon as many concerns will permit me, are the *Life of Lessing*, and the *Essay on Poetry*." Rather ominous is the remark which follows: "The latter is still more at my heart than the

---

[1] Letter to Thomas Poole, January 4, 1799. *Letters*, E. H. C., vol. I, p. 268. In a letter to Josiah Wedgwood, from Keswick, November 1, 1800 (Cottle, *Reminiscences*, p. 442), he writes: "You will in three weeks see the letters on the 'Rise and Condition of the German Boors.' I found it convenient to make up a volume out of my journey, etc. in North Germany—and the letters (your name of course erased) are in the printers' hands. I was so weary of transcribing and composing, that when I found those more carefully written than the rest, I even sent them off as they were." It is almost certainly to this book that he refers in a letter to Davy (Coleridge, *Letters*, Turnbull, pp. 205 f.), where he speaks of publishing a volume of letters from Germany, which will be "a decent *lounge* book, and not an atom more" (October 9, 1800). The book does not seem to have been published after all.

[2] *Letters*, E. H. C., vol. I, pp. 267 ff.

[3] Cottle, *Reminiscences*, pp. 427–428.   [4] idem, p. 431.

[5] Coleridge, *Letters*, Turnbull, pp. 206–207.

former." But we learn a little more of the project from what might be called its obituary notice in an exchange of remarks on the subject between William Taylor of Norwich and Southey: W. T. of N. to R. S., March 7, 1805, "I believe I shall now set about a 'Sketch of the Life and Writings of Lessing.' It was a project of Coleridge's never begun, I suspect." R. S. to W. T. of N., March 9, 1805, "Coleridge never began his 'Life of Lessing.' He made very ample collections for the introduction, which would have been a history of German literature,—*very ample*, for I have seen them; but concerning Lessing nothing was ever written, and in all probability never will. He has certainly given up the intention altogether."[1] Southey, in saying that nothing of the Life of Lessing was written was too absolute, since in the letter to Poole (Jan. 4, 1799; see p. 117) Coleridge makes a clear statement to the contrary; but he may have lost the little compilation referred to, as he seems subsequently to have lost the "very ample collections" for the Introduction.

While at Ratzeburg he wrote the adaptation of the German folk-song *Wenn ich ein Vöglein wär'*, his poem *Something Childish but Very Natural*. He sent it to his wife from Göttingen in April 1799. It is noticeable that while he describes his feelings when writing the poem, he makes no mention of its derivation[2].

He moved from Ratzeburg to Göttingen early in 1799. Here he took German lessons with Benecke, who afterwards told Beddoes that he had a very superficial knowledge of the language[3]. Professor Heyne, whom he ungratefully described to his wife as a "little, hopping, over-civil sort of thing" gave him permission to take out in his own name an indefinite number of books from the Göttingen Library, and he set to work to study the older German authors; he also attended Lectures on Physiology, Anatomy and Natural History. There were lectures held on Kant at the time of Coleridge's stay in Göttingen, and Bouterwek's lectures were strongly Kantian in inspiration. To what extent did Coleridge study Kant at this time? Leslie

[1] Robberds, *Memoir*, vol. II, pp. 74 ff.
[2] Coleridge, *Letters*, E. H. C., vol. I, p. 294.
[3] *Letters of T. L. Beddoes*. Edited by Edmund Gosse, London and New York, 1894. Limited edition.

Stephen places his first serious study of Kant in 1801, and this agrees closely with *Biographia Literaria* (1817) I, p. 145, where he speaks of his "fifteen years familiarity" with Kant's works[1]. But he was interested in metaphysics as well as in his literary studies at Göttingen, if we may believe Carlyon's account. Carlyon was one of a party of young Englishmen who were at Göttingen at the same time as Coleridge, and in his book *Early Years and Late Reflections*, he has recorded his recollections of the poet. A remark in *Early Years* suggests that Coleridge impressed his companions as being at that time an adherent of Kant's doctrines; and Carlyon tells us that "Coleridge was much amused at a young lady who expressed her surprise that he, not being a German, could understand Kant's writings 'which were not even intelligible to *her*!'"[2] We can hardly believe that Coleridge, with his strong metaphysical proclivities, would have missed this opportunity of studying, in favourable circumstances, a thinker who as we have seen, had long since attracted his attention. At the same time, Leslie Stephen seems positive, and gives his reasons, which appear cogent[3]. Perhaps the evidence that appears to contradict Leslie Stephen's opinion may be reconciled with it if we give sufficient weight to his epithet *serious*, and regard Coleridge's study of Kant in Germany as preliminary and insufficient to give him a comprehensive grasp of the subject.

He wrote at this time translations and adaptations of various German poets (see p. 122, note, for a list of his minor translations from German). In spite of Benecke's opinion of the superficiality of Coleridge's knowledge of German, there is no doubt that he steeped himself in the language and literature of the country during his residence at Ratzeburg and Göttingen. He left the latter place for England in June, 1799, and was again at Stowey in August, with £30 worth of German books[4].

The outward events of Coleridge's life do not greatly concern us further. The expedition to Germany and the studies under-

[1] Coleridge, *Letters*, E. H. C., p. 351, note.
[2] Carlyon, *Early Years*, vol. I, p. 162.
[3] See *Letters of S. T. Coleridge*, edited by E. H. Coleridge, London, 1895, vol. I, p. 351, note, for a letter in which Leslie Stephen discusses the question.
[4] See Cottle, *Reminiscences*, pp. 428, 431.

taken there are almost the last instance of steady and consecutive effort over a considerable period of time on his part. The rest of his life presents a singularly fitful and fragmentary appearance; the habit of taking opium becomes more and more fixed, and a kind of paralysis lames his faculties.

Early in 1800 Coleridge was in London, working for the publisher Longman at the translation of *Die Piccolomini* and *Wallensteins Tod*[1]. According to Brandl[2] he sat close at his task for six weeks, from the beginning of March onwards, but in a letter to Godwin of May 21, 1800[3], he says that the translation of *Wallenstein* has *hitherto* prevented him writing, which, if taken literally, extends the time accorded to the task beyond the date given by Professor Brandl; Coleridge adds moreover, "not that it (the translation) engrossed my time, but that it wasted and depressed my spirits, and left a sense of wearisomeness and disgust which unfitted me for anything but sleeping or immediate society." We hear much in his letters of the depression this work produced in him—"the accursed Wallenstein," he calls it, writing to Josiah Wedgwood some months later (Nov. 1, 1800) and complains of "deep, unutterable disgust" suffered in the work. A further indication of his state of mind about the play after his translation of it may be found in a letter to the Editor of the Monthly Review, written in panic fear lest he should be regarded as an admirer of the German Theatre, which by this time, after the Kotzebue deluge, was in bad repute. Coleridge wrote as follows:

To the Editor of the Monthly Review, Greta Hall, Keswick, November 18, 1800. In the review of my translation of Schiller's *Wallenstein* (Review for October), I am numbered among the partisans of the German theatre. As I am confident there is no passage in my preface or notes from which such an opinion can be legitimately formed, and as the truth would not have been exceeded if the direct contrary had been affirmed, I claim it of your justice that in your

---

[1] The MS from which Coleridge translated had been prepared by Schiller, and sent to Bell, who sold it to Longman, who commissioned Coleridge. The MS differs in many respects from the printed play; cp. Prof. K. Breul's Introduction to *Wallenstein* (*Wallenstein*, ed. by Karl Breul, Litt.D., 2 vols., Cambridge University Press, 1894 and 1896, vol. II, pp. xlix–li).

[2] Brandl, *Coleridge*, p. 271.

[3] Coleridge, *Letters*, Turnbull, p. 193.

Answers to correspondents you would remove this misrepresentation. The mere circumstance of translating a manuscript play is not even evidence that I admired that one play, much less that I am a general admirer of the plays in that language. I remain, etc. S. T. Coleridge.

His ardour towards the "Bard tremendous in sublimity" seems to have abated considerably by this time. We shall refer again in some detail to the variations in Coleridge's opinion of Schiller.

Coleridge's reasons for not translating the *Lager*, as stated in the preface to the first edition[1], were that it is not necessary as a preliminary explanation, that the difficulties of a translation in the same form are insuperable, and that a translation into prose or any other metre than that of the original would give "a false notion both of its style and purport."

Coleridge's translation of the two other parts of *Wallenstein*, in spite of the refractory mood in which it seems to have been written, gives to some extent a worthy notion of Schiller's drama. It lacks, no doubt, something of the vigour, of the sharpness of outline of the original, but it is a dignified performance, and on the whole a very faithful and fairly successful attempt to render Schiller's manner and thought. Roscher, and especially Machule (see Bibliographical Note to this Chapter), have made a long analysis of the inaccuracies of translation. This list of mistakes has a somewhat formidable appearance; and although many of them are trivial, and some erroneously ascribed to Coleridge[2], I think one must agree with Machule when he says (p. 238) that the comparison reveals a considerable number of gross errors of translation. Coleridge has also a tendency to emphasise and amplify, which impairs the fidelity of his translation. But the high level of the style compensates for many defects; the play as thus presented to the English reader does

---

[1] Coleridge, *Poetical Works*, vol. II, p. 724.

[2] Machule's imperfect acquaintance with English has led him to attribute error at times where it does not exist: e.g. p. 212 "Ich darf nicht länger schweigen, muss die Binde—Von deinen Augen nehmen"; is translated by Coleridge:

"I dare no longer stand in silence—dare
No longer see thee wandering on in darkness
Nor pluck the bandage from thine eye...",

where *nor* etc. has the value of "without plucking the bandage etc.", and is not, as Machule imagines, an erroneous translation.

not offend literary taste, and gives, if an incomplete and blurred, not a degraded idea of the original. And claiming this for it, is to claim for it a high place among translations[1]. Coleridge's translation of *Wallenstein* was published at an unfortunate moment. The prodigious success of Kotzebue, more perhaps than the easy advantage which the Anti-Jacobin had taken of his absurdities, had discredited the German drama in the opinion of the more cultured public. Coleridge's translation was very coldly received. It was not until German literature was regaining its hold on the public favour that interest in Coleridge's version revived; Gillies points out, says Rea, that the existence of Coleridge's *Wallenstein* was forgotten until Scott used it to furnish mottoes for the chapter-headings of the Waverley novels[2].

Apart from *Wallenstein*[3], Coleridge translated or adapted a considerable number of shorter poems from German. Most of these renderings are from writers of slight merit[4]; and do not

---

[1] For Brandl's very favourable opinion—more favourable perhaps than that given in the text—see his *Coleridge*, pp. 274–280. Carlyle's opinion, given in the *Life of Schiller*, may also be worth quoting: "...Judging from many large specimens, we should pronounce it, excepting Sotheby's *Oberon*, to be the best, indeed the only sufferable translation from the German with which our literature has yet been enriched."

[2] T. Rea, *Schiller's Dramas*, etc., p. 73.

[3] For a translation of Arndt's *Geist der Zeit*, announced by Coleridge in 1808, but probably never made, see Haney, *Influence*, p. 27.

[4] Translated or adapted are: from Matthison: *Catullian Hendecasyllables* (no date) (a fairly close translation of lines from the *Milesisches Märchen*); from Stolberg: (a) *Tell's Birthplace* (date unknown) (translation of *Bei Wilhelm Tells Geburtstätte*), (b) *The British Stripling's War-Song* (published August 17, 1799) (translation, with adaptations, of the *Lied eines deutschen Knaben*), (c) *Hymn to the Earth* (date uncertain) (adaptation of part of the *Hymne an die Erde*), (d) Conclusion of *Fancy in Nubibus* (1817) (imitation of lines in *An das Meer*), (e) *On a Cataract* (date?) (some lines translated from "Unsterblicher Jüngling, u.s.w."); from Schiller: (a) *The Homeric Hexameter described*, and *The Ovidian Elegiac Metre described* (1799?) (translated from *Distichen auf den Hexameter und Pentameter*), (b) *The Visit of the Gods*, imitated from Schiller (first published 1817) (a partly close translation of the *Besuch der Götter*); from Friederike Brun: *Hymn before Sunrise, in the Vale of Chamouni* (first published 1802) (free imitation of *Chamouni vor Sonnenaufgang*); from Goethe: from the German, *Know'st thou the Land* (1799?) (fragment of translation of *Kennst du das Land*); from Folk-song: *Something Childish but Very Natural* (1799) (adaptation of *Wenn ich ein Vöglein wär'*). The conception of the Lover's Resolution (*The Picture*, 1802) was borrowed from Gessner's *Der Feste Vorsatz*. To these must be added epigrams from Lessing, Wernicke, and less-known epigram-writers, of which some twenty

occupy a place of much importance in Coleridge's work. We must except *Something Childish but Very Natural*, which has caught in some degree the naïve charm of the original; the *Hymn before Sunrise*, which is at any rate an attempt in a large style; and a lyric, not so well-known as *Kubla Khan*, but belonging perhaps to Coleridge's finest inspiration. I refer to *Glycine's Song*, first published in *Zapolya* (1817, written 1815), Act II, Scene 1:

GLYCINE'S SONG

> A sunny shaft did I behold,   1
> From sky to earth it slanted:
> And poised therein a bird so bold—
> Sweet bird, thou wert enchanted!
>
> He sank, he rose, he twinkled, he trolled   5
> Within that shaft of sunny mist;
> His eyes of fire, his beak of gold,
> All else of amethyst!
>
> And thus he sang: "Adieu! adieu!
> Love's dreams prove seldom true.   10
> The blossoms they make no delay:
> The sparkling dew-drops will not stay.
>   Sweet month of May,
>   We must away;
>   Far, far away!   15
>   To-day! to-day!"

Various readings of certain lines of the *Song*[1]:

  1. A pillar grey did I behold.
  4. A faery Bird that chanted.
  6. For *sunny*: shiny.

In E. H. Coleridge's edition of S. T. Coleridge's *Poetical Works* (1912), vol. I, p. 426, a note to *Glycine's Song* refers the reader to the Appendices for a prose-version of the *Song*, "probably a translation from the German." After reading the

have been identified by Professor H. G. Fiedler and Miss Schlesinger (see Coleridge, *Poetical Works*, vol. II, p. 951, note). In a notebook containing entries of an early date, there are some forty-eight numbered specimens of various metres derived from German and Italian sources (see *Poetical Works*, vol. II, p. 1014). Finally, the adaptation of Tieck's *Herbstlied*, fully dealt with in the text.

[1] Coleridge, *Poetical Works*, vol. I, p. 427.

PROSE VERSION OF GLYCINE'S
SONG IN "ZAPOLYA"[1]

1

On the sky with liquid openings of Blue,
The slanting pillar of sun mist,
Field-inward flew a little Bird.
Pois'd himself on the column,
Sang with a sweet and marvellous voice,
    Adieu! adieu!
I must away, Far, far away,
    Set off to-day.

2

Listened—listened—gaz'd—
Sight of a Bird, sound of a voice—
It was so well with me, and yet so strange.
    Heart! Heart!
Swell'st thou with joy or smart?
But the Bird went away—
    Adieu! adieu!

3

All cloudy the heavens falling and falling—
Then said I—Ah! summer again—
The swallow, the summer-bird is going,
And so will my Beauty fall like the leaves
From my pining for his absence,
And so will his Love fly away.
    Away! away!
Like the summer-bird,
    Swift as the Day.

4

But lo! again came the slanting sun-shaft,
Close by me pois'd on its wing,
The sweet Bird sang again,
And looking on my tearful Face
    Did it not say,
    "Love has arisen,
True Love makes its summer,
    In the Heart"?

[1] Coleridge, *Poetical Works*, vol. II, p. 1109.

TIECK'S "HERBSTLIED"

1

Feldeinwärts flog ein Vögelein,
Und sang im muntern Sonnenschein
Mit süssem wunderbarem Ton:
Ade! ich fliege nun davon,
 Weit! Weit!
 Reis' ich noch heut.

2

Ich horchte auf den Feldgesang,
Mir ward so wohl und doch so bang
Mit frohem Schmerz, mit trüber Lust
Stieg wechselnd bald und sank die Brust:
 Herz! Herz!
 Brichst du vor Wonn' oder Schmerz?

3

Doch als ich Blätter fallen sah,
Da sagt' ich: Ach! der Herbst ist da,
Der Sommergast, die Schwalbe, zieht,
Vielleicht so Lieb' und Sehnsucht flieht,
 Weit! Weit!
 Rasch mit der Zeit.

4

Doch rückwärts kam der Sonnenschein,
Dicht zu mir drauf das Vögelein
Es sah mein thränend Angesicht
Und sang: Die Liebe wintert nicht,
 Nein! Nein!
 Ist und bleibt Frühlingsschein.

prose-version, I hunted, at a lucky venture, through Tieck's poems[1] and was rewarded by the discovery (p. 25) of the poem which is printed above (pp. 124–125), parallel to the prose-version of *Glycine's Song*. This poem of Tieck's is classed in the edition I used among those written between 1793 and 1799.

There are some rather puzzling differences between the original and the translation. Lines translated literally are interspersed with others that seem to bear no relation to the German text. It is possible, of course, that another version of the poem lay before Coleridge when he made his translation. This is not a probable explanation, however, especially in view of the unequal length of the strophes in the prose-version, which suggests interpolation. Another suggestion may be more acceptable, and has a trifle of evidence in its favour. This alternative sugges-tion is that Coleridge, requiring a song for Glycine in *Zapolya*, had noted down certain lines or ideas for lines before he came across Tieck's *Herbstlied*; that reading it, he was struck by the metrical arrangement, and the theme of the bird that sings farewell at the summer's end, and resolved to blend so much of the *Herbstlied* with his own previous idea as might be convenient: hence the prose-version, in which lines literally translated from the *Herbstlied* alternate with some drawn from the earlier scheme. The fragment of evidence in support of this theory is that more than once (in 1799 and 1803), long before the probable date of the composition of the poem, Coleridge had been struck by the nature-picture of the first and second lines of the *Song* (the second of the prose-version). In a note of 1799 occurs the expression: "Slanting pillars of misty light moved along[2] under the sun hid by clouds," and on October 21, 1803, he observes how "slanting pillars travel across the lake at long intervals."[3]

---

[1] Ludwig Tieck, *Gedichte*, Berlin, 1841.

[2] cp. the prose-version: "The slanting pillar of sun mist."

[3] Coleridge, *Anima Poetae*, p. 9. The Phoenix in Tieck's *Elfen* may have given some touches to the picture. Coleridge knew *Phantasus*, in which *Die Elfen* is included, in 1820 at any rate (see letter to Allsop, April 8, 1820, quoted on p. 79, note). The Phoenix has a wonderful song, and its gorgeous colouring is emphasised: "Sein Gefieder war purpurn und grün, durch welches sich die glänzenden goldenen Streifen zogen, auf seinem Haupte bewegte sich ein Diadem von so hellleuchtenden kleinen Federn, dass sie wie Edelgesteine blitzten. Der Schnabel war rot, und die Beine glänzend blau." There appears to me to be, in spite of the differences, a suggestion

If this suggestion is correct, it opens an exceptionally large rift into the poet's workshop, at a moment when a masterpiece is on the frames; the psychological critic may peer through and observe one stage of the transmutation of borrowed elements, of the process by which they are purged of the dross of the commonplace and wrought into the miracle of beauty.

Little further direct influence from German sources on Coleridge's purely literary work remains to be noted. *Remorse*, which was played at Drury Lane in 1813, and had a run of twenty nights, is a recast of *Osorio*, written in 1797. The first three acts of *Remorse* are taken with some modifications from the Sicilian's *Story of Jeronymo and Lorenzo* in Schiller's *Geisterseher*, a translation of which had appeared in 1795. There are points of resemblance between the reasoning villain Ordonio and Franz Moor, though Margraf[1] goes too far, I think, in calling him "ein erschütterndes Abbild des Franz Moor." Ordonio is not a crass self-seeking materialist and cynic like Franz, but a more subtle and less powerful figure. In Coleridge's preface to the earlier form of the play, in which Ordonio is named Osorio, there is an analysis of the personage which I reproduce here, underlining the traits which appear to me to constitute important deviations in Ordonio's character from that of Franz Moor:

A man, who *from constitutional calmness of appetites*, is seduced into pride and the love of power, by these into misanthropism, or rather a contempt of mankind, and from thence, by the co-operation of envy, and a curiously modified love for a beautiful female (which is nowhere developed in the play), into a most atrocious guilt. A man who is in truth *a weak man, yet always duping himself into the belief that he has a soul of iron.* Such were some of my leading ideas[2].

Rea mentions two points of resemblance of detail which may not be accidental[3]:

of Coleridge's enchanted bird here, and throughout the passage in *Die Elfen*, where the bird sings to the throng. The resemblance will not bear pressing, I admit, particularly in view of remarks made in various parts of this study on undue readiness to discover originals in German writers!

[1] E. Margraf, *Einfluss*, p. 20.
[2] Coleridge, *Poetical Works*, vol. II, p. 1114.
[3] T. Rea, *Schiller's Dramas*, etc., p. 25.

In Act II, Sc. I, where Osorio urges Ferdinand to deceive Maria with the portrait, we are reminded of the scene in *The Robbers*, where Franz incites Hermann to do a similar thing (*Räuber*, Act II, Sc. I and 2). The words of Velez to Maria in Act IV, "Repent and marry him—or to the convent," seem to be suggested by the scene where Franz threatens Amalia with a similar fate.

That the secret assembly of the Moors in which the death of Ordonio is decreed is a reminiscence of the Femgericht is perhaps rather probable than not[1]. When Coleridge recast *Osorio* in its later form, which he named *Remorse*, he embodied, as Margraf points out, some lines of his *Wallenstein* in it without much modification[2]. Margraf holds that there is influence from *Wallenstein* on the character of Emerick in *Zapolya* (1817). I doubt whether a comparison of the two will confirm his opinion in a careful reader's mind[3].

I will conclude this sketch of Coleridge's relation to German literature with some account of his later reading in German and of his opinions of German writers of greater and less eminence. It is a little surprising to find how fragmentary Coleridge's reading in German appears to have been, or, if this conclusion, in view of the imperfect means we have of gauging the extent of his reading, be not fully justified, at least how completely he failed to grasp the fact of the revival of German literature as a whole[4]. He makes little reference to the older German

[1] Margraf's remark (*Einfluss*, p. 20) seems couched in about the right strain of uncertainty: "(während) die Scene, in der die Mauren zusammenkommen, um über die Bestrafung des Bösewichts Osorio zu beratschlagen, an das in den deutschen Schauerromanen jener Zeit so häufig wiederkehrende Ceremoniell bei Abhaltung von Femgerichten erinnert."

[2] Margraf (*Einfluss*, p. 21) gives three instances of lines in *Remorse* palpably borrowed from the *Wallenstein* translation. His remark (pp. 20–21): "Auch Schillers 'Wallenstein,' den Coleridge inzwischen übersetzt hatte, machte in der neuen Fassung seinen Einfluss geltend, wie einige Stellen zeigen, die fast wörtlich herübergenommen sind," implies a singular latitude of meaning in the word *Einfluss*.

[3] I quote Margraf (loc. cit. p. 22): "Auch in dem dramatischen Gedicht 'Zapolya' (1817) lassen sich gewisse verwandte Züge auffinden; wenigstens scheint der Tyrann Emerick mit seinem soldatischen Wesen, seinem Hochverrat und vor allem mit seinem versteckten frevelhaften Streben nach der Krone von der Figur des Wallenstein beeinflusst zu sein, der ja gleichfalls sein Streben nach der höchsten Gewalt geschickt zu verbergen verstand." Such general resemblances have little value.

[4] As Haney, *Influence*, p. 40, has pointed out.

writers at any time, although he had studied Gothic and Old and Middle High German when in Germany (*Biographia Literaria*, vol. I, p. 203). He brought some of the older German literature back with him to England, or acquired them after his return; for Southey, in a letter to Rickman, June 6, 1804 (Southey, *Life*, vol. II, p. 290), mentions sending to Sharon Turner "a parcel of old German or Theotistic books of Coleridge's." *Theotistic* probably means Old High German, as Coleridge (*Biographia*, loc. cit.) evidently uses *Theotiscan* for O.H.G.

Hans Sachs, whom he read in Germany, appears alone of older German writers to have made a lasting impression on him. In *Biographia Literaria* (1817, p. 204) he speaks of the "rude, yet interesting strains of Hans Sachs the cobbler of Nuremberg." Crabb Robinson, in his notes on Coleridge's Lectures at the beginning of 1808, says: "Mr Coleridge met with an ancient MS at Helmstadt, in which God was represented visiting Noah's family; the descendants of Cain did not pull off their hats to the great visitor." In the *Lectures and Notes on Shakspere and Other English Poets, by Samuel Taylor Coleridge*[1] we have a report of Coleridge's words thus referred to which rectifies a slight error of Robinson's: "I have myself a piece of this kind, which I transcribed a few years ago at Helmstadt, in Germany, on the education of Eve's children, in which, after the fall and repentance of Adam, the offended Maker, as in proof of his reconciliation, condescends to visit them, and to catechise the children." He goes on to describe the piece more fully. It is, of course, the Comedia of Hans Sachs entitled *Die Ungleichen Kinder Eve* (for the ill-mannered conduct of Cain, who offers the Almighty his left hand to shake and keeps his hat on his head, see ll. 368–375). Here we probably have the solution of a little problem which has puzzled commentators. Perry, in his essay on *German Influence in English Literature*[2], remarks that "it is likely that Coleridge had read *Faust* at about that time (1800), for in a letter to him, dated August 6, 1800, Lamb, enumerating some things he had sent him, mentions 'one or two small German books, and that drama in which Got-fader

---

[1] Now first collected by T. Ashe, B.A., 1885, p. 108.
[2] Atlantic Monthly, August 1877.

performs.'" Haney points out that this can hardly be taken as referring to *Faust*, since the *Prolog im Himmel* (the only scene to which this characteristic description of Lamb's might apply) is not found in *Faust, Ein Fragment* 1790, which was the only form in which *Faust* was known at that time. There seems a strong probability that Lamb is referring to Coleridge's transcription of *Die Ungleichen Kinder Eve*; Lamb did not know German, but Coleridge, impressed as he was by this play (he talked about it at Göttingen to his English companions, see Carlyon, *Early Years*, vol. 1, pp. 93–94), had not improbably given Lamb an outline of it.

We have already noted Coleridge's early interest in Gessner (see p. 99), whose *Tod Abels* he had imitated in the fragmentary *Wanderings of Cain*. At about the same time as he published his adaptation of *Der Feste Vorsatz*, he was writing a translation of another poem of Gessner's, which has been lost. This was a blank verse rendering of *Der Erste Schiffer*, in the summer of 1802, apparently at the request of Sotheby, the translator of Wieland's *Oberon*. It was to be included in a book, to be published in a "gay livery" by an unidentified Mr Tomkins, a friend of Sotheby's. The letters to Sotheby which give us the history of this translation are full of bitter contempt for Gessner as author of *Der Erste Schiffer*; he likes the idea of the poem but hopes to discover that this is not original in Gessner, "he has so abominably maltreated it; the story is artificially constructed, the machinery contemptible, the moral tone objectionably suggestive." The translation was probably never sent to Mr Tomkins, and was ultimately lost. The title would have been *The First Navigator*[1]. Writing to Godwin, on March 26, 1811, Coleridge says: "I told dear Miss Lamb that I had formed a complete plan of a poem, with little plates for children, the *first* thought, but that alone, taken from Gessner's First Mariner; and this thought, I have reason to believe [the reason may well have been purely subjective, cp. the letters to Sotheby] was not an invention of Gessner's." In the same letter he says " ...I once translated into blank verse about half of the poem,

---

[1] See Letters to Sotheby, July 13, 19, August 26, September 10, 1802, in Coleridge, *Letters*, E. H. C. vol. 1, pp. 369 ff.

but gave it up under the influence of a double disgust, moral and poetical."[1] Apparently his memory failed him here, for in a letter to Sotheby of August 26, 1802, he tells him: "I have finished the 'First Navigator,' and Mr Tomkins may have it whenever he wishes."

Miss Bertha Reed, in her book on the *Influence of Solomon Gessner upon English Literature*[2] attributes influence with a recklessness unusual even in this branch of research; she finds the influence of Gessner on Coleridge extending even to *Christabel* and *The Ancient Mariner*.

Coleridge regarded Wieland as a poet with admiration, to judge at least by the only reference to him which I have noted, from the Recollections of May 1811 communicated by Mr Justice Coleridge (*Table Talk*, p. 344): "The Germans were not a poetical nation in the very highest sense. Wieland was their best poet: his subject was bad, and his thought often impure; but his language was rich and harmonious, and his fancy luxuriant. Sotheby's translation had not at all caught the manner of the original."

Fouqué's masterpiece *Undine* he appreciated warmly, reading it several times in German and once in an English translation (that of E. Littell, of Philadelphia, published 1824, in the opinion of the editor of the *Table Talk*)[3].

The meeting with Klopstock finally dispelled any feeling of admiration towards him, and from the date of his visit he has scarcely a good word to say for him. Thus, in Crabb Robinson's *Diary*, July 28, 1811: "Coleridge, talking of German poetry, represented Klopstock as compounded of everything bad in Young, Hervey, and Richardson"; a remark which we find in a somewhat amplified form in the Recollections of Mr Justice Coleridge, and which cannot be called penetrating[4]. At times

---

[1] Coleridge, *Letters*, Turnbull, vol. II, pp. 68, 69.
[2] Philadelphia, 1905.   [3] Coleridge, *Table Talk*, vol. I, p. 158.
[4] It is interesting to compare this remark with one in *Biographia Literaria*. I will quote both passages:
(a) (*Table Talk*, vol. II, p. 344): "Mr Coleridge was asked what he thought of Klopstock. He answered, that his fame was rapidly declining in Germany; that an Englishman might form a correct notion of him by uniting the moral epigram of Young, the bombast of Hervey, and the minute description of Richardson."
(b) (*Biographia Literaria*, vol. II, p. 258): "But to understand the true character of the *Robbers*, and of the countless imitations which were its

Coleridge is at some pains to indulge in heavy pleasantries on the subject of "Klubstick," the liveliest of which is contained in a letter to Sotheby of July 13, 1802:

> I must, though, tell you the malicious motto which I have written in the first part of Klopstock's "Messias":
>
> "Tale tuum carmen nobis, divine poeta!
> Quale sopor!"
>
> Only I would have the words *divine poeta* translated "verse-making divine."

Coleridge in a facetious mood is almost inhuman in his clumsiness.

We have already seen Coleridge making use of a poem of Tieck's for the song in *Zapolya*. In his last conversation with Allsop he quoted from Tieck's *Gemälde*[1]. From a passage in *Old Mortality* he concluded (see p. 79) that Scott had been reading *Phantasus*[2]. It seems probable that he read *William Lovell*; at least, on June 20, 1817, he has obtained "Tieck's William Lovell and his friend Wagenröder's (sic) Phantasien," and has already read a few pages of the latter, which interested him much, but not to enthusiasm[3]. *Sternbald* he thought "too

---

spawn, I must inform you, or at least call to your recollection, that about that time, and for some years before it, three of the most popular books in the German language were the translations of Young's *Night Thoughts*, Hervey's *Meditations*, and Richardson's *Clarissa Harlowe*. Now we have only to combine the bloated style and peculiar rhythm of Hervey...with the strained thoughts, the figurative metaphysics and solemn epigrams of Young on the one hand; and with the loaded sensibility, the minute detail, the morbid consciousness of every thought and feeling in the whole flux and reflux of the mind, in short, the self-involution and dream-like continuity of Richardson on the other hand; and then to add the horrific incidents, and mysterious villains...to add the ruined castles, the dungeons, the trap-doors, the skeletons, the flesh and blood ghosts and the perpetual moonshine of a modern author, (themselves the literary brood of the Castle of Otranto...),—and as the compound of these ingredients duly mixed, you will recognize the so-called German Drama."

These two remarks taken in conjunction almost amount to saying that *The Robbers* is Klopstock plus Anne Radcliffe, a formula which, while showing a certain ingenuity, is certainly not wide enough to cover this phase of *Sturm und Drang*.

[1] Allsop, *Letters*, vol. I, pp. 65 ff.
[2] Coleridge, *Letters*, Turnbull, vol. II, p. 185.
[3] Carré, *Quelques Lettres*, p. 38. Carré says that the letter of Coleridge to Henry Crabb Robinson, in which this occurs, has never been published,

like an imitation of Heinse's 'Ardinghello'"[1] (to Green, Dec. 13, 1817). The latter he had known for at least five years. He either used it or intended to use it for his third series of Lectures, begun in May 1812, as appears from a letter to his wife from London, April 21, 1812: "There is one (book) scarcely a book, but a collection of loose sheets tied up together, at Grasmere, which I want immediately...It is a German Romance with some name beginning with an A, followed by 'oder Die Glückliche (sic) Inseln'...If sent off immediately it would be of serious benefit to me in my lectures."[2] In Lessing he was interested on the critical and philosophical side rather than from the literary point of view. He admired his style; his writings "for *manner*, are absolutely perfect" he remarked in 1833[3]. And he thought he had, of all Germans, "the best notion of blank verse"(!) He has the following sensible if not profound remarks on Lessing's dramas:

Their deficiency is in depth and in imagination: their excellence is in the construction of the plot; the good sense of the sentiments; the sobriety of the morals; and the high polish of the dialogue. In short, his dramas are the very antipodes of all those which it has been the fashion of late years at once to abuse and to enjoy, under the name of the German Drama (*Biographia Literaria*, vol. II, p. 257)[4].

The first unqualified and uncritical admiration of Schiller, based on his reading of *The Robbers*, was to be modified by more extensive reading, and it may be worth while to trace the phases of his opinion. By 1797 the enthusiasm with which he regarded the "convulser of the heart" whose "human beings agitate and astonish more than all the *goblin* rout—even of Shakespere," as we read in the Note, printed 1796, to the *Sonnet to the Author of the Robbers*, has considerably subsided. He counts but three or four of "those profound touches of the human heart" in *The Robbers*, which are to be found in Shakespeare often, and

although marked *copied* by Sadler. But part of it at least is quoted by Brandl, *Coleridge und die englische Romantik*, p. 397.
    [1] Coleridge, *Letters*, E. H. C. vol. II, p. 683.
    [2] idem, p. 582.   [3] Coleridge, *Table Talk*, pp. 116, 323.
    [4] Haney (*Influence*, p. 41), points out the importance of Lessing as furnishing a basis for Coleridge's Shakespeare criticism, and gives a reference to Lowell's *Literary and Political Addresses*, p. 71.

continually, it would seem from the context, in Wordsworth's *Borderers* (Letter to Cottle, June 1797)[1]. The *Wallenstein* translation, with the drudgery it involved, did not induce in him a frame of mind favourable to the appreciation of Schiller. In his preface, indeed, he places it above *The Robbers*, and mentions individual beauties in the commendatory spirit suitable in a translator; but other public and private utterances of his at this time reveal a very unfavourable opinion of the play (cp. p. 120) or at least one quite divested of enthusiasm. Later, however, he formed a more considered and favourable judgment of it. In 1812, he praised *Wallenstein* to Crabb Robinson, while censuring Schiller for a "sort of ventriloquism in poetry." "By the by, a happy term to express that common fault of throwing the sentiments and feelings of the writer into the bodies of other persons, the characters of the poem," Robinson adds[2]. Another remark, made towards the end of his life, seems to show a further stage of understanding and admiration. Speaking of Schiller's second manner, he says:

> After this he outgrew the composition of such plays as *The Robbers*, and at once took his true and only rightful stand in the grand historical drama—the *Wallenstein*; not the intense drama of passion,—he was not master of that—but the diffused drama of history, in which he had ample scope for his varied powers. The *Wallenstein* is the greatest of his works: it is not unlike Shakespeare's historical plays—a species by itself.

In 1817 he characterises *The Robbers* as the "pledge, and promise, of no ordinary genius," and although he holds this work responsible for Kotzebue and all the monstrosities of the "German Drama" as it was transplanted to England at the end of the eighteenth century, yet he considers Schiller's later censure of his work unnecessarily severe: "...In his latter years his indignation at the unwonted popularity of the *Robbers* seduced him into the *contrary* extremes, viz. a studied feebleness of interest (as far as the interest was to be derived from incidents and the excitement of curiosity); a diction elaborately metrical; the affectation of rhymes; and the pedantry of the

---

[1] Cottle, *Early Recollections*, p. 250.
[2] H. C. Robinson, *Diary*, vol. I, p. 396.

chorus."[1] He thought ill of Schiller's blank verse, "he moves in it like a fly in a glue-bottle," though his thoughts have connection and variety[2]. A remark of 1822 characterises Schiller's earlier manner with some felicity: "Schiller has the material sublime; to produce an effect, he sets you a whole town on fire, and throws infants with their mothers into the flames, or locks up a father in an old tower. But Shakespeare drops a handkerchief, and the same or greater effects follow."[3] He adopted this happy expression "material sublime" and used it again in 1833, when differentiating between Schiller's earlier and later work: "Schiller had two legitimate phases in his intellectual character: the first as author of the *Robbers*—a piece which must not be considered in reference to Shakespeare, but as a work of the mere material sublime, and in that line it is undoubtedly very powerful indeed. It is quite genuine, and deeply imbued with Schiller's own soul..."[4]. Finally must be mentioned a remark from the notebooks of 1808 or 1809, which may be read with some curiosity.

If I have leisure [he writes], I may, perhaps, write a wild rhyme on the *Bell*, from the mine to the belfry, and take for my motto and Chapter of Contents, the two distichs, but especially the latter:

"Laudo Deum verum, plebem voco, congrego clerum:
Defunctos ploro, pestem fugo, festa decoro.
Funera plango, fulgura frango, sabbata pango:
Excito lentes, dissipo ventos, paco cruentes."

Not a hint that he was aware that a "wild rhyme" on the same theme and taking the motto *Vivos voco. Mortuos plango. Fulgura frango* had been public property for some ten years!

---

[1] Coleridge, *Biographia Literaria*, vol. II, p. 258. Presumably it was likewise the *Braut von Messina* that called forth the pained exclamation in 1805: "Schiller, disgusted with Kotzebuisms, deserts from Shakspere!" (*Anima Poetae*, p. 150). And in 1833 he again expressed his distaste for the *Braut*: "After this point it was, that Goethe and other writers injured by their theories the steadiness and originality of Schiller's mind; and in every one of his works after the *Wallenstein* you may perceive the fluctuations of his taste and principles of composition. He got a notion of introducing the characterlessness of the Greek tragedy with a chorus, as in *The Bride of Messina*, and he was for infusing more lyric verse into it" (Coleridge, *Table Talk*, vol. II, p. 116, February 16, 1833).

[2] Coleridge, *Table Talk*, vol. II, p. 323, June 1834.

[3] idem, vol. I, p. 2.

[4] idem, vol. II, p. 114.

However qualified his admiration for Schiller may have been, it was whole-hearted compared with his feeling towards Goethe: "The young men in England and Germany who admire Lord Byron," he is reported to have remarked in 1833, "prefer Goethe to Schiller; but you may depend upon it, Goethe does not, nor ever will, command the common mind of the people of Germany as Schiller does."[1] On the same occasion he reproaches both Goethe and Wordsworth with their objective attitude towards the characters of their fictitious personages; his expression is that they are always "spectators *ab extra*; feeling *for*, but never *with*, their characters." He finds Schiller "a thousand times more *hearty* than Goethe." Robinson, ever Goethe's champion, notes with disapproval, after an evening spent with Coleridge, that the latter sets "Goethe far below Schiller."[2] He praised, however, Goethe's lyrics highly on more than one occasion[3]. *Werther* he numbered at one time among *larmoyant* novels[4], but in 1813 he spoke of it as a fine portrayal of a man in a state of exalted sensibility, and thought that Goethe later under-rated the talent so eminently displayed in *Werther*[5]. *Wilhelm Meister* Coleridge liked best of Goethe's prose works; but he preferred Lessing's prose style to that of either Schiller or Goethe[6]. In March 1813 Robinson, calling on Coleridge one evening, found him in raptures over *Wilhelm Meister*, though he thought the conclusion bad, and Mignon's death and the scenes in the Castle "a sort of Ratcliffe scenes unworthy the exquisite earlier parts. He repeated *Kennst du das Land* with tears in his eyes, and he praised the Song of the Harper which Walter Scott told Coleridge was the original of his (a favourite scene) Minstrel in the Lay" (Crabb Robinson, *Typed Diary*, March 20, 1813). Coleridge denied merit to *Torquato Tasso*[7]. He censured in general

[1] Coleridge, *Table Talk*, vol. II, p. 114, February 16, 1833.
[2] H. C. Robinson, *Diary*, vol. II, p. 274.
[3] Coleridge, *Table Talk*, vol. II, p. 116, February 16, 1833, and p. 187, May 18, 1833.
[4] So Brandl, *Coleridge und die englische Romantik*, p. 125. He gives *The Watchman*, No. IV, as a reference.
[5] H. C. Robinson, *Diary*, vol. I, p. 407.
[6] Coleridge, *Table Talk*, vol. II, p. 116.
[7] H. C. Robinson, *Diary*, vol. I, p. 388, May 29, 1812.

Goethe's want of religion and enthusiasm, applying the term "picturesque" to Goethe's later manner, because "in after life he delighted to exhibit objects in which a pure sense of the beautiful was chiefly called into exercise. These purely *beautiful* objects, not objects of desire or passion, he coldly delighted to exhibit as a statuary does his succession of marble figures."[1] A favourite criticism of Coleridge's on Goethe was that he "wrote from an idea that a certain thing was to be done in a certain style, not from the fulness of sentiment on a certain subject."[2] Coleridge on one occasion excused his seeming depreciation of Goethe on the ground that "he compared him with the greatest of poets."[3] But it must be acknowledged that the high standard is less in evidence than the unfavourable comments to which it gives rise. There seems to be in Coleridge an antagonistic frame of mind concerning Goethe, and he fails to appreciate his literary personality as a whole. This may have been due partly to insufficient study of his works[4].

According to J. M. Carré he read *Faust* in 1809, and meditated writing an Anti-Faust in 1812[5]. The 1809 reading must have been that of the 1790 *Fragment*, and not the 1808 *Erster Teil*; for on August 13, 1812, Robinson reads him a "number of scenes out of the new 'Faust.' He (Coleridge) had before read the earlier edition."[6] This reading of *Faust* led to some discussion of the drama between Robinson and Coleridge. Coleridge considered the additions the finest part; he admired the *Zueignung*, and did not take offence at the *Prolog im Himmel*, as Robinson had expected him to do. He did not think Mephistopheles a character, but had nothing to oppose to Robinson's

---

[1] H. C. Robinson, *Diary*, vol. I, p. 305, November 15, 1801, and (Third edition) March 2, 1813.

[2] idem, vol. II, p. 274, June 10, 1824.

[3] idem, vol. I, p. 407.

[4] It is true that in 1816 he projected writing a work "on Goethe as poet and philosopher, with a bibliographical and critical analysis of his writings, with translations," as appears from a letter to Crabb Robinson edited by Carré (*Quelques Lettres inédites de William Taylor, Coleridge et Carlyle*, etc., p. 38). But this proves only that he intended to make a thorough study of Goethe's works, and Coleridge's intentions, even the most definite, had a way of evaporating without leaving a trace.

[5] Carré, *Quelques Lettres*, p. 37. Carré gives Quarterly Review, 1834, p. 52, as reference for the Anti-Faust.

[6] H. C. Robinson, *Diary*, vol. I, p. 395.

remark that Mephistopheles ought to be a mere abstraction. Less comprehensibly he objected that it is not explained how Faust is thrown into the state of mind that led to the catastrophe, meaning apparently by the catastrophe the pact with Mephistopheles[1].

It may have been Crabb Robinson who proposed to Murray that Coleridge would be a suitable translator of *Faust*: at least he offered to approach Coleridge in the matter, as appears from the *Typed Diary*, July 6, 1814: "...He (Murray) wishes to have *Faust* translated and I proposed to write to Coleridge on the subject." Shelley (v. p. 144 note) regarded Coleridge as the ideal translator of *Faust*. Robinson does not seem to have written to Coleridge on the subject of the *Faust*-translation; but Coleridge at Bristol received a letter from Lamb written at Robinson's request and containing Murray's proposal. Coleridge wrote to Murray from Bristol on August 23, 1814, to the effect that he would not be averse from making the translation, "thinking, as I do, that among many volumes of praiseworthy German poems the 'Louisa' of Voss, and the 'Faust' of Goethe, are the two, if not the only ones that are emphatically *original* in their conception, and characteristic of a new and peculiar sort of thinking and imagining..."[2]. Coleridge, while expressing his willingness to attempt the translation, says in the same letter that he will require all Goethe's works, which he cannot procure in Bristol; "for to give the 'Faust' without a preliminary critical Essay would be worse than nothing, as far as regards the public." Murray offered £100 for the translation, and Coleridge wrote promptly in reply, expressing his opinion of this inadequate offer. He pointed out that persons "of the highest accredited reputation" considered his translation of *Wallenstein* superior to the original: "the parts most admired were substitutions of my own, on a principle of compensation," a rather surprising remark. Whether Murray feared that Coleridge would unduly apply the principle of compensation to *Faust*, or was unwilling to agree to the conditions proposed by Coleridge, is not clear; only it is certain that nothing came of the proposal[3]. Are we to

---

[1] H. C. Robinson, *Diary*, vol. I, pp. 395 ff.
[2] Coleridge, *Letters*, E. H. C. p. 625.
[3] Nor of one made to Murray by Coleridge in 1816, for a periodical for

believe Coleridge, who said in 1833 that on being "pressed" to translate *Faust*, he "so far entertained the proposal as to read the work through with great attention," but decided that he might be better employed in composing a work of his own on similar lines (a project to which we shall return later); and secondly "debated within myself whether it became my moral character to render into English—and so far, certainly, lend my countenance to language—much of which I thought vulgar, licentious, and blasphemous. I need not tell you that I never put pen to paper, as the translator of Faust."[1] Crabb Robinson's version is different; he says in a letter to Goethe, Jan. 31, 1829: "Coleridge, too, the only living poet of acknowledged genius, who is also a good German scholar, attempted 'Faust,' but shrunk from it in despair."[2] At any rate, one capable of misunderstanding *Faust* as thoroughly as Coleridge seems to have done would hardly have made a good translator, and the flowing redundancy of Coleridge's style save at rare moments of supreme poetic excitement, would almost inevitably have inflated and weakened the tense nervous outline of *Faust* past recognition—especially if he applied his principle of compensation here.

To the end of his life he remained purblind to the significance of *Faust*, as the following extract from the *Table Talk* of 1833 makes clear:

The intended theme of the Faust is the consequences of a misology, or hatred and depreciation of knowledge caused by originally intense thirst for knowledge baffled. But a love of knowledge for itself, and for pure ends, would never produce such a misology, but only a love of it for base and unworthy purposes. There is neither causation nor progression in the Faust; he is a ready-made conjurer from the very beginning; the *incredulus odi* is felt from the first line. The sensuality and the thirst after knowledge are unconnected with each

the review of old books, "foreign writers, though alive, not to be excluded, if only their works are of established character in their own country, and scarcely heard of, much less translated, in English literature. Jean Paul Richter would supply two or three delightful articles" (S. Smiles, *A Publisher and his Friends*, vol. I, pp. 299 ff.). It may have been in consequence of this offer being rejected by Murray, that in August 1816 he proposed to Boosey and Co. the establishment of a periodical on German literature up to the present time (from Gellert and Klopstock) in the form of letters to his friends (Campbell, *Coleridge*, p. 224).

[1] Coleridge, *Table Talk*, vol. II, p. 117.
[2] H. C. Robinson, *Diary*, vol. II, p. 390.

other. Mephistopheles and Margaret are excellent; but Faust himself is dull and meaningless. The scene in Auerbach's cellars is one of the best, perhaps the very best; that on the Brocken is also fine; and all the songs are beautiful. But there is no whole to the poem; the scenes are mere magic-lantern pictures and a large part of the work is to me very flat.

A conclusion which is hardly surprising in the circumstances[1]. I find only one reference to *Faust II*, which is commendably short; he merely refers, on July 6, 1833, to "this continuation of Faust, which they tell me is very poor."[2]

Records of Coleridge's intention to write a play on the Faust-theme, or on one closely allied to it, exist in Crabb Robinson's *Diary* and in the second letter to Murray on the subject of the proposed *Faust*-translation. In the former[3] Robinson, who has recorded discussions with Coleridge, occasioned by the reading of *Faust Erster Teil*, remarks: "Coleridge talks of writing a new Faust! He would never get out of vague conceptions—he would lose himself in dreams!" On August 31, 1814, Coleridge, writing to Murray, enumerates the conditions on which he would accept Murray's terms: "And third that if (as I long ago meditated) I should re-model the whole [of Faust], give it a finale, and be able to bring it, thus re-written and re-cast, on the stage, it shall not be considered a breach of the engagement between us...". He adds that the case is possible, but not probable, and that he is confident that he would not repeat one-fifth of the original[4].

But in 1833 Coleridge gave an account of this plan which presents it as something far more developed than the above notices indicate, and assigns an early date to its conception. According to the report of this statement in the *Table Talk* (Feb. 1833)[5], Coleridge, before he had seen any part of Goethe's *Faust*, though being already familiar with Marlowe's, conceived and drew up the plan of a work, a drama "which was to be to his mind what the *Faust* was to Goethe. He had chosen

[1] Coleridge, *Table Talk*, vol. II, p. 114, February 16, 1833.
[2] idem, p. 222.
[3] H. C. Robinson, *Diary*, vol. I, p. 397, August 20, 1812.
[4] S. Smiles, *A Publisher and his Friends*, vol. I, p. 302.
[5] Coleridge, *Table Talk*, vol. II, pp. 108 ff.

Michael Scott, the wizard, for his protagonist, whom he considered a much better and more likely original than Faust." Michael Scott, in the midst of a College of enthusiastic disciples, is possessed of the lust of power, and pursues knowledge in order to attain it. He raises the Devil. Coleridge's Devil "was to be, like Goethe's, the universal humorist, [this seems to be an advance in comprehension on that shown in his conversation with Crabb Robinson in August 1812, see p. 137] who should make all things vain and nothing worth, by a perpetual collation of the great with the little in the presence of the infinite." "Michael flings himself into sensual excess, feeling himself hopelessly damned by his pact with the Devil, and his soul is finally redeemed by Agatha [Coleridge's Margarete] and he ends in the conviction of a salvation for sinners through God's grace." It is perhaps doubtful whether this plan existed at so early a date as Coleridge implies; it is to be noticed that he apparently revealed nothing of it in his conversation with Crabb Robinson in 1812, for if he had done so, Robinson would hardly have remarked that "he would never get out of vague conceptions," since the plan as given in 1833 is quite tangible and definite. Possibly the plan developed soon after the conversation with Robinson, which (given Coleridge's curious inaccuracy of mind) would account for the expression "long ago" used in his letter to Murray, where he mentions the original plan. If this supposition seems to assume an incredible vagueness on Coleridge's part in recalling past events, the assumption receives some support from his note on the projected composition of a poem on the subject of the Bell, quoted above. Coleridge's memory was notoriously irretentive, as his kinsman and early editor, H. Nelson Coleridge, points out to account for what must otherwise appear to be shameless plagiarism[1].

With the exception of certain early enthusiasms, and his constant admiration for Kant, the impression we receive from Coleridge's expressed opinions on German writers is that of a rather grudging admiration. A carping spirit is evident, too, in his more general comments on the German people and

[1] Coleridge, *Table Talk*, vol. I, Preface, pp. lxii–lxiii.

mentality. On learning, in 1805, that "the French stage is to be re-introduced" into Germany, he exclaims pathetically: "O Germany! Germany! why this endless rage for novelty? why this endless looking out of thyself?...Leibnitz, Lessing, Voss, Kant, shall be *Germany* to me, let whatever coxcombs rise up, and *shrill* it away in the grasshopper vale of reviews."[1] The *Table Talk* offers the following opinions: "Hahnemann... like most Germans, is not altogether wrong, and like them also, is never altogether right."[2] "There is a nimiety—a too-much-ness—in all Germans. It is the national fault."[3] "The Germans were not a poetical nation in the very highest sense. Wieland was their best poet...But the Germans were good meta-physicians and critics: they criticised on principles previously laid down."[4] We may add this fragment of a conversation with Allsop:

> The German writers have acquired a style and an elegance of thought and of mind, just as we have attained a style and smartness of composition...so that if you were to read an ordinary German author as an English one, you would say—"This man has *something in him*, this man thinks"; whereas it is merely a method acquired by them as we have acquired a style[5].

Summing up, we may venture on the following generalisations. Coleridge had a mind closely akin to the contemporary critical and philosophical thought of Germany. On the literary side his affinities with German writers are much less strongly marked than on the philosophical side, and his knowledge of the literature, though excelled by few of his English contemporaries in the first twenty years of the nineteenth century, was by no means thorough. The discernible German influence on his literary work is in general slight. He translated or adapted a number of poems, but with few exceptions the originals are by authors of little note. His opinions of German literature are for the most part rather superficial; they represent an outside,

---

[1] Coleridge, *Anima Poetae*, p. 150.
[2] Coleridge, *Table Talk*, vol. II, p. 54.
[3] idem, p. 323.
[4] Recollections of May, 1811, communicated by Mr Justice Coleridge (*Table Talk*, vol. II, p. 344).
[5] Allsop, *Letters*, vol. II, p. 4.

unsympathetic, and in many cases a very insular point of view. His fairly abundant utterances on German literature leave us with the impression that, while he had read widely in it, at least in comparison with most of his contemporaries, yet he had no grasp of the literature as a whole, and little comprehension of the development it was undergoing in his lifetime. In Romanticism, as a literary movement, he seems to have taken little or no interest, though he was keenly interested in Romantic philosophical speculation. His failure to appreciate Goethe and Schiller at their true value is striking, more especially in the case of the former. Doubtless he encouraged in some degree interest in German literature by his conversation, and at an earlier period by his active preoccupation with it; but the latter is mainly previous to his visit to Germany, and his later conversations were directed mainly to metaphysical speculations. Coleridge contributed chiefly to the understanding of German literature in England by his translation, in many respects excellent, of Schiller's *Piccolomini* and *Wallenstein's Tod*; for the rest, his real though rather distorted and limited interest in it probably served to impress people with a sense of its importance. But he had fewer opportunities of making his opinions on the subject known than had Crabb Robinson, who preached German literature (and with much more knowledge and understanding of it) in the market-place; whereas Coleridge the conversationalist was like a recluse, whose word is vouchsafed only to those who make the pilgrimage to his cell.

CHAPTER VI

Percy Bysshe Shelley (1792–1822)

THE date of Shelley's earliest German studies must be considered uncertain, though I am inclined to place them, as does Medwin, in his last year at Eton (1809–10). (For the evidence, see Appendix IV.) It is at least certain that from 1815 onwards his interest in German literature was constant and intelligent, without apparently leading him at any time to devote himself to a profounder study of the subject. His knowledge, indeed, of the literature seems to have been very limited. Adolf Droop, in his dissertation: *Die Belesenheit Percy Bysshe Shelley's*, has collected most of the available direct evidence of Shelley's reading of German works; his list numbers in all the names of some twenty authors, including those read in translation. His most extensive reading appears to have been in Wieland (three, possibly four novels[1]), Schiller (*Robbers, Jungfrau von Orleans, Wallenstein, Maria Stuart*[2], possibly *Der Geisterseher*) and Goethe (*Werther, Faust I*, probably *Dichtung und Wahrheit*[3]).

---

[1] Asanger's supposition (*Sprachstudien*, p. 19) based on Shelley's letter in Dowden's *Life of Shelley*, vol. II, p. 201, that Shelley had read *Aristippus* in the original as well as in the French translation, is not a legitimate inference. Shelley blames the "impudent translator" for omitting much of the original, but he knew that he had done so from the translator's preface.

[2] Droop (*Belesenheit*) does not mention either *Maria Stuart* or *Wallenstein* as having been read by Shelley. With regard to *Maria Stuart*, a remark of Medwin's (*Life of Shelley*, vol. II, p. 32) leads me to infer that he had read the play, probably in the winter of 1820. As to *Wallenstein*, the evidence that he had read it in Coleridge's translation seems to me to be conclusive: see Medwin's *Conversations*, p. 330: "(Shelley) said that the translator of 'Wallenstein' was the only person living who could venture to attempt (the translation of *Faust*)." See further a letter in Medwin's *Life of Shelley*, vol. II, p. 263, and a letter quoted by Droop (*Belesenheit*, p. 124): "Ask Coleridge if their (the translators of *Faust*) stupid misintelligence of the deep wisdom and harmony of the author does not spur him to action." Droop seems to have missed the inference, but perhaps he had not noticed the other passages. I am inclined to reject an alleged influence of Schiller's *Glocke* on the *Epithalamium* (Droop, *Belesenheit*, p. 131).

[3] Byron (Medwin's *Conversations*, p. 330) says that Shelley "has sometimes explained part of (*Dichtung und Wahrheit*) to me." But Medwin's unsupported testimony must be received with caution.

Although we may fairly assume that the direct evidence gives us a very incomplete list of the German books read by Shelley, yet it probably represents a large proportion of the works that chiefly interested him; and we must infer that the range of his German reading was narrow. Nor does his linguistic knowledge of German appear to have been even approximately perfect. In spite of all this, his translation of some scenes from Goethe's *Faust* shows that he had a real understanding of the genius of the German language.

Germany's literature appealed first to the boy Shelley, as to so many other immature minds of the day, in its merely sensational or sentimental aspects, chiefly through English translations or imitations of the *Schauerroman* order of fiction. Shelley, at his first meeting with Hogg at Oxford in 1810, expresses "an enthusiastic admiration for the poetical and imaginative works of the German school," but confesses afterwards, according to his biographer, that he had only read the works of the Germans in translation. What these works were, we cannot say; according to Droop (*Belesenheit*) he had probably read Zschokke's *Abbälino* in 1808, and Peacock[1] classes Schiller's *Robbers* and Goethe's *Faust* among the works "which took deepest root in his mind, and had the strongest influence on the formation of his character." The latter expression suggests that Peacock supposed Shelley to have read the works at an early period of his life. But 1815 is the generally accepted date for his first reading in *Faust*; and if the above interpretation of Peacock's meaning is correct, he is probably mistaken with regard to *Faust*; however profound its influence in later years, it would hardly have appealed strongly, one imagines, to the Shelley of *Zastrozzi* and *St Irvyne*, or even of *Queen Mab*. The *Wandering Jew*, *Zastrozzi* and *St Irvyne* serve to indicate the probable direction of Shelley's literary tastes in this early period of his imaginative production (1808?–1810)[2].

<hr>

[1] ~ock, *Memoirs*, p. 36.

[2] The date of *Zastrozzi* and that of the *Wandering Jew* are a little uncertain (see Dowden, *Life of Shelley*, vol. I, p. 44, note, and p 46). *Zastrozzi* was in great part written by May of the year 1809, Dowden tells us, and perhaps considerably earlier. Medwin contradicts himself about the date of the *Wandering Jew*; the later date given by him (1809–10) is certainly prefer-

The *Wandering Jew* is a rather important personage historically among the creations of Shelley's imaginative world. He appears not only in the earliest work (*The Wandering Jew*, *Original Poetry of Victor and Cazire*, *Queen Mab*) but also in the delightful prose-fragment *The Assassins*, in *Alastor*, and in *Hellas*[1].

Now [says Dowden] he rises beside those airy battlements that surmount the universe, to reveal forbidden lore to Ianthe's spirit; now he hangs, a mangled ruin of manhood, yet calm and triumphant, in the cedar-tree of the Assassins' valley...and now he comes forth by moonlight from his sea-cavern of a foamless isle...to show as in a dream to the Turk the mutability of empire and the ever-new renascence of liberty[2].

For the origination of the figure of the Wandering Jew in Shelley's mind we must look, I think, to M. G. Lewis's *Monk* (1795)[3], where the unfortunate Wanderer makes his appearance. Taking into consideration Shelley's tastes in literature at this time, as revealed by his own literary endeavours, and the notoriety of Lewis's *Schauerroman*, we can hardly doubt that

able. *St Irvyne*, also published in 1810, probably followed immediately on the *Wandering Jew*.

[1] See Zettner (*Shelley's Mythendichtung*, Inaug.-Diss. Leipzig, 1902), p. 48, where he remarks: "Auffällig ist es, dass der versöhnende Schluss von Schubart's Gedichte in der Übersetzung fehlt. Fehlte der Schluss schon in Shelley's Exemplar, oder liess er ihn beiseite, um die wirkungsvolle Gestalt des revolutionären Helden, der mit recht als das erste Bild des Prometheus hingestellt wird, nicht zu schwächen?" The latter surmise is probably correct; for the conclusion, which is wanting in the Notes to *Queen Mab*, is given by Hogg (*Life of Shelley*, vol. I, p. 194) from a paper in his possession in Shelley's handwriting. It is perhaps worth noting in this connection that Shelley appears to have been in doubt at one time whether he should call his poem *The Wandering Jew* or *The Victim of the Eternal Avenger*. The latter title smacks of an heretical tendency, perhaps. (See *The Wandering Jew*, a Poem by P. B. Shelley, edited by Bertram Dobell, London, p. xx.) Middleton (*Shelley and his Writings*) is very inaccurate in his statements about *The Wandering Jew*.

[2] Dowden, *Life of Shelley*, vol. I, pp. 44–45. In Dobell's edition of *The Wandering Jew*, p. 36, there is a long passage, agreeing in substance with the translated fragment (see below) but couched in abominably inflated language; to it is appended the following Author's (Shelley's) Note: "I have endeavoured to deviate as little as possible from the extreme sublimity of idea which the *style* of the German author, of which this is a translation, so forcibly impresses."

[3] *The Monk* was an especial favourite of Shelley's according to Medwin, *Life of Shelley*, vol. I, p. 31.

Shelley had read it, and Dobell, the Editor of *The Wandering Jew*, considers that "several of the circumstances of Shelley's poem are derived from Lewis's romance."[1]

It was probably in the winter 1809–10 that Shelley designed his metrical romance, *The Wandering Jew*. Some cantos, according to Medwin[2], had already been written, when a further impulse was supplied by a lucky find of Medwin's who picked up in Lincoln's Inn Fields a fragmentary translation of a German poem on the same subject, "probably part of the German Museum[3] for June 1801, or some journal which had reprinted from it the translations from Schubart given on its pp. 424–426" Dowden thinks[4]. We have seen above that the German Museum printed a translation of Schubart's *Ewige Jude* (see p. 37). Medwin asserts that seven or eight cantos were written by Shelley and himself, the first three almost entirely by Medwin; but Dobell[5] regards this as a mis-statement, and thinks that the poem as published in Fraser's Magazine 1831 in 4 cantos is complete, and entirely from Shelley's hand. However that may be, the value of the poem does not lie in its literary merit, but in its position as a landmark in the development of Shelley's ideas and interests.

The same may be said of the novels *Zastrozzi* and *St Irvyne, or the Rosicrucian*, which belong to the same period of immaturity[6]. They are crude imitations of the sensational fiction

---

[1] *The Wandering Jew* (see Bibliographical Note, pp. xxviii–xxix).

[2] Medwin, *Life of Shelley*, vol. I, p. 57.

[3] Droop (*Belesenheit*, p. 124) mentions also a translation by Clarence Mangan in the Dublin University Magazine, 1809.

[4] Hogg (*Life of Shelley*, vol. I, pp. 193–194), with characteristically shallow scepticism and in a characteristically amusing manner, treats the finding of this fragment as imaginary, "an integral part of the fiction." He is, of course, mistaken.

[5] *The Wandering Jew*, pp. xxiv ff.

[6] Herford calls them imitations of Mrs Radcliffe; Medwin specifies Rosa Matilda's (Mrs Byrne's) *Zofloya* as a model; Arthur B. Young finds direct influence of Lewis's *Monk* (but fails to convince us of any notable resemblance between the personages and events of that tale and those of *Zastrozzi*; see Arthur B. Young, *The Life and Novels of Thomas Love Peacock*, Norwich, 1904, note to p. 68). Margraf mentions, rather at random, I think, Vulpius, Zschokke, Goethe's *Faust* as sources. *Quot homines, tot sententiae*. But Margraf is almost certainly wrong so far as *Faust* is concerned. There is not a scrap of evidence to show that Shelley had read it in 1810, and the strongest presumption to the contrary.

which had flourished with increasing virulence, lately enhanced by foreign inoculation, since the publication of Walpole's monstrous and absurd *Castle of Otranto* in 1765.

It has been suggested that *St Irvyne, or the Rosicrucian* is a composite translation based on German originals. The question deserves to be briefly discussed[1]. Of the two early novels, *Zastrozzi*, the earlier, is also by far the better; there is a boyish freshness and enthusiasm in its absurdity which lend it charm, and the story is fairly coherent. *St Irvyne* is heavier, clumsier, and incredibly ill-constructed. It falls into two parts, each with a different set of personages and localities, the connection between them being rapidly indicated at the close of the story in a few sentences, which do little to justify the association of the incongruous portions. In Fraser's Magazine, June 1841, an anonymous Newspaper Editor, giving some reminiscences of Shelley, tells of his meeting with him in London, probably in 1810 or 1811[2], and how they formed a temporary acquaintance, which lasted about twelve months, terminating with the Newspaper Editor's departure from London. During this time, Shelley paid three or four visits to London, and they corresponded frequently. On the last of these visits (loc. cit. p. 703) Shelley

had brought with him the MS of three tales, one original, the other two translations from the German, which were written in a common school ciphering book. He offered them to three or four booksellers for ten pounds, but could not find a purchaser. On the evening which preceded my departure, he insisted on my accepting them as a token of remembrance. They were of a very wild and romantic description, but full of energy... Two years ago, taking up by chance a paper called The Novelist, I saw in it one of those tales as a reprint.

---

[1] For Dowden's discussion of the question, see *Life of Shelley*, vol. 1, pp. 93 f. As to the enigmatic sentence (quoted by him from Hogg) occurring in a letter of Shelley's of May 17, 1811: "Why will you compliment *St Irvyn*? I never saw Delisle's but mine must have been pla...". If the uncompleted word be "plagiarized," as Dowden supposes, I still fail to read this as meaning "that his German original must have been plagiarized from some romance or drama by Delisle," as Dowden suggests we may do. The link is so slight, so flawed, that it were perhaps better to omit it altogether from the chain of evidence.

[2] Since he mentions (p. 700) that Shelley was in London on a few days' visit from Oxford, at the time of their first meeting.

Buxton Forman, in his Preface to Shelley's *Prose Works*, mentions his reasons for suspecting influence beyond that of Mrs Byrne's *Zofloya* on *St Irvyne*, these reasons being (1) a notable frequency of foreign idioms, (2) the precocity of certain descriptions of scenes of passion, (3) the double story and double set of characters. He concludes "that in fact a good deal in these two juvenilities was translated or paraphrased from another tongue." He takes then the narrative of the Newspaper Editor as a striking confirmation of this view. He identifies *The Novelist* with the *Romancist and Novelists Library*, in the tenth number of which *Zastrozzi* is reprinted; this he believes to have been the original tale of the three MSS given by Shelley to the Newspaper Editor; and he regards *St Irvyne* as an amalgamation of the two other MSS. The evidence with regard to *Zastrozzi* seems strong, it must be admitted. But it appears to me that all this fits together very ill chronologically. *Zastrozzi* and *St Irvyne* were published in 1810[1]. The Newspaper Editor says that Shelley at the time of their first meeting was in London on a few days' visit from Oxford; this seems to place the first meeting as not earlier than April 10, 1810, when Shelley signed his name on the books of University College; he did not indeed go into residence until the Michaelmas Term, 1810. The visit on which Shelley brought the MSS in question with him (p. 703) took place about twelve months later, which would be after the publication of both the novels. But of the MSS the Newspaper Editor says (loc. cit.) "He offered them to three or four booksellers for ten pounds, but could not find a purchaser." Even allowing for considerable errors of time in the Newspaper Editor's narrative, it would be difficult, I think, to bring it into line with Buxton Forman's theory. But had this difficulty not existed, I should, while admitting the evidence for the identification of *Zastrozzi* with one of the MSS to be very strong, still be disinclined to admit Buxton Forman's second suggestion, that we may suppose that Shelley amalgamated the

---

[1] *Zastrozzi* is mentioned among publications of the month in the British Critic for April 1810. It was reviewed in the Critical Review for November 1810. *St Irvyne* was published December 1810. Dowden, *Life of Shelley*, vol. I, p. 46, note, and p. 93.

other two MSS and that *St Irvyne* was the outcome of the process. Neither in Medwin, Hogg, Middleton nor elsewhere is there any suggestion of such an origin for the tale. Medwin, on the contrary (*Life of Shelley*, vol. I, p. 31) says that both *Zastrozzi* and *St Irvyne* were modelled on Mrs Byrne's *Zofloya*. With regard to alleged foreign idioms in *St Irvyne*, A. Koszul (*Jeunesse de Shelley*, note to p. 35) remarks: "...Les germanismes qu'on a relevés dans ses romans ne prouveraient quelque chose que s'ils étaient rares dans le roman populaire anglais de l'époque."[1] Again, the supposed German originals have never been traced, although the question has been open for nearly forty years. Finally, I think that the following passages from letters in which Shelley gives an account of his mental development for Godwin's benefit, bear rather strongly against the assumption: Hogg, *Life of Shelley*, vol. II, p. 55. Shelley to Godwin, Jan. 10, 1812: "From a reader, I became a writer of romances; before the age of seventeen[2] I had published two, 'St Irvyn' and 'Zastrozzi,' *each of which, though quite uncharacteristic of me as now I am, yet serves to mark the state of my mind at the period of their composition.*" (The italics are mine.) He sends Godwin copies of the novels, and writes to him (Jan. 16, 1812): "You will perceive the 'Zastrozzi' and 'St Irvyn' were written prior to my acquaintance with your writings...I had, indeed, read 'St Leon' before I wrote 'St Irvyn'; but the reasonings had then made little impression."

The years 1811–15 form a transitional stage in Shelley's development. He finds peace neither without nor within. In the Spring of 1811 came the expulsion from Oxford, followed by the marriage with Harriet, swift wild journeys significant of the inner restlessness, and the gradual process of disillusionment leading to the final separation from Harriet in 1814. The interest he had previously shown in German literature seems to have lapsed during the period in question; and this is natural

---

[1] Koszul agrees with Medwin as to the influence of *Zofloya* (*Jeunesse de Shelley*, p. 22, note): "On aurait sans doute mieux vu l'importance du *Zofloya* de 'Rosa Matilda' comme source des *deux* romans de Shelley, si le livre n'était devenu si rare (il n'est pas au British Museum, mais on le trouve à la Bodléienne)." See also Zeiger, *Beiträge*, p. 58, note 2.

[2] An error of fact.

enough, since the Notes to *Queen Mab* (published 1813) and other indications make it clear that he had turned for a while, with his usual completeness and enthusiasm, to the rationalistic doctrine of the *Encyclopédistes*. His reading of *Werther* (see below) probably occurred, however, in the early part of this interval[1].

Shelley's serious study of German seems to have begun in 1815[2] at a moment of no small importance in his life. The stormy, feverish existence with Harriet was over; in Mary Godwin he had found a companion who could interest herself in his studies and share them with him; and he was experiencing the relief from the worst of his harassing pecuniary difficulties. After his first crude attempts, after the sour promise of *Queen Mab*, he is now about to write *Alastor*. "At this time dawns the tranquillity of soul which, though sorely tried by storms within and without, beamed more and more throughout the remainder of his life" (Richard Garnett).

These and other circumstances peculiarly favoured his approach to Goethe's masterpiece in a spirit at once receptive and penetrating. His acquaintance with Goethe, in minor works, had begun some time before this. In 1813, while on a stolen visit to Field Palace, he is reported to have read aloud a translated ballad of Goethe's[3]; earlier still[4] he had read *Werther*; Hogg says that he was fascinated by it. At the same time his approval was not unqualified; Albert, he thought, played an undignified part, and he projected and partially wrote an amplification of the novel, in which Albert was to abandon his rôle of passive spectator and to take poor Werther's sentimental education into his own hands; the instruction was to take the form of letters, long and tedious, to judge by a specimen rescued from oblivion by Hogg[5], who declares it to be "cold, bald, didactic, declamatory, rigid, frigid," an accumulation of epithets requiring neither addition nor qualification.

[1] He mentions it in a letter of June 2, 1811.
[2] Zeiger (*Beiträge*, p. 59) remarks: "Wahrscheinlich hat Shelley wie Byron Frau von Staëls Buch 'De l'Allemagne' veranlasst, der deutschen Litteratur wieder seine Aufmerksamkeit zuzuwenden."
[3] Dowden, *Life of Shelley*, vol. I, p. 390.
[4] He mentions it in a letter of June 2, 1811.
[5] It is to be found in Hogg, *Life of Shelley*, vol. II, pp. 490 ff.

His study of *Faust* in 1815 bore fruit in the translations of the *Erdgeistscene* and the *Osterspaziergang* in the same year. His interest in Goethe's drama remained with him till the end of his life, though it may have lapsed somewhat between 1815 and 1821. In July of the latter year, writing to the Gisbornes, he asks whether they observe any trace of *Faust*-influence on an enclosed poem of his own[1]. There are many references to *Faust* in his letters of the ensuing months. In the Spring of 1822 he saw Retzch's *Outlines*, a book of illustrations to Goethe's *Faust*. This aroused his enthusiastic admiration. "What etchings those are!" he writes to Gisborne from Pisa, on April 10, 1822[2]. "I am never satiated with looking at them, and, I fear, it is the only sort of translation of which Faust is susceptible. I never perfectly understood the Hartz Mountain scene, until I saw the etching; and then Margaret in the summer-house with Faust!" We may feel surprised at such extravagant praise of Retzch's bold but only crudely imaginative designs; Shelley's taste in the pictorial art would seem to be nearly akin to a child's: probably what he liked about the *Outlines* was the unmistakable way in which they told their story. In the same letter he adds

---

[1] See the letter to Mr and Mrs Gisborne, July 13, 1821, in Shelley, *Prose Works*, ed. by R. H. Shepherd, p. 329. The poem referred to is probably *Adonais*, though the text of the letter leaves this in some doubt. It is rather singular that in September of the same year (ibid. p. 349) he should ask Horatio Smith to send him, among other works, a "German Faust." Possibly he had, before this, been reading the specimen translations published in Blackwood's Magazine in 1820, or those in de Staël's *Germany*; or had simply lost his copy of the original. Droop (*Belesenheit*, p. 125) says: "Nach Medwin's Angabe befinden sich Goethe's Werke in Shelley's Bibliothek 1820," and gives as a reference Medwin, *Life of Shelley*, vol. II, p. 31. But this is a disputable inference from the passage in Medwin, which runs as follows: "He (Shelley) used to say that a good library consisted not of many books, but of a few chosen ones; and asking him what he considered such, he said, 'I will give you my list—catalogue it can't be called: The Greek Plays, Plato, Lord Bacon's Works, Shakespeare, The Old Dramatists, Milton, Göthe and Schiller, Dante, Petrarch and Boccaccio, and Machiavelli and Guicciardini, not forgetting Calderon; and last, yet first, the Bible'." Medwin adds: "I do not mean that this was all his collection"; but it seems hardly safe to infer that all the books mentioned were in his library, especially as Medwin's language is far from precision at most times. Droop repeats his inference with regard to Schiller's works (*Belesenheit*, p. 131). The passage indicates at any rate in what high estimation Schiller and Goethe were held by Shelley at this time.

[2] Shelley, *Prose Works*, ed. R. H. Shepherd, p. 354.

that he has already translated several scenes from *Faust* and Calderon. "I am well content with those from Calderon, which, in fact, gave me very little trouble, but those from Faust—I feel how imperfect a representation, even with all the licence I assume to figure to myself how Goethe would have written in English, my words convey." The latter part of the foregoing sentence is interesting, as an indication of Shelley's method of translation; and bearing it in mind, we shall not be surprised at the vigour and beauty of some portions of his *Faust*-translation.

His mind at this time seems to have been full of the subject, and in the letter to Gisborne of April 10, 1822, he describes his impressions of *Faust* in a passage which is worth quoting in full:

I have been reading over and over again *Faust*, and always with sensations which no other composition excites. It deepens the gloom and augments the rapidity of ideas, and would therefore seem to me an unfit study for any person who is a prey to the reproaches of memory, and the delusions of an imagination not to be restrained. And yet the pleasure of sympathising with emotions known only to few, although they derive their sole charm from despair, and the scorn of the narrow good we can attain in our present state, seems more than to ease the pain which belongs to them. Perhaps all discontent with the *less* (to use a Platonic sophism) supposes a sense of a just claim to the *greater*, and that we admirers of *Faust* are on the right road to Paradise.

Shelley was probably never possessed of the German language in a scholarly fashion, and Asanger[1] points out that there are many errors in the *Faust*-translations. But their freshness, vigour, and fidelity to the spirit of the original entitle them to a very high place in their order of literature[2]. The opening choruses of the *Prologue in Heaven*, where the original comes nearest to the spirit of Shelley's own poetry, are most success-

---

[1] Florian Asanger, *Sprachstudien*, p. 18. See also Zeiger's parallel passages from *Faust* and the translation (*Beiträge*, pp. 69–70) which show that Shelley was surprisingly unfamiliar with common German expressions.

[2] H. C. Robinson, in a letter to Goethe, January 31, 1829, refers to the "splendid fragments from 'Faust' by Shelley..." (*Diary*, vol. ii, p. 390).

ful; the *Walpurgisnacht* is vigorous; but the discussion between Mephisto and The Lord God of the *Prologue in Heaven*, has lost its verve in Shelley's rendering[1].

Although Shelley's interest in *Faust* was so considerable both in duration and intensity, traces of direct influence of the drama on his works are not, I think, abundant, nor strongly marked save in a few cases. "Poets—the best of them," says Shelley in a letter to the Gisbornes of July 13, 1821, "are a very cameleonic race; they take the colour not only of what they feed on, but of the very leaves under which they pass." It is *Faust*-influence of this kind, of colour, of tone, rather than imitation, that must be looked for in Shelley's works, particularly of the last period[2]. In a certain number of cases, however, a more tangible effect of Shelley's *Faust*-study may be pointed to. The first in date is the influence on *Alastor*. This poem was written in the Autumn of 1815, and it was probably in this year, as we have seen, that Shelley first read *Faust*. This coincidence of dates makes the influence probable. The youth in *Alastor* who "drinks deep of knowledge, and is still insatiate," has, in his vain pursuit, his "sacred thirst of doubtful knowledge," a near kinship with Faust. And the Preface, the invocation (ll. 1–49) and the earlier portion of the narrative (ll. 50–128) have a Faustish quality, sensible as a strong undercurrent, now more, now less definitely felt. A *Faust*-influence of form appears in the fragmentary prologue to *Hellas*[3], in which Christ, Mahomet, Satan and an angelic chorus take part. While differing widely in tone from its prototype (we may notice in particular the absence of the ironic element, which had already puzzled

---

[1] For a discussion of the *Faust*-translation, see Zeiger, *Beiträge*, pp. 65–71.

[2] In this connection may be quoted a critical observation of Richard Ackermann's (*Shelley's Epipsychidion und Adonais. Mit Einleitung etc. herausgegeben von Richard Ackermann*, Berlin, 1900, Einleitung pp. xxvii–xxviii): "Mit Recht als einer der Subjektivisten unter den Lyrikern bezeichnet, liebt er es bei seinen Dichtungen, eingestandnermassen oder nicht, bewusst oder unbewusst, von einem Vorbilde auszugehen, das ihm die Anregung giebt, manchmal nur den Namen, (*Alastor*), oder die Idee, die Stimmung, das äussere Gewand. Aber selbst wenn er auch im ersten Teile dem Vorbilde nachfolgt, wird er allmählich immer selbstständiger, so dass die weitere Ausführung ein durchaus eigenartiges, modernes, subjektives Gepräge erhält."

[3] Pointed out by Ackermann (*Quellen*).

Shelley in his translation of the *Prolog im Himmel*), its agreement with it in structure is very noticeable[1]. Zettner[2] notes a resemblance pointed out by Sweet (*Shelley Society's Papers*, Part II, p. 307) between a passage in the *Fragment of an Unfinished Drama*, and the chant of the *Erdgeist* (*In Lebensfluten*, etc.); the passage in question is the Earth-Spirit's answer to the Enchantress[3]. It is clearly a modification of the same theme[4]. Finally, Droop notes two reminiscences of *Faust* in the poem *To Edward Williams*[5].

In conclusion a brief account may be given of other possible sources of German influence on Shelley. His taste for the grotesque and fantastic in literature, which seems to have been predominant in his boyhood, did not leave him in more mature years. In 1816, at the Villa Diodati on Lake Geneva, Byron and the Shelleys read aloud a collection of German ghost-stories in

[1] The date of the composition of *Hellas* is 1821, and the prologue-fragment occurs in the same note book as the original MS of *Hellas*, "and so blended with this as to be barely separable after very minute examination" (Shelley, *Poetical Works*, 2 vols., London, 1870 (edited by W. Rossetti), note to p. 582). I take this to imply a probability that they were written about the same time. There are references to *Faust* in letters of July and September of that year, and in a letter to John Gisborne, October 22, 1821, in which he announces the completion of *Hellas*, Shelley makes a gallant but not altogether successful attempt, to quote from memory a line of ˌthe original text of *Faust*.

[2] Zettner, *Shelley's Mythendichtung*, Inaug.-Diss. Leipzig, 1902.

[3] Shelley's *Poetical Works*, ed. Hutchinson, 1912, p. 529.

[4] Zettner (*Mythendichtung*, pp. 3, 4) remarks: "Es liegt die Annahme nahe, dass Shelley zu der Darstellung [of the earth-Spirit] im Prometheus durch den Erdgeist in Goethes *Faust*, den er zur Entstehungszeit seines Dramas (1819) wohl gekannt haben kann [in fact did, as we have seen] angeregt wurde." But it is a question at most, I think, of such an initial suggestion as Ackermann (see p. 154, n. 2) alludes to; and personification of this type is met with so frequently in Shelley, that we need hardly look for its origin in the particular case outside his own shaping intellect.

[5] Droop, *Belesenheit*, p. 130. Many more instances of alleged *Faust*-influence are given by Droop (*Belesenheit*), but those mentioned in the text are the only ones which have come to my notice in which the evidence appears strong. Mr Buxton Forman (see *Note Books of P. B. Shelley*, pp. 108 ff.) thinks that the *Herne's Feast* fragments, which probably belong to 1822, may have been a sort of exercise in rendering a Walpurgisnacht theme in English. The fragments, given in the *Note Books of P. B. Shelley*, vol. III, do not seem to me to support this view. The poem, if completed, would probably have consisted in the fairies' narrative of the sights and wonders of their travels. The fantastic element in the earlier lines hardly recalls, even faintly, the diabolical marvels of the *Walpurgisnacht*. Zeiger has the following note (*Beiträge*, p. 71, note 2): "Auf eine fast wörtliche

a French translation[1]. Some novels of Wieland (*Agathon*, *Peregrinus Proteus*, and *Aristipp* at any rate) he seems to have read with approval, and calls him "a very tolerable pagan." Of Schiller he thought so well as to place his works, with Goethe's, in his very short list of books that should go to make up a good library (see p. 152, note 1). He read the *Jungfrau von Orleans* in 1820 or 1821, and probably *Maria Stuart* about the same time[2]. There is some divergence of opinion as to the extent to which he became acquainted with Kant's works. Hogg speaks of a Latin translation, uncut, on the poet's shelves and does not believe that he had read a word of him[3]; but then Hogg would believe whatever it amused him to believe. Asanger[4] says that according to Dowden (*Life of Shelley*, vol. II, p. 446), he read Kant in 1821 in a French edition; but that he read him at all is hardly a legitimate deduction from Dowden's only mention of Kant at the place referred to "Here (in Pisa) in his pensive citadel he hoped to gather his books around him—Calderon, Goethe, Kant, Plato, and the Greek dramatists." Middleton, however[5], speaking of Übereinstimmung einer Stelle der 'Faustübersetzung' mit einer Stelle des 'Prometheus Unbound' sei hingewiesen:

'Faustübersetzung.'
Sweet notes of love. . .

.   .   .   .   .   .

Resound around, beneath, above. (II, 55 ff.)
'Prometheus Unbound.'
(*a*) And one sound, above, around,
One sound beneath, around, above,
Was moving; 'twas the soul of love. (First Spirit, I Akt.)
(*b*) And from beneath, around, within, above

.   .   .   .   .   love

Bursts in like light on caves cloven by thunder-ball. (IV Akt.)"

Margraf (*Einfluss*) points out an almost literal translation from the *Osterspaziergang* ("Der alte Winter, in seiner Schwäche, zog sich in rauhe Berge zurück") in *The Dirge*: "Old winter was gone in his weakness back to the mountains hoar."

[1] See also p. 163.

[2] Medwin, *Life of Shelley*, vol. II, p. 32, and letter to J. Gisborne, October 22, 1821.

[3] See Asanger, *Sprachstudien*, p. 13, and Hogg, *Life of Shelley*, vol. II, p. 311. See also Hogg, *Life of Shelley*, vol. II, p. 176, for letters of Shelley, Winter 1812–13, asking Hogg to procure a translation of Kant for him. Scythrop, in *Nightmare Abbey* (see below, p. 157) studies transcendental philosophy. (Thomas Love Peacock, *Works*, Bentley and Son, 1875, vol. I, p. 314.)

[4] Asanger, *Sprachstudien*, p. 13.

[5] Middleton, *Shelley and His Writings*, vol. II, p. 302.

the residence at Pisa, says that "the study of Calderon, and the philosophy of Kant seem at this period mostly to have engaged his attention." And the following passage from a letter of Shelley's to Claire Clairmont, February 1821, may be worth quoting, as supporting Middleton's statement. Shelley remarks that she is "Germanising" very fast, and that she makes distinctions

in the choicest style of the criticism of pure reason. There is a great deal of truth in it [her distinction], of truth surrounded and limited by so many exceptions as entirely to destroy its being...Their philosophy [the Germans'] as far as I understand it, contemplates only the silver side of the shield of truth: better in this respect than the French, who only see the narrow edge of it.

Shelley, like most of his contemporaries, fell under the spell of Bürger's *Lenore*. Medwin, who mentions the powerful effect it produced upon Shelley, states that he had in his possession "a copy of the whole poem, which he made with his own hand,"[1] and Dowden tells us that one Christmas Eve Shelley entertained a little guest by narrating the *Lenore*-story, "working up the horror to such a height of fearful interest that Polly quite expected to see Wilhelm walk into the drawing-room."[2] *Lenore* may have influenced the ballad *Sister Rosa* in *St Irvyne* (see particularly the 15th stanza)[3].

Thomas Love Peacock parodied Shelley's Germanising tendencies in *Nightmare Abbey* (1817) in the person of Scythrop.

---

[1] Medwin, *Life of Shelley*, vol. I, p. 62.

[2] Dowden, *Life of Shelley*, vol. II, p. 123.

[3] Zeiger, *Beiträge*, p. 61, sees further influence of *Lenore* on the poem from *St Irvyne* beginning: "Ghosts of the dead!" But the only instance he adduces would rather suggest influence of *Der Wilde Jäger*. And this type of gruesome verse rather testifies to the writer's delight in the grotesque and the horrible, than reveals any particular influence. Margraf, *Einfluss*, p. 54, says: "Einer seiner Biographen Ch. Mittleton (sic!) (1858, vol. I, p. 47) sagt geradezu: 'the "Lenore" of Burgher first awakened his poetic faculty'." Middleton makes no such affirmation, but says on the contrary: "*It is hinted, somewhat plausibly,* that the 'Leonora' of Burgher first awakened his poetic faculty. A tale of such beauty and terror *might well* have kindled his lively imagination, *but his earliest pieces, written about this time,* and consisting only of a few ballads, are deficient in elegance and originality, and *give no evidence whatever of the genius which soon after declared itself.*" (My italics, F. W. S.) What Margraf has to say of Shelley is almost entirely valueless. He affirms without stating his sources, and is careless and superficial.

We may summarise as follows the results of our inquiry: Shelley was first attracted to the sensational type of German literature and to its imitations; it must be considered doubtful whether he was able to read these in the original previously to 1815, but the question is not of the first importance to us, since most of his writings up to this date are of very slender merit. Among these, the novels *Zastrozzi* and *St Irvyne* are influenced directly or indirectly by the *Schauerromane*. In 1815 he began to take his German studies seriously, and henceforth to the end of his life his interest in German literature probably never lapsed entirely though evidence of it is not forthcoming for the years 1817–20. From the end of 1820 to his death in 1822 this interest appears to have been most constant and intense. The evidence does not lead us to suppose his German reading to have been extensive, nor did he master the language at all thoroughly. Of the German works with which he was acquainted, *Faust* made by far the deepest impression upon him, and in the case of *Faust* alone, I think, can we point with any confidence to direct German influence on the work of his maturer years. Even here, the instances of such influence are not numerous or important. That Goethe's poem had considerable effect upon him, we may judge from the frequency with which he refers to it in his correspondence, from the excellent translations he made from it, and from a remarkable passage in a letter to Gisborne of April 10, 1822, quoted on p. 153.

CHAPTER VII

Byron (1788–1824)

BYRON'S interest in German literature was more superficial than Shelley's, and his enthusiasm for Goethe, the
preponderating German influence in his case as in Shelley's,
was less intelligent and perhaps less disinterested[1]. But it was
also noisier, taking the form of prefaces and dedications to the
sage of Weimar, and of exchanges of compliments with him.
It need not surprise us that direct influence from German
sources is to be more surely and directly traced in Byron's
works than in Shelley's: the more superficial the influence, the
more obvious the forms are likely to be in which it is manifested.

The rudiments of German he learnt as a boy were completely
forgotten in after years. "Of the *real* language," he wrote in
his Diary, January 12, 1821, "I know absolutely nothing,—
except oaths learned from postillions and officers in a squabble!
I can *swear* in German potently...".

When a child of eight, he read Gessner's *Tod Abels* with a
German master—and while the German master was "crying his
eyes out over its pages, I thought that any other than Cain had
hardly committed a crime in ridding the world of so dull a
fellow as Gessner made Brother Abel."[2] This early reading was
not without influence on his writings, the extent of which we
shall have to discuss later. The German studies just referred

---

[1] Though it is but fair to note that his high opinion of Goethe was formed
before he had learnt with what flattering interest Goethe regarded him. See
his letter to R. B. Hoppner, sending him the article by Goethe on *Manfred*
in *Kunst und Alterthum*, and requesting him to translate it for Byron's benefit.
He is unable to read the German, but judges, from "*two* notes of *admiration*
(generally put after something ridiculous by us) and the word 'hypochondrisch'..." that the remarks on his poem are unfavourable. "I shall regret
this, for I should have been proud of Goethe's good word; but I shan't
alter my opinion of him, even though he should be savage" (Byron, *Works,
Prose*, vol. v, p. 33).

[2] Medwin, *Conversations*, p. 150. Elsewhere, however, he has recorded
that his general impression of the book is one of delight (*Letters and Journals*,
vol. v, pp. 208–209).

to were not, apparently, followed up[1], and all his later knowledge of the literature he derived from hearsay, from criticism, and from translations. Of these last, one that made a most vivid impression on him in his boyhood, an impression that persisted in later years, was Schiller's unfinished romance, *Der Geisterseher*; we have his emphatic testimony to the effect it produced on his mind; in a letter to Murray from Venice, April 2, 1817, he mentions "Schiller's *Armenian*, a novel which took a great hold of me when I was a boy. It is also called the *Ghost Seer*, and I never walked down St Mark's by moonlight without thinking of it, and 'at nine o'clock he died'."[2] In a note to the early and insipid ballad *Oscar of Alva*, he acknowledges that the *Geisterseher* suggested the catastrophe of that poem, where the murdered brother appears at the wedding-festivities[3]. Further points of *Geisterseher*-influence have been alleged. Kraeger[4] and Margraf[5] suppose that the reported mysterious

---

[1] Though Elze (*Lord Byron*) seems to imply, I know not on what authority, that he studied it at Harrow (K. Elze, *Byron*, p. 42): "Deutsch lernte er noch weniger [than French] und auch dieses Wenige vergass er bald wieder."

[2] Compare also in *Childe Harold*, Canto IV (written 1817), Stanza xviii, where speaking of Venice, he says: "I loved her from my boyhood...—And Otway, Radcliffe, Schiller, Shakespeare's art,—Had stamped her image in me." In a note to this is an explanatory reference to the *Geisterseher* (Byron, *Works, Poetry*, vol. II, p. 342). In Roger's *Italy: St Mark's Place*, this incident from Schiller's romance referred to in the text is likewise recalled: "Who answered me just now! Who, when I said, 'Tis nine,' turned round and said so solemnly—'*Signor, he died at nine.*' 'Twas the Armenian;— The mask that follows thee, go where thou wilt." See Byron, *Works, Prose*, vol. IV, p. 92, note.

[3] Heinrich Kraeger (*Der Byronsche Heldentypus*, p. 20) supposes ingeniously that Byron's Armenian studies in Venice were an effect of his early interest in Schiller's *Armenian*. But cp. the letter to Moore (Byron, *Works, Prose*, vol. IV, pp. 9-10): "Venice, December 5, 1816. By way of divertisement, I am studying daily, at an Armenian monastery, the Armenian language. I found that my mind wanted something craggy to break upon; and this— as the most difficult thing I could discover here for amusement—I have chosen, to torture me into attention." Cp. also (*Works, Prose*, vol. IV, pp. 43-45) the fragment found among Byron's papers, which contains a statement of his reasons for undertaking the study. It will be recalled, also, that the Armenian in the Ghost-Seer is but a sham Armenian, after all. It appears then that Kraeger's suggestion, somewhat emphatically worded, rests upon nothing but its ingenuity. For an investigation of the extent of *Geisterseher*-influence on *Oscar of Alva*, see Kraeger, *Heldentypus*, pp. 20-25.

[4] Kraeger, *Der Byronsche Heldentypus*, p. 26.

[5] Margraf, *Einfluss*, p. 45.

disappearance of the Armenian during one hour of the twenty-four suggested the trances of Lara. But a comparison of the passages in question will not, I think, tend to confirm the supposition[1]. Margraf states further that the meeting of the Count with the Hungarian in *Werner* is also influenced by an incident in the *Geisterseher*. I have been unable to trace the incident in Schiller's romance to which Margraf refers here; as usual, he gives no reference, and the bare assertion, coming from this source, has little weight.

He read *The Robbers* in 1814, as a note in his *Journals* testifies. "Feb. 20, 1814: ...Redde the Robbers. Fine,—but *Fiesco* is better; and Alfieri, and Monti's Aristodemo, *best*."[2]

Besides these three works of Schiller, of which the *Geisterseher* seems to have made the deepest impression, I find specific mention of a "French translation of Schiller," read, as his Diary shows, in September 1816[3]. He had read *Don Carlos*, however, we may suppose, since in the introduction to *Parisina* he alludes to Schiller's treatment of incestuous passion. Rea[4] points out that Byron may have been influenced by *Don Carlos* in deviating in *Parisina* from his authority for the story, Gibbon's *Antiquities of the House of Brunswick*, by the introduction of a betrothal of the lovers, previous to the marriage of Parisina to the Marquis of Este. Hermann Schiff[5] notes a resemblance between *Fiesco* (2 Aufzug, Schlussmonolog) and the Doge's "I will resign a crown and make the state renew its freedom..." in *Marino Faliero*. Kraeger[6] traces a number of resemblances between the two poets, but makes a good deal more of them than they are worth, in my opinion. Another favourite of early days was the *German's Tale*, in the *Canterbury Tales* of Sophia and Harriet Lee, which may be regarded as a German influence at second-hand (see below, p. 169).

---

[1] Lara's fit or swoon ("that fevered moment of his mind's disease") is not one which recurs at regular intervals, or at a certain hour of the twenty-four: lacking this resemblance in the peculiar characteristics of the Armenian's fabled trance, its connection with it is at least problematical.

[2] Byron, *Letters and Journals*, vol. II.

[3] idem, vol. III, September 20, 1816.

[4] T. Rea, *Schiller's Dramas*, p. 45.

[5] H. Schiff, *Über Lord Byrons Marino Faliero*, Marburg, 1910.

[6] H. Kraeger, *Heldentypus*, pp. 27–30.

But it was apparently Madame de Staël's *De l'Allemagne*, published in 1813, that first turned his thoughts seriously to German literature, and especially to Goethe, whose *Faust* was to leave so many traces of influence in his later work. Byron and Madame de Staël, as became two of the most distinguished lions of the day, met in London society, and exchanged somewhat feline amenities. References to her and to her work occur in his letters, journals, and in notes to his poems[1]. For her work he seems to have entertained a deservedly high opinion. There can be little doubt that the line: "Know ye the land where the cypress and myrtle" in Byron's *Bride of Abydos* is derived from Mignon's Song in *Wilhelm Meister*, probably through the medium of a translation, though Byron declared that he was unconscious of this origin. His disclaimer is characteristic if not convincing[2]:

"In all the charges of plagiary brought against me in England [said Byron], did you hear me accused of stealing from Madame de Staël the opening lines of my 'Bride of Abydos'? She is supposed to have borrowed her lines from Schlegel, or to have stolen them from Goethe's 'Wilhelm Meister'; so you see I am a third or fourth hand stealer of stolen goods. Do you know de Staël's lines? [continued Byron] for if I am a thief, she must be the plundered, as I don't read German, and do French; yet I could almost swear that I never saw her verses when I wrote mine, nor do I even now remember them. I think the first began with 'Cette terre,' etc. etc., but the rest I forget; as you have a good memory, perhaps you could repeat them." I did so, and they are as follows: "Cette terre, où les myrtes fleurissent,— Où les rayons des cieux tombent avec amour,—Où des sons enchanteurs dans les airs retentissent,—Où la plus douce nuit succède au plus beau jour." "Well [said Byron], I do not see any point of resemblance, except in the use of the two unfortunate words land and myrtle, and for using these new and original words I am a plagiarist!...Does not this charge prove the liberal spirit of the hypocrites of England?"

It appears, however, that the *Épître sur Naples* cannot be regarded as the link between Mignon's Song and the *Bride of Abydos*, as appears from the following considerations, which I reproduce,

---

[1] References to Madame de Staël occurring in Byron's *Works*, and in the *Conversations*: Byron, *Works, Poetry*, vol. III, p. 164, note; *Works, Letters and Journals, Prose*, vol. II, p. 326; idem, p. 354; (Countess of Blessington), *Conversations of Lord Byron*, 1834, p. 326.

[2] Blessington, *Conversations*, p. 326.

by kind permission of Professor J. G. Robertson, from his unpublished study of the literary relations of Goethe and Byron[1].

It appears that Byron could not have imitated these lines (*Épître sur Naples*) as the Épître was not printed until 1821. If Madame de Staël comes into the question at all, it was thus rather the mention of Goethe's poem in *De l'Allemagne* or Corinne's *Improvisation sur le Capitole* that Byron was thinking of[2]. As, however, the characteristic echo of Goethe is less the reference to the myrtle than the repetition of the phrase "Know ye the land?" it is more likely Byron had in his memory an English translation of the German poem.

Professor Robertson notes two versions by Cyrus Redding[3] and a translation in *The German Erato*[4] which was reprinted in the German Museum.

It is legitimate to suppose that he obtained his first notion of *Faust* from *De l'Allemagne*[5], on its publication in 1813. It was three years later, in the early summer of 1816, soon after Byron had turned his back on England for ever, that the historic meeting between him and the Shelleys took place, at Geneva. The two poets, both in some degree outcasts from the society of their native land, immediately formed a close alliance—it was that rather than friendship—which endured until Shelley's death in 1822. On the present occasion his Lordship took up his residence at the Villa Diodati, on the shore of Lake Leman, the Shelleys living in a more humble abode close by. One of their intellectual amusements was to abandon their imagination to the lure of supernatural tales. During a spell of rainy weather, they read aloud from a collection of stories claiming to be translated from the German—*Fantasmagoriana, ou Recueil*

[1] J. G. Robertson's exhaustive study of the relations of Goethe and Byron has now appeared in the Publications of the English Goethe Society, New Series, vol. II.

[2] Attention was drawn to the latter by A. Knobbe, *Die Faust-Idee in Lord Byrons Dichtungen* (Programm), Stralsund, 1906, p. 7.

[3] Monthly Magazine, vol. XXXVIII, p. 45, August 1814, and *Yesterday and To-day*, vol. II, pp. 14–15.

[4] Fiedler in Modern Language Review, vol. XVIII, pp. 55 ff.

[5] Sinzheimer (*Goethe und Byron*), pp. 13–14, goes so far as to say that thanks to *De l'Allemagne*, Byron had already at the end of 1813 "eine sehr klare und richtige Kenntnis von Goethe." But I do not know where he can have found evidence of this. Presumably the reference by Byron to "a sorry French translation" reported in Medwin's *Conversations* (p. 170) is an allusion to the translated passages from *Faust* in *De l'Allemagne*.

d'histoires d'apparitions, de spectres, revenans, etc., Traduit de l'allemand par un Amateur, Paris, 1811—a title that suggests that the book was suited to their purpose. Byron related or partly recited the tale of *Christabel*, which he had seen in manuscript; and one evening Shelley's imagination so wrought upon him, that he fled shrieking with terror from the company, at the thought of a woman whose breasts had eyes in the place of nipples. When the tranquillity of Shelley's mind had been restored, Byron proposed that each of the party should write a tale of the supernatural, and Mary's *Frankenstein* was the not insignificant outcome of this proposal. Byron's own effort, *The Vampire*, was not carried by him beyond a few pages; his physician, Polidori, afterwards completed the story and published it. But a more important incident of Byron's sojourn at the Villa Diodati was the viva voce translation of part of *Faust* made by M. G. Lewis, who was for a time Byron's guest. Before he left Switzerland Byron visited the Bernese Oberland and the impressions received there coalesced with the recent memories of Lewis's version of *Faust*, and were incorporated in a marked degree in *Manfred*[1], which was begun in the summer of 1816, published June 1817.

We assumed above that Byron became first acquainted with Goethe's *Faust* through the medium of Madame de Staël's *De l'Allemagne*. In a conversation with Medwin[2], which from the reference to Shelley must have taken place in 1822, Byron said, speaking of *Faust*: "All I know of that drama is from a sorry French translation, from an occasional reading or two into English of parts of it by Monk Lewis when at Diodati, and from the Hartz mountain scene that Shelley versified the other day. Nothing I envy him so much as to be able to read that astonishing production in the original." As this conversation related to the influence of *Faust* on his own work, somewhat of a sore point with him[3], his statement here as to the extent of

[1] "...It was the *Staubach* (sic) and the *Jungfrau*, and something else, much more than Faustus, that made me write *Manfred*." Letter to Murray, June 7, 1820.   [2] Medwin, *Conversations*, p. 170.

[3] That Byron resented the imputation of German or other influence on *Manfred* appears from the tone as well as from the comparative frequency of his references to the subject. To Murray, October 12, 1817 (Byron, *Works, Poetry*, vol. IV, p. 80): "*I never read, and do not know that I ever saw*, the

Lewis's translation may be usefully collated with another, occurring in a letter to Murray of June 7, 1820[1]. "Faust I never read, for I don't know German, but Matthew Monk Lewis, in 1816, at Coligny, translated *most of it*[2] to me *viva voce*."

Manfred is one who, removed from human sympathies by pride and the consciousness of superior faculties, and by the remorseful memory of a past mysterious crime committed by him, seeks to obtain power over the spirit-world. The first scene of *Manfred*, that in the Gothic Gallery at Midnight, consists, as does the first scene in *Faust*, in a monologue and the evocation of elemental spirits[3]. The direct influence of *Faust* on the machinery of the poem in this first scene is palpable[4]. The more difficult question is of the closeness of the resemblance of Manfred, as a person or type, to Faust. In Goethe's review of *Manfred* in *Kunst und Alterthum* he says[5]: "Dieser seltsame, geistreiche Dichter hat meinen Faust in sich aufgenommen, und, hypochondrisch, die seltsamste Nahrung daraus gesogen. Er hat die seinen Zwecken zusagenden Motive auf eigne Weise benutzt, sodass keines mehr dasselbige ist, und gerade deshalb kann ich seinen Geist nicht genugsam bewundern." This statement is flattering indeed to Byron, but it lays, perhaps, too little stress on the fundamental nature of the differences between *Faust* and *Manfred*; nor does it suggest that the resemblances are superficial. Yet there is nothing in *Manfred* that suggests to me that Byron realised at all fully the significance of the *Faust*-theme; there is all the difference between *Faust* and

Faustus of Marlow...As to the *Faustus* of Marlow, I never read, never saw, nor heard of it." To John Murray, October 23, 1817 (*Works, Letters and Journals, Prose*, vol. IV, p. 177): "An American, who came the other day from Germany, told Mr Hobhouse that *Manfred* was taken from Goethe's *Faust*. The devil may take both the Faustuses, German and English,—I have taken neither." See also letter to Murray, June 7, 1820 (*Works, Poetry*, vol. IV, p. 81), and Medwin, *Conversations*, p. 170.

[1] Byron, *Works, Poetry*, vol. IV, p. 81.   [2] The italics are mine.
[3] In a later scene Manfred attempts to commit suicide, but the suicide-theme is so common (especially in Romantic literature) that it is undesirable to emphasise the question of influence in this case, especially as the accompanying circumstances are very dissimilar in *Faust* and *Manfred*.
[4] For some other resemblances between *Manfred* and *Faust*, see J. G. Robertson, *Goethe and Byron* (Publications of the English Goethe Society, New Series, vol. II, 1925).
[5] As quoted by Ackermann, *Lord Byron*, Heidelberg, 1901, p. 102.

Manfred that distinguishes the desire for knowledge for its own sake and the pursuit of it for the sake of the power it confers[1]. There is little indeed to remind us of Faust's Titanic spirit of revolt against the boundaries of intelligence in Manfred's irritable desire for forgetfulness. "Forgetfulness," he says to the Witch of the Alps:

> I sought in all, save where 'tis to be found,
> And that I have to learn—my sciences,
> My long-pursued and superhuman art,
> Is mortal here...

I cannot even agree with Kraeger that Manfred shares the "geniale Verzweiflung des Übermenschen Faust."[2] Manfred's grief, rebellion, despair, is personal and pettish, not, as with Faust, the reaction from superhuman aspiration thwarted. Faust is mankind, European mankind at least; Manfred is Byron[3].

The influence of *Faust* on Byron's work was not confined to *Manfred*. It reappears next in *Cain*, begun July 16, finished September 9, 1821. Cain's desire for knowledge, which induces him to accept Lucifer's guidance through the Abyss of Space, is, indeed, based on a sense of personal grievance; yet it is nearer the disinterested passion of Faust than is Manfred. And Lucifer has caught something, I think, of Mephisto's cynical humour, which appears especially in Act II.

In 1822, as we have seen, Shelley was busied with his translations from *Faust*. Byron was at this time in Pisa. Medwin tells us[4] that one day, handing a MS to Shelley, he said: "Shelley, I have been writing a *Faustish* kind of drama: tell me what you think of it." Shelley, after reading it, pronounced it to be a bad imitation of *Faust*. This was *The Deformed Trans-*

---

[1] H. Kraeger, *Heldentypus*, p. 88, points out this distinction.

[2] Kraeger, *Heldentypus*, p. 88.

[3] Kraeger (*Heldentypus*, p. 88) and Sinzheimer (*Goethe und Byron*, p. 38) agree in the main with these conclusions. Eberty (*Lord Byron*, p. 31) points out the similarity between Manfred's invective against patience, and Faust's famous "Fluch vor allem der Geduld." Manfred's utterance is in Act II, Sc. 1:

> "Patience—and patience! Hence—that word was made
> For brutes of burthen, not for birds of prey!
> Preach it to mortals of a dust like thine,—
> I am not of thine order."

[4] Medwin, *Conversations*, p. 183.

formed[1]. Dr H. Varnhagen[2] has made an exhaustive and admirable comparison of this drama with its sources, which are acknowledged by Byron in the Advertisement to *The Deformed Transformed*. These are *Faust* and Pickersgill's *Three Brothers*. Referring those interested in the subject to Dr Varnhagen's work, I will mention briefly here the points where *Faust*-influence is most patent. As in *Faust*, the Devil appears without being summoned, and emerges from a vapour. The will-o'-the-wisp and the coal-black horses in the *Deformed Transformed* may well be a reminiscence of those in *Faust*. As in *Faust*, Arnold sets out to see the world under the Devil's guidance. The metre of the Stranger's Song ("Shadows of beauty," towards the end of the first scene) was probably suggested by that of the chorus "*Christ ist erstanden*." All the resemblances just mentioned are found in the first scene. Arnold and Faust are almost completely dissimilar from one another; and Dr Varnhagen sees little resemblance between Mephistopheles and the Stranger (Caesar in Scene II). Here I must emphatically disagree. The Stranger or Caesar has throughout a strain of the cynical humour, almost good-humour, that characterises the Mephisto of *Faust I*.

The interest in Goethe and his *Faust* felt by Byron was stimulated, no doubt, by his reception in May 1820 of Goethe's enthusiastic review of *Manfred* in *Kunst und Alterthum* (II, 2. 191)[3]. Goethe's reputation was European, and Byron was naturally flattered by his praise of *Manfred*[4]. He designed dedications to Goethe for *Marino Faliero* (1821) and for *Sardanapalus* (1821). The former was chiefly devoted to abuse of Wordsworth and Southey, but the following passages addressed to Goethe are noteworthy:

[1] Probably begun and finished between April 20 and July 8, 1822: see Byron, *Works, Poetry*, vol. v, p. 469.
[2] Dr Hermann Varnhagen, *Über Byrons dramatisches Bruchstück: Der Umgestaltete Missgestaltete*, Erlangen, 1905.
[3] See p. 159, n. 1.
[4] The letter to his publisher, John Murray, of June 7, 1820, testifies to his jubilation. "Enclosed is something which will interest you, (to wit), the opinion of *the* Greatest man of Germany—perhaps of Europe—upon one of the great men of your advertisements...in short, a critique of *Goethe's* upon *Manfred*."

My principal object in addressing you was to testify my sincere respect and admiration of a man, who, for half a century, has led the literature of a great nation, and will go down to posterity as the first literary Character of his Age...Considering you, as I really and warmly do, in common with all your own, and with most other nations, to be by far the first literary character which has existed in Europe since the death of Voltaire, I felt, and feel, desirous to inscribe to you the following work...

The dedication to *Sardanapalus* was even more flattering, and more gracefully so.

To the illustrious Goethe, a stranger presumes to offer the homage of a literary vassal to his liege lord, the first of existing writers, who has created the literature of his own country, and illustrated that of Europe. The unworthy production which the author ventures to inscribe to him is entitled *Sardanapalus*.

Neither of these dedications appeared with the published plays, John Murray apparently not regarding them as suitable[1]. Byron's letters show him to have been indignant at Murray's omission of the latter dedication at any rate[2]. With *Werner* (1823) there appeared at last a dedication to Goethe. On the day on which he sailed from Leghorn for Greece (July 24, 1823) he wrote to Goethe in reply to a letter and copy of verses from him which he had received through his friend Stirling.

Besides *Faust*, he had read at any rate a translation of *Die Wahlverwandtschaften*, as appears from the Extracts of Letters from Mr George Finlay to Colonel Stanhope, given by Karl Elze[3].

---

[1] Byron, *Works, Poetry*, vol. IV, pp. 340, note and ff., and vol. V, p. 7.

[2] Byron, *Works, Prose*, vol. VI *passim*.

[3] K. Elze, *Byron*, p. 480. "We then conversed about Germany and its literature, and I found, to my astonishment, Lord Byron knew nothing of the language, though he was perfectly (!) acquainted with its literature; with Goethe in particular, and with every passage of 'Faust.' He said nothing could be more sublime than the words of the Spirit of the Earth to Faust, 'Thou resemblest the spirit of thy imagination, not me.' I involuntarily repeated it in German, and he said, 'Yes, those are the words.' The scene of the monkeys had made a considerable impression on him, and I remember, on my saying I supposed Goethe meant to represent men transformed into monkeys, he exclaimed, 'Suppose no such thing—suppose them veritable monkeys, and the satire is finer and deeper.' After a few words on *Wilhelm Meister*, I asked if he had read the *Wahlverwandtschaften*. He said he did not recollect the hard word, but inquired the signification of it. I gave

Mention has already been made of his admiration of Harriet Lee's *The German's Tale*[1]. According to Medwin[2] he thought it as fine as anything of Scott's. By his own account[3], it contained the germ of much that he wrote. "I had begun a drama upon this tale as far back as 1815 (the first I ever attempted, except one at thirteen years old, called *Ulric and Ilvina*, which I had sense enough to burn), and had nearly completed an act, when I was interrupted by circumstances."[4]

In October 1821 he was again thinking of taking *Kruitzner* (*The German's Tale*) as the subject of a drama, and wrote to Murray asking him "to cut out Sophia Lee's [an error for Harriet Lee] *German's Tale* from the Canterbury Tales, and send it in a letter." As he acknowledges in his preface, he "adopted the characters, plan, and even the language of many parts of this story," adding only the character of Ida of Stralenheim. The whole question of the relation of *Werner* to *The German's Tale* has been carefully investigated by W. Kluge, whose work supersedes that of K. Stöhsel[5].

some stupid translation, as the 'Choice Relationships.' Lord Byron said, 'Yes, yes, the Affinities of Choice—I recollect reading a translation, which I should think was not a very good one, for some parts seemed to border on the unintelligible'."

[1] *Kruitzner, The German's Tale*, was one of a series named *The Canterbury Tales*, by Sophia and Harriet Lee, successive volumes of which appeared in 1797 and 1798, according to the *Cambridge History of English Literature*, vol. XI, p. 461. But I think that the fourth volume, which contained *The German's Tale*, must have appeared in 1801; it was reviewed 1802 (July) in the Monthly Review (and see Byron, *Works, Prose*, vol. v, p. 325).

[2] Medwin, *Conversations*, p. 326.

[3] Byron, *Works, Poetry*, vol. v, p. 338, Preface to *Werner*.

[4] It has been assumed that *Ulric and Ilvina* was a play written on the subject of *Werner*. But, as W. Kluge (*Lord Byron's Werner*, p. 10, note 1) has pointed out, Byron's statement really proves the contrary, if it is to be taken as exact; for he says in the preface that he first read *The German's Tale* "when I was young (about fourteen, I think)," and he gives his age at the time he wrote the play as thirteen. This seems conclusive, in the absence of a scrap of evidence to the contrary; none is brought forward by E. H. Coleridge, Byron's editor (see Introduction to *Werner*, Byron, *Works, Poetry*, vol. v, p. 325), nor by Kraeger (*Heldentypus*, p. 41), who accept the other view; nor have I been able to discover any in Byron's *Letters and Journals*. The coincidence of the name Ulric has presumably misled Coleridge and Kraeger, though of course it proves nothing but that the name appeared to Byron suitable to a dramatic hero.

[5] Walther Kluge, *Lord Byron's Werner or The Inheritance, Eine dramentechnische Untersuchung mit Quellenstudium*, Inaug. Diss. 1913.   Karl

He read, as we have seen, Gessner's *Tod Abels* in early days. In his preface to *Cain* he asserted that he had not read it since the age of eight, and that of the contents he remembered only that Cain's wife was called Mahala, and Abel's, Thirza. The name Thirza he had used in early poems to designate a mysterious lady, whose tragic fate he hints at in the verses. Nothing definite is known about her identity. When he took, in *Cain*, a subject closely allied to Gessner's, more recollections of his early reading recurred than he was aware, in the opinion of E. H. Coleridge, Byron's editor:

Not only in such minor matters as the destruction of Cain's altar by a whirlwind, and the substitution of the Angel of the Lord for the *Deus* of the Mysteries, but in the Teutonic domesticities of Cain and Adam, and the evangelical piety of Adam and Abel, there is a reflection, if not an imitation, of the German idyll[1].

We may question, however, whether the domesticities could well have been other than "Teutonic"—if by that term, as I suppose, Byron's editor means primitive, unsophisticated; the first family must almost necessarily be represented as living in a passably simple, unsophisticated fashion. Bertha Reed (in *The Influence of Solomon Gessner upon English Literature*, Philadelphia, 1905) has much to say on the subject of Gessner's influence on Byron. Some of her instances appear to me to be disputable, as for instance her likening of Cain's vision in Byron's drama to the dream in Gessner; others appear too slight to be taken as evidence of influence: that Cain in both cases should be a loving father and affectionate husband is perhaps not singular enough to require to be explained by foreign influence.

Stöhsel, *Lord Byrons Trauerspiel Werner und seine Quelle*, Inaug. Diss., Erlangen, 1891. Kraeger, in his work on *Der Byronsche Heldentypus*, traces Byron's predilection for robber-heroes (Lara, the Corsair, etc.) back to Schiller's *Räuber* via Lee's *German's Tale*, which he considers to be influenced by *Die Räuber*. It is preferable to say that the popularity of this type of adventurer probably encouraged Byron to introduce it in leading parts in his own fictions. Byron's own somewhat defiant attitude towards conventions and the social code generally, the result of deeply-rooted characteristics, accounts in the main for his choice of hero. This much being granted, it may be readily admitted that the same peculiarities of character and situation would attract him towards the works of other writers manifesting a rebellious spirit towards the present constitution of society.

[1] Byron, *Works, Poetry*, vol. v, p. 200.

Nor, taking all the circumstances into account, can we endorse her remark (p. 102) that "It is of importance to note that Cain and Abel marry their own sisters, as in the *Death of Abel.*" She discovers similarity between the characters of Gessner's *Tod Abels* and those of Byron's *Cain* (loc. cit. p. 105). But one may object to this that the personages in Gessner's idyll have next to no characters at all. Byron, by adding, as Bertha Reed says "that unquenchable thirst for knowledge" has given his Cain at least a semblance of reality, which is lacking in the unfortunate victim of inscrutable decrees in Gessner. If Byron had never read *Der Tod Abels* he might not have chosen the theme of *Cain*, and a few details and possibly certain "domesticities" and "pieties" of the drama show traces of Gessner's influence. More than this it is hardly safe to affirm.

A few scattered notes may be added with regard to some other occasional reading of German authors by Byron. In 1821 he read with great admiration Guido Sorelli's Italian translation of Grillparzer's *Sappho*[1], and remarked that the author's was

a devil of a name, to be sure, for posterity, but they *must* learn to pronounce it...The tragedy of *Sappho* is superb and sublime! There is no denying it. The man has done a great thing in writing that play. And *who* is he? I know him not; but *ages will.* 'Tis a high intellect.

This, from his Diary of January 12, 1821[2], is in a strain of enthusiasm unusual in Byron; and what follows may be worth copying here.

I have read *nothing* of Adolph Müllner's (the author of *Guilt*) and much less of Goethe, and Schiller, and Wieland, than I could wish. I only know them through the medium of English, French and Italian translations...(I like) all that I have read, translated, of their writings...Grillparzer is grand—antique—*not so simple* as the ancients, but very simple for a modern—too Madame de Staëlish, now and then [whatever Byron precisely means by that]—but altogether a great and goodly writer[3].

---

[1] There was an English translation of *Sappho* in 1820.

[2] Byron, *Letters and Journals*, vol. v, pp. 171 f.

[3] It has been suggested that the anachronism in *Sardanapalus*, Act III, Scene 1: "Sing me a song of Sappho," etc., may be due to the impression made on him by Grillparzer's *Sappho*. *Sardanapalus* was published December 1821.

A few weeks later he is reading a work of Friedrich Schlegel's, to which some entries in his Diary for January 28 and 29 refer[1]. He finds nothing in him which one can take hold of, "he always seems on the verge of meaning, and lo! he goes down like sunset, or melts like a rainbow, leaving a rather rich confusion." Later, however, he finds him "not such a fool as I took him for," but he objects to his assumption of omniscience. Next day, the improvement of his opinion of Schlegel apparently continued. From references to Wilhelm Schlegel we may infer that he had read him also[2].

Thomas Moore, in his *Life of Byron*[3], mentions noticing when at Venice a book in Byron's gondola "with a number of paper marks between the leaves. I enquired of him what it was?— 'Only a book,' he answered, 'from which I am trying to crib, as I do wherever I can'...On taking it up and looking into it, I exclaimed, 'Ah, my old friend, Agathon!' 'What!' he cried archly, 'you have been beforehand with me there, have you?'" On the next page Moore mentions that Byron was at that time writing the third Canto of *Don Juan*, and we may note one or two small resemblances, that may not be accidental, between the two works. The first is the similarity between Juan's fate and that of the hero of Wieland's *Agathon*, both being sold as slaves (*Agathon*, Book I, Chap. VII, and *Don Juan*, Fourth Canto); another between the independent attitude of Danae as slave of the amorous Cyrus, and that of Juan as slave of the no less amorous Gulbeyaz; both Cyrus and Gulbeyaz are accustomed to find their slightest advances received rapturously, and both are disappointed (*Agathon*, Book XV, Chap. II). There is further a coincidence of imagery which is probably not accidental; we may well believe that one of the paper slips stood at the following passage, especially in view of Wieland's express recommendation, which I have put in italics[4]. "Die Wuth

---

[1] Byron, *Letters and Journals*, vol. V, pp. 191 f.

[2] To Madame de Staël, August 25, 1816: "I received the works of Mr Schlegel, which I presume is the book to which you allude, and will take great care of it." W. Schlegel's *Lectures on Dramatic Literature*, translated by John Black, had appeared in 1815; F. Schlegel's *Lectures on the History of Literature*, by an anonymous translator, appeared in 1818.

[3] Thomas Moore, *Life, Letters and Journals of Lord Byron*, 1838, pp. 420–421.

[4] Wieland's *Sämmtliche Werke*, Leipzig, 1839, Vol. VI, p. 81.

einer stürmischen See—einer zur Rache gereizten Hornisse—
oder einer Löwin, der ihre Jungen geraubt worden, sind Bilder,
*deren sich in dergleichen Fällen sogar ein epischer Dichter mit
Ehren bedienen könnte*; aber es sind nur schwache Bilder der
Wuth, in welcher Kleonissens tugendhafter Busen u.s.w."*;
and *Don Juan*, III, lviii:

> The cubless tigress in her jungle raging
> Is dreadful to the shepherd and the flock;
> The ocean when its yeasty war is waging
> Is awful to the vessel near the rock...

and *Don Juan*, V, cxxxii:

> A tigress robbed of young, a lioness,
> Or any interesting beast of prey,
> Are similes at hand for the distress
> Of ladies who can not have their own way.

The type of imagery is common enough. The fact that two out
of three of the images proposed by Wieland are used by Byron
shortly after reading the book where they occur, makes it highly
probable that he borrowed them. (Cantos III–IV were written
in the winter of 1819–20, Canto V after an interval of five months[1].)
A more careful examination, were it worth while, of Wieland's
Agathon might yield further discoveries of the kind.

Byron, we have seen, was friendly towards German literature,
though he never troubled to learn the language beyond the
rudiments acquired in boyhood and subsequently forgotten.
There is little evidence that he read much beyond a few works
of Wieland, Schiller, Goethe and Grillparzer; the last was only
beginning his career when Byron died. His borrowings from
German, and especially from Goethe's *Faust*, are well-defined,
and more important in character perhaps than any of those we
have noticed in the case of other writers. In *Manfred* we have
similarities of situation and of some details, with a remote
parallelism of character to Goethe's *Faust*. Both the Stranger
in *The Deformed Transformed* and Lucifer in *Cain* have traits
in common with Mephistopheles, and the former drama has
details of resemblance to *Faust*. The subject of *Cain* is closely

---

[1] Byron, *Works, Poetry*, vol. VI. *Introduction to Don Juan.*

allied to that of Gessner's *Tod Abels*, which appears to have supplied some inconsiderable details to Byron's work[1].

In conclusion, we may say that both Byron and Shelley manifest a much more intelligent appreciation of German literature than did either Coleridge or Scott, in the sense that they did not hedge about their approval of it with a thousand reserves. The boldness of speculation which alarmed the older generation was welcomed by the younger, the representatives of a more radical intellectual revolt. Furthermore, the lapse of time, and the publication of De Staël's *Germany*, had rendered the appreciation of German literature an easier matter than it was when the older poets began their career.

[1] M. Eimer (*Byrons persönliche und geistige Beziehungen zur den Gebieten deutscher Kultur*, Anglia, 1912, Bd. xxxvi, pp. 313, 397) has collected very completely the available information concerning Byron's interest in and knowledge of German literature.

Scott's German Books

THE *Catalogue of the Library at Abbotsford* (Edinburgh, 1838, Bannatyne Club) shows that Scott had assembled a notable collection of German books. They number over 300 volumes, of which 42 are accounted for by Wieland's *Sämmtliche Werke*, Leipzig, 1794–1801. Lessing does not appear at all. Goethe is represented by the 1787–90 Leipzig edition of the *Schriften* in 8 vols., the last missing[1]; and by the *Neue Schriften*, 6 vols., Berlin, 1792–96[2]. There is also a Latin translation of *Hermann und Dorothea* by Fischer (1822), which perhaps contained the German text as well; and a French translation of Goethe's poems published in 1825, picked up for curiosity's sake, we may suppose, during Scott's visit to Paris in 1826. Schiller's *Sämmtliche Werke* (12 vols., 8vo., Stuttgart, 1812–15) are mentioned in the catalogue, besides a separate edition of his tragedies (*Die Räuber, Fiesko, Kabale und Liebe*, Mannheim, 1788) and the three volumes of Schiller's *Musenalmanach* for 1797, 1799 and 1800. Bürger's *Sämmtliche Schriften* are the only other edition of collected works (2 vols., 12°, Göttingen, 1796). De la Motte-Fouqué is very fully represented by more than 30 volumes. There are half-a-dozen plays besides other works of Oehlenschläger. Of the Grimms he had the *Hausmärchen*, and *Altdeutsche Wälder* and *Deutsche Heldensagen*. On the whole the leading Romantics appear sparsely, Tieck with two volumes of poems, three of *Volksmärchen, Kaiser Octavianus*, the Novelle *Der Geheimnisvolle* and *Minnelieder*; and Brentano, Arnim, Hoffmann, the Schlegels, by two or three volumes each. The bulk of the remaining German books consists of volumes and collections of medieval legends and tales of chivalry, with some volumes of history and antiquarian lore.

[1] The seventh volume of this edition contained *Faust, Ein Fragment*.
[2] The *Neue Schriften* were complete in seven volumes, appearing from 1792 to 1800.

APPENDIX II

The Date of the Lenore-reading by Mrs Barbauld

SCOTT (*Minstrelsy*, vol. IV, p. 37) gives "about the summer of 1793 or 1794" as the date of the visit to Edinburgh of "the celebrated Miss Laetitia Aikin," who, as a matter of fact, had been married to the Rev. Rochemont Barbauld for some twenty years at this time. Although Lockhart (*Memoirs*, vol. I, p. 204) hesitatingly places the visit in 1795, 1794 is almost certainly the correct date. It is the one given by Robberds (*Memoirs*, vol. I, p. 92), and a letter from Mrs Barbauld to Mrs Beecroft, dated from Buxton, October 1794, gives an account of a recent visit to Scotland, presumably that in question (*Works of Anna Laetitia Barbauld, with a Memoir by Lucy Aikin*, 2 vols., London, 1825, vol. II, p. 86). Scott was not present when Mrs Barbauld read Taylor's version of *Lenore*. Countess Purgstall, formerly Miss Cranstoun, claimed the honour of having described the event to Scott (Captain Basil Hall, *Schloss Hainfeld; or, a Winter in Lower Styria*, Edinburgh, 1836, p. 332), and Lockhart admits her claim. But Scott refers more than once to her brother, Mr Cranstoun, in this connection; for instance, in a letter to William Taylor of Norwich (in which, as may be observed, occurs an awkward construction that comes surprisingly from the pen of the future author of *Waverley*): "Edinburgh, 25 November, 1796. My friend Mr Cranstoun, brother-in-law to Professor Stewart, who heard your translation read by a lady in manuscript, is the gentleman...to whose recollection I am indebted for the two lines which I took the liberty to borrow." This does not necessarily invalidate Countess Purgstall's statement. But in his Introduction to *The Chase and William and Helen* (Edinburgh, 1807), p. iv, Scott says: "In justice to himself, the Translator thinks it his duty to acknowledge, that his curiosity was first attracted to this truly romantic story by a gentleman, who, having heard *Lenore* once read in manuscript, could only recollect the general outlines, and part of a couplet, which, from the singularity of its structure, and frequent recurrence, had remained impressed on his memory."[1] The lines for which Scott acknowledges his indebtedness to Taylor's version, are those occurring in stanzas XLVII and LVII:

> "Tramp! tramp! along the land they rode,
> Splash! splash! along the sea."

[1] This reference also appeared in the first edition of *William and Helen* (1796). See the letter to William Taylor of Norwich from which an extract is quoted above (Robberds, *Memoirs*, vol. I, p. 94).

APPENDIX III

Scott's Unpublished Translations

THE extent to which Scott translated from the German is some-what doubtful. Scott, as already quoted (p. 68), speaks of translating "various dramatic pieces" from German (*Minstrelsy*, vol. IV, p. 42). We can scarcely believe Gillies when he says that Scott "very sedulously set to work and translated right through" the works of Goethe, Schiller, Bürger and some of the romances of Spiess to boot! Gillies adds, it is true, that he did not trouble to polish his versions, being content to transfer to paper in a broad outline the sense of the German author[1]. It is noticeable that Gillies does not mention any of the three unpublished translations, the exist-ence of which is indisputable. Lockhart (*Memoirs*, vol. I, p. 215) says: "He was thenceforth [i.e. from the time when *The Wild Huntsman* was published, in 1796] engaged in a succession of versions from the dramas of Meier and Iffland, several of which are still extant in his MS, marked 1796 and 1797." He further mentions two of the translations by name (though not by the right ones), as "Steinberg's Otho of Wittelsbach" and "Meier's Wolfred of Dromberg, a drama of Chivalry." In the *Catalogue of the Library of Abbotsford*, p. 104, they appear as "(MS translation of) Steinberg's Otho of Wittelsbach, a Tragedy, (1796–7) MS, 4to. 1797," and "Translation of Meier's Wolfred of Stromberg, a Drama of Chivalry (1797) MS 4to. 1797." Hohlfeld[2] says that for "Meier's Wolfred von Dromberg," we should read Jakob Maier's "Fust von Stromberg," and that the name of the author of "Otto von Wittelsbach" is Babo, not Steinberg[3]. Hohlfeld further points out that there is no evidence that Scott undertook a translation of Gerstenberg's *Braut*, as Margraf (*Einfluss*, p. 14) has assumed to be the case. The expressions in Scott's Diary of July 5 and 6, 1797, are no evidence of translation, and Margraf does not adduce any other. A third translation, however, mentioned by Brandl and by Margraf, was undoubtedly made by Scott about the same time: namely, that of Iffland's *Mündel*. Hohlfeld (loc. cit. p. 501, note) wonders how Brandl and Margraf came to include this

---

[1] Gillies, *Recollections*, Fraser's 1835, p. 265.

[2] *Studien zur vergleichenden Litteraturgeschichte*, 1903, p. 500.

[3] Hohlfeld, loc. cit. p. 501: "Was den bei Lockhart fälschlich genannten Steinberg betrifft, so ist damit zweifellos Karl Steinberg gemeint, und wir können wohl mit Sicherheit annehmen, dass sich Scott auch mit diesem Schriftsteller beschäftigt und Lockhart dazu die Angaben verwechselt hat." The name Steinberg appears, however, both in Lockhart and in the Cata-logue, which Lockhart probably followed.

among Scott's translations, and adds the comment: "Belege gibt keiner von beiden." The existence of this translation is established, however, by the notice on p. 104 of the *Catalogue etc.*, "MS translation of Iffland's Wards, a Drama in 5 Acts"; Margraf probably followed Brandl, who may have found the entry in the Catalogue.

APPENDIX IV

The Date of Shelley's earliest German Studies

THE date of Shelley's earliest German studies remains in some doubt. Are we to believe with Medwin (*Life*, vol. i, pp. 45, 118; and *Conversations*, p. 306) that during his last year at Eton, which he left Midsummer 1810, he "worked hard at German—in which... he soon made great advances," or to accept Hogg's statement that Shelley knew no German before 1815 (Hogg, *Life of Shelley*, vol. i, pp. 51 ff., 193; vol. ii, p. 178)? Neither Medwin nor Hogg is to be trusted as an uncorroborated witness, Medwin being, it appears, constitutionally incapable of adhering to facts, while Hogg is perhaps too much busied with rounding off a consistent and amusing narrative to be worried by any deviation from the truth involved in the process. There appears to be some evidence in support of either assertion. Let us take Hogg's side first. He was certainly in a position to know whether Shelley had learnt German and whether he read or possessed German books between 1810 and 1815; and there is no obvious inducement to him to pervert the truth in this case. The fact that there is no trace of German studies in Shelley's letters previous to 1815 is rather significant, but no great number of these is preserved, which further weakens this merely negative evidence. But writing in January 1813, asking Hogg to send him one of Kant's works, Shelley says: "I have no choice between a Latin, a French, and an English translation." He thus pointedly omits here to allude to the possibility of his reading Kant in the original; had such a possibility existed, and had he merely preferred the translation on account of his imperfect knowledge of the language, we should have expected him to explain the latter circumstance to his correspondent. So much for the evidence for the negative contention. For the affirmative, there is considerably stronger evidence; but the *onus probandi* lies on this side. Asanger (*Shelleys Sprachstudien*, p. 14) points out that Medwin (*Life*, vol. i, p. 118) maintains his assertion against Hogg. Asanger (loc. cit. p. 15), repeating

Druskowitz (*P. B. Shelley*, Berlin, 1884), remarks further that it is unlikely that Shelley should have begun German in 1815 and have undertaken translations from *Faust* in the same year. But a fragment of this translation, given in W. M. Rossetti's edition of Shelley's *Poetical Works* (London, 1894, vol. III, pp. 436–437) shows how imperfect was Shelley's knowledge of German at this time. According to the same source (Druskowitz, *Shelley*, p. 242) Shelley read also Schiller's *Räuber* in this year. I have not seen the book of Druskowitz. Medwin (*Life*, vol. I, p. 118) speaks of seeing translations made by Shelley from German, on the occasion of his visit to Shelley at Oxford, in November 1810. This statement receives some confirmation from an independent source, for the anonymous Newspaper Editor, whose reminiscences appeared in Fraser's Magazine in 1841, likewise states that he has seen and formerly had in his possession, translations by Shelley from German, of about the same date (see p. 148). Dowden regards the Newspaper Editor as trustworthy "inasmuch as he writes with an evident desire to state the facts truly." Two further points in Medwin's favour may be cited. When Shelley first visited the Bodleian, he asked to see the German original of *The Wandering Jew*. Although we have only Medwin's word for this (Medwin, *Life*, vol. I, p. 59) it has some evidential value from the fact that Medwin does not mention it in support of his contention, but in quite a different connection. Assuming the report to be correct, it seems unlikely that Shelley would ask to see a German work, unless he had at least a slight knowledge of the language. The second point emerges from a passage in De Quincey's article on Shelley (De Quincey, *Works*, Edinburgh and London, 1857, vol. VI, pp. 19–20). It relates to Shelley's residence near Keswick, in the winter 1811–12. De Quincey was living near by in a cottage at Grasmere (p. 20): "Some neighbourly advantages I might certainly have placed at Shelley's disposal...[among others] my own library, which being rich in the wickedest of German speculations, would naturally have been more to Shelley's taste than the Spanish library of Southey." But De Quincey may very well base his assumption on evidence no more reliable than Medwin's statement.

This, I think, concludes the evidence on the affirmative side. The fact that one of the poems in the volume *Original Poetry. By Victor and Cazire* (1810) has the subtitle: *Translated from the German*, has probably no bearing on the subject; poems "translated from the German" had been in vogue within recent years, and Shelley and his collaboratress may have inserted the subtitle as an attractive flourish. The poem in question is of incredible vagueness and vapidity, and bears every mark of belonging to the more strictly "original" productions of Victor or Cazire. There is one case at least of a shameless theft from M. G. Lewis among the contents of the volume.

For Dowden's discussion of the date of Shelley's earliest German studies, see Dowden, *Life of Shelley*, vol. I, p. 61, note, and pp. 93–94. He inclines to think that Shelley knew little or nothing of German before 1815. Zeiger (*Beiträge*, p. 60) holds the same opinion. Droop (*Belesenheit*, p. 122) leaves the question open. Asanger (*Sprachstudien*, pp. 14–15) inclines to the earlier date, accepted also by Margraf (*Einfluss*, p. 53). The evidence, as I have stated it above, appears to me to bear in favour of the earlier date; though, on the showing of the 1815 translations, his knowledge of German even at the latter date was very imperfect.

APPENDIX V

Books translated, adapted or imitated from German; Parodies; and German Grammars; published between 1789 and 1805

THE following lists are compiled from the reviews in periodicals. They must not be regarded as even approximately complete. The notes were collected hastily and at a late period of the investigation. I include them as having a certain interest as an illustration and comment to Chapter IV, and indeed to the whole book. As the periodicals do not always give the date of publication of works reviewed, it is possible that in some cases the books have been placed in the year subsequent to that in which they appeared—or even later, though this is less likely; but I believe that these errors are not sufficiently numerous to affect the lists from the point of view mentioned above. There seems to be an undue disparity between the list for 1797 and those for the years preceding and following it. For this, I fear, the insufficiency of my notes is to blame.

1789

The Sorrows of Werter. A Poem. By Amelia Pickering.
Goethe. *A tribute to the Memory of Ulric of Hutton.*

1790

Heerfort and Clara. (Given as being *From the German.*)
The German Hotel. Tr. by Mr Marshal.
An Introduction to German Grammar. By the Rev. Dr Wendeborn.

1791

Musäus. *Popular Tales of the Germans.*
The Authentic Memoirs and Suffering of Dr William Stahl, a German Physician. (Tr. from the German.)

1792

Schiller. *The Robbers.* (A. F. Tytler's translation.)
Dramatic Pieces from the German: (1) *The Sister, a Drama*, by Goethe.
(2) *The Conversation of a Father with his Children*, by Gessner, Author of the Death of Abel. (3) *The Set of Horses, a dramatic piece*, by Emdorff.
Charlotte, or a Sequel to the Sorrows of Werter. By Mrs Farrell.

1793

Goethe. *Iphigenia in Tauris.* (Taylor's translation.)
Knigge. *The German Gil Blas, or The Adventures of Peter Claus.* 3 vols.
A Vocabulary of the German Tongue. By E. Hesse.
The Castle of Wolfenbach, a German Story. By Mrs Parsons. 2 vols.
Frederica Risberg, a German Story. 2 vols.

I take these last two to be, not translations, but attempts to imitate the German style of narrative, or to produce a German atmosphere. This rather suggests that stories translated from German had already appeared in considerable numbers.

1794

Grosse. *The Dagger.*
(Cramer.) *Herman of Unna.* (For the real author, Benedikte Naubert, cf. W. Sellier, *Kotzebue in England*, p. 5.)
The Necromancer, or the Tale of the Black Forest. Translated from the German of Lawrence Flammenberg (pseudonym of K. F. Kahlert.)
Haller. *The Poems of Baron Haller*, translated into English by Mrs Howarth.

1795

Schiller. *Cabal and Love.*
—— *The Ghost-Seer, or Apparitionist.*
The Victim of Magical Delusion; or the Mystery of the Revolution of P...l. Translated from the German of Cajetan Tschink.

Monthly Review, August 1795, says: "One of the numberless imitations to which the Ghost-Seer of the celebrated Schiller has given rise in Germany."
The Secret Tribunal; a Play. In Five Acts. By James Boaden.

Obviously based on the *Femgericht* idea, developed in Naubert's *Herman of Unna*, published the preceding year.

The Modern Arria; a Tragedy in Five Acts. Translated from the German of F. M. Klinger.

Dialogues of the Gods. Originally written in German by C. M. Wieland.

1796

Bürger. *Leonora. A Tale*, translated freely from the German of G. A. Bürger. By J. T. Stanley. (2s. 6d., Miller.)

—— *Leonora, a Tale*, translated and altered from the German of G. A. Bürger. By J. T. Stanley. A new edition. (5s., Miller.)

—— *Lenora, a Tale.* Tr. by Henry James Pye.

—— *Ellenore, a Ballad.* (Taylor's translation.)

—— *The Chase, and William and Helen.* (Scott's translation.)

—— *Leonora.* Translated from the German etc. by W. R. Spencer.

Gessner. *Laura, or the Influence of a Kiss.*

Grosse. *The Genius.* Tr. by Joseph Trapp.

Haller. *The Alps, a Moral and Descriptive Poem of the Great Haller.* Tr. by Henry Barrett.

Kant. *Project for Perpetual Peace.*

—— *A General and Introductory View of Professor Kant's Principles* etc. by F. A. Nitsch.

Kotzebue. *Negro Slaves.*

Nicolai. *The Life and Opinions of Sebaldus Nothanker.* Tr. by T. Dutton (Vol. I).

Schiller. *Fiesco, or the Genoese Conspiracy.* Tr. by G. H. N(oehden) and J. S(toddart).

Weber. *The Black Valley; a Tale*, from the German of Veit Weber.

Wieland [?]. *Select Fairy Tales from the German of Wieland.* By the Translator of The Sorcerer.

—— *Private History of Peregrinus Proteus the Philosopher.*

The German Miscellany; consisting of Dramas, Dialogues etc., translated from that Language, by A. Thomson.

Varieties of Literature, from Foreign Literary Journals and Original Manuscripts. 2 vols. (Included translations from German.)

Maurice, a German Tale by Mr Schulz. Translated from the French.

Albert of Nordenshild, or the Modern Alcibiades. Translated from the German. 2 vols.

A Concise Review of Original German Books. No. 1. 8vo. 84 pages. Price 1s. Printed in Edinburgh.

Grosse. *Horrid Mysteries. A Story.* From the German of the Marquis of Grosse. Tr. by P. Will.

1797

Bürger. *The Wild Huntsman's Chase.* From the German of Bürger, Author of Lenore.

(Bürger.) *Miss Kitty; a Parody on Lenora, a Ballad.* Translated from the German, by several Hands.

Goethe. *Stella,* translated from the German of M. Goethe, Author of The Sorrows of Werter.

Kotzebue. *Appearances Deceive.* Tr. by Benjamin Thompson.

Schiller. *The Minister,* by M. G. Lewis. (Translator of *Kabale und Liebe.*)

All's Well that ends Well, or Alvaro and Ximines. A Spanish Tale. Translated from the German.

Count Donamar; or the Errors of Sensibility. A Series of Letters written in the Time of the Seven Years' War. Translated from the German. 3 vols.

Interesting Tales, selected and translated from the German.
    Critical Review, May 1798, doubts whether they are from the German.

1798

Bürger. *Eleonora.* Novella Morale scritta sulla traccia d' un Poemetto Inglese tradotto dal Tedesco. Trattenimento Italico di Mrs Taylor. In Londra.

Goethe. *Clavidgo.*

Kant. *Elements of the Critical Philosophy.* By A. F. M. Willich.

Kotzebue. *The Stranger.* Tr. by George Papendick.

—— *The Stranger.* Tr. by Schink, according to the European Magazine, May 1798.

—— *Count Benzowski.* Tr. by Rev. W. Render.

—— *The History of My Father...A Romance...*Translated from the German of Kotzebue.

—— *Lovers' Vows, or the Child of Love.* Stephen Porter.

—— *Lovers' Vows.* Mrs Inchbald. (Adaptation.)

—— *Adelaide of Wulfingen.* Benjamin Thompson.

—— *Count of Burgundy.* Anne Plumptre.

—— *Ildegerte, Queen of Norway.* Benjamin Thompson. 2 vols.

Kratter. *Natalia and Menzikof...A Tragedy...*From the German of Kratter.

—— *The Maid of Marienburg, a Drama...*From the German of Kratter.

Nicolai. *Sebaldus Nothanker.* Vols. II and III. Tr. by Thomas Dutton.

The Midnight Bell, a German Story, founded on Incidents in real life. 3 vols.

The German Erato, or a Collection of favourite Songs, translated into English, with their original Music. Berlin. (Beresford.)

The German Songster, or a Collection of favourite Airs, with their original Music, done into English by the Translator of *The German Erato*. (Place of publication not given.) (Beresford.)

Schiller. *Don Carlos, a Tragedy*. Tr. by G. H. Noehden and J. Stoddart. (Publ. by Mills.)

—— *Don Carlos*. (Anonymous, published by Richardson.)

1799

Goethe. *Gortz of Berlingen*. Rose d'Aguilar.

—— *Goetz of Berlichingen*. By William Scott, Esq.

Iffland. *The Bachelors*.

—— *The Lawyers*. Tr. by C. Ludger.

—— *The Foresters*. Tr. by Bell Plumptre.

Kotzebue. *The Constant Lover* (a Novel).

—— *Sighs; or the Daughter. A Comedy*. Tr. by Prince Hoare.

—— *The Noble Lie*. Tr. by M. Geisweiler.

—— *The Noble Lie*. (Anonymous.)

—— *The Stranger*.

—— *Pizarro. The Spaniards in Peru or the Death of Rolla*. Tr. by Anne Plumptre.

—— *Pizarro in Peru*. Tr. by Thomas Dutton.

—— *Pizarro*. (Sheridan's adaptation.)

—— *Pizarro*. (Yet another translation.)
  Monthly Review, Feb. 1800, says that it is an ungrammatical and ridiculous translation by a North Briton.

—— *The Virgin of the Sun*. Tr. by James Lawrence, Esq.

—— *Rolla*. Tr. by M. G. Lewis.

—— *Self-Immolation*. Tr. by Henry Nouman, Esq.

—— *The Widow and the Riding-Horse*. Tr. by Anne Plumptre.

—— *The Horse and the Widow*. Tr. by Dibdin.

—— *Poverty and Nobleness of Mind*. Tr. by M. Geisweiler.

—— *False Shame*.

—— *The Peevish Man*. Tr. by C. Ludger.

—— *The Corsicans*.

—— *La Peyrouse*. Tr. by Anne Plumptre.

—— *La Peyrouse*. Tr. by B. Thompson.

—— *The East Indian*. Tr. by A. Thomson.

—— *The Writing-Desk*.

—— *The Wise Men of the East*. Tr. by Mrs Inchbald.

—— *The Happy Family*. Tr. by B. Thompson.

—— *The Escape, A Narrative*. Tr. by B. Thompson.

—— *The Reconciliation*. Tr. by Ludger.

—— *The Force of Calumny*. Tr. by Anne Plumptre.

—— *The Natural Son*. Tr. by Anne Plumptre.

Sheridan and Kotzebue. (British Critic calls it a compilation wholly beneath the notice of Criticism.)

More Kotzebue! The Origin of my own Pizarro. A Farce.

Knigge. *The History of the Amtsrath Gutman.*

Lessing. *The School for Honour, or the Chance of War.* (*Minna von Barnhelm.*)

Matthisson. *Frederick Matthisson's Letters.* Tr. by Anne Plumptre.

Miltenburg. *The Man of Nature, or Nature and Love,* from the German of Miltenburg. William Wennington.

Schiller. *The Red-Cross Knights.* (Holcroft's adaptation of *The Robbers.*)

A Complete Introduction to the Knowledge of the German Language. By George Crabb. (Another edition 1800.)

A Concise Practical Grammar of the German Tongue. By W. Render.

Sigevart, a Tale. Translated from the German.

1800

Campe. *Cortez.* Tr. by Elisabeth Helme.

—— *Pizarro.* Tr. by Elisabeth Helme.

Iffland. *The Nephews.* Tr. by Hannibal Evans Lloyd.

—— *Crime from Ambition.* Tr. by M. Geisweiler.

Kotzebue. *Johanna of Montfaucon.*

—— *Johanna of Montfaucon,* upon the Plan of the German Drama of Kotzebue, adapted to the English Stage by Richard Cumberland. (Was based upon the above translation.)

—— *The Birthday,* by T. Dibdin, adapted from Kotzebue's *Reconciliation.*

—— *The Sufferings of the Family of Ortenberg, a Novel.* Tr. by P. Will.

—— *Sketch of the Life and Career of A. von Kotzebue.* Tr. by Anne Plumptre.

—— *Pizarro; ein Trauerspiel.* (Retranslated by Constantine Geisweiler from Sheridan's adaptation of Kotzebue.)

—— *The Beauties of Kotzebue*; containing the most interesting scenes etc., in all his admired Dramas. By W. Chamberlain Oulton.

Critical Remarks on (Sheridan's) Pizarro. By S. A. Bardsley.

A. La Fontaine. *Romulus.* Tr. by P. Will.

Musäus. *Physiognomical Travels.* Tr. by Anne Plumptre.

Schiller. Coleridge's *Piccolomini and Death of Wallenstein.*

Stolberg. *Hymn to the Earth* etc. Tr. by the Rev. John Whitehouse.

Vulpius. *The History of Rinaldo Rinaldini.* Tr. by J. Hinckley.

German Grammar. By G. H. Noehden.

A Complete Introduction to the Knowledge of the German Language. By George Crabb. (New edition, see 1799.)

Elements of German Conversation. By George Crabb.

Selections of German Prose and Poetry, with a Small Dictionary and Other Aids for Translating. By George Crabb.

The Tournament. A Tragedy; imitated from the celebrated German Drama, entitled Agnes Bernauer, which was written by a Nobleman of high Rank etc., by Mariana Starke.

1801

Goethe. *The Sorrows of Werter.* Tr. by William Render, D.D.

The Sacred Meditations of John Gerhard, translated into Blank Verse by W. Papillon.

Goethe. *Herman and Dorothea.* Tr. by Thomas Holcroft.

Schiller. *Mary Stuart.* Tr. by J. C. M(ellish), Esq.

Tales of Wonder; written and collected by M. G. Lewis.

Tales of Terror. (Published, as the above, by Bell. No author's name. It consists in part of a collection similar to the *Tales of Wonder*, in part of parodies of this kind of fiction.)

Tales of the Devil, from the Original Gibberish of Professor Lumpwitz, S.U.S. and C.A.C. in the University of Snoringberg. (Parody of Lewis's collection or collections.)

Leonhard and Gertrude, a popular story; written originally in German; translated into French, and now attempted in English.

1802

Gessner. *The Works of Solomon Gessner*, translated from the German. 3 vols.

Kotzebue. *The Guardian Angel.* (A Narrative.)

—— *The Female Jacobin Club: a Political Comedy.* Tr. by J. Siber.

—— *The Most remarkable Year in the Life of Kotzebue.* Tr. by Rev. Benjamin Beresford.

La Fontaine. *The Reprobate.* Tr. by the Author of The Wife and the Mistress, etc.

1803

La Fontaine. *The Village Pastor and His Children.*

—— *New Moral Tales.* Tr. by Ni...ce.

1804

Gessner. *The Letters of Gessner and His Family.* From the German.

Kotzebue's *Travels from Berlin to Paris.*

La Fontaine. *Henrietta Bellman.*

Wieland. *Confessions in Elysium.* Tr. by J. B. Elrington.

Translations from the German, Danish, etc. Herbert.

A Complete Analysis of the German Language. By Dr W. Render.

1805

Gellert. *The Life of Professor Gellert*; with a Course of Moral Lessons
...taken from a French Translation of the Original German.
By Mrs Douglas. 3 vols.

Schiller. *The Piccolominis.* (Includes translation of the *Lager*.)

La Fontaine. *Love and Gratitude, or Traits of the Human Heart.*
Tr. by Mrs Parsons.

Lessing. *Nathan the Wise.*

The Venetian Outlaw, A Drama. By R. W. Elliston. (Translated
from a French piece: *Abeline le Grand Bandit ou l'Homme à
trois Visages*, founded on Zschokke's *Aballino*.)

The Bravo of Venice. A Romance translated from the German by
M. G. Lewis.

Chapter II

Althaus, Friedrich. *Beiträge zur Geschichte der deutschen Colonie in England.* Unsere Zeit, N.F., 9. Jahrgang, Erste Hälfte. Leipzig, 1873.

Carré, J. M. *Goethe en Angleterre. Bibliographie de Goethe en Angleterre.* 1920.

Cooke, Margaret W. *Schiller's Robbers in England.* Modern Language Review, vol. XI, no. 2 (April 1916).

Haney, J. L. *German Literature in England before 1790.* Americana Germanica, vol. IV.

Kluge, J. *Henry Mackenzie.* Anglia XXXIV, N.F. Band XXII. Hefte I and II (Jan. 1911).

Mackenzie, H. *Account of the German Theatre.* Transactions of the Royal Society of Edinburgh, vol. II, 1790, part II.

Morgan, B. Q. *A Bibliography of German Literature in English Translation.* University of Wisconsin Studies in Language and Literature, No. 16. Madison, 1922.

Rea, Thomas. *Schiller's Dramas and Poems in England.* London, 1906.

Richmond, H. M. *Mackenzie's Translations from the German.* Modern Language Review, vol. XVII, Oct. 1922, p. 412.

Schaible, K. H. *Geschichte der Deutschen in England.* Strassburg, 1885.

Schwarz, Hans. *Henry Mackenzie.* Inaug. Diss. Winterthur, 1911.

Turner, A. E. Review of Carré's *Goethe en Angleterre.* Modern Language Review, vol. XVI, July–October 1921.

Willoughby, L. A. *English Translations and Adaptations of Schiller's Robbers.* Modern Language Review, July–October 1921.

—— *Die Räuber. Ein Trauerspiel von Friedrich Schiller.* pp. 1–101. Humphrey Milford, 1922.

See also the General Bibliography.

Chapter III

Andrews, Alexander. *The History of British Journalism.* 2 vols. London, 1859.

Clarigny, Cucheval. *Histoire de la Presse en Angleterre et aux États-Unis.* Paris, 1857.

Drake, Nathan. *Essays etc., illustrative of the Rambler, Adventurer and Idler.* 2 vols. London, 1810.

Fiedler, H. G. *Goethe's Lyric poems in English Translation.* Modern Language Review, vol. XVIII, Jan. 1923, pp. 51 ff.

(Grant, James.) *The Great Metropolis.* 2 vols. London, 1836.

Jaeck, Emma G. *Madame de Staël and the Spread of German Literature.* New York, 1915.

Sellier, Walter. *Kotzebue in England. Ein Beitrag zur Geschichte der englischen Bühne und der Beziehungen der deutschen Litteratur zur englischen.* Leipzig, 1901.

Staël-Holstein. *Germany.* By the Baroness Staël-Holstein. Translated from the French. In Three Volumes. London, 1813.

Stevens, A. *Life and Times of Madame de Staël.* 2 vols. London, 1881.

Whitford, R. C. *Madame de Staël's Literary Reputation in England.* University of Illinois Studies in Language and Literature, vol. IV, no. 1, Feb. 1918. Published by the University of Illinois.

Crabb Robinson.

Carré, J. M. *Un Ami et Défenseur de Goethe en Angleterre. Henry Crabb Robinson. Avec des documents inédits.* Extrait de la Revue Germanique de juillet-août 1912.

—— *Goethe en Angleterre.* (1920.)

—— *Madame de Staël, H. C. Robinson et Goethe.* Modern Language Review, vol. XI, no. 3 (July 1916).

Eitner, K. *Ein Englander über deutsches Geistesleben im ersten Drittel dieses Jahrhunderts. Aufzeichnungen Henry Crabb Robinson's nebst Biographie und Einleitung.* Weimar, 1871.

Margraf, E. *Einfluss* etc. (see General Bibliography), pp. 38 ff.

Mayer, Ellen. *Begegnungen eines Engländers mit Goethe.* Deutsche Rundschau, August 1899. Heft 11.—Separatabdruck.

Robinson, H. Crabb. *Diary, Reminiscences and Correspondence.* Edited by Thomas Sadler. 3 vols. London, 1869. Also the 3rd edition. 2 vols. 1872.

Todt, W. *Lessing in England.* p. 27. Heidelberg, 1912.

William Taylor of Norwich.

Carré, J. M. *Quelques Lettres inédites de William Taylor, Coleridge et Carlyle à Henry Crabb Robinson sur la littérature allemande.* Extrait de la Revue Germanique de janvier-février 1912.

Herzfeld, G. *William Taylor of Norwich.* (Studien zur englischen Philologie.) Halle, 1897.

Margraf, E. *Einfluss* etc. (see General Bibliography), pp. 7 ff.

Robberds, J. A. *Memoir of the Life and Writings of the late William Taylor of Norwich.* 2 vols. London, 1843.

Taylor, William. *Historic Survey of German Poetry*, by William Taylor of Norwich. 3 vols. London 1828–30.

Chapter IV

Abramczyk, R. *Über die Quellen zu Walter Scott's Roman: Ivanhoe.* Inaug. Diss. Halle a. S. 1903.

Ball, Margaret. *Sir Walter Scott as a Critic of Literature.* New York, 1907.

Barbauld. *Works of Anna Laetitia Barbauld, with a Memoir* by Lucy Aikin. 2 vols. London, 1825.

Bernays, M. *Schriften zur Kritik und Litteraturgeschichte.* 4 vols. Vol. I. Stuttgart, 1895.

Blumenhagen, K. *Sir Walter Scott als Übersetzer.* Dissertation. Rostock, 1900.
> Uncritical comparison of texts. Criticised with merited severity by Hohlfeld, *Koch's Studien zur vergleichenden Litteraturgeschichte,* 1903, v. infra.

Carré, J. M. *Goethe en Angleterre* and *Bibliographie.* 1920.

Catalogue of the Library at Abbotsford. Edinburgh, 1838 (Bannatyne Club).

Ellis, Grace A. *Memoirs, Letters etc. of Anna Laetitia Barbauld.* Boston, 1874.

Freye, W. *The Influence of "Gothic" Literature on Sir Walter Scott.* Rostock, 1902.

Gillies, R. P. *Recollections of Sir Walter Scott.* Fraser's Magazine, September 1835.
> Published in book form, with some alterations, 1837.

—— *Memoirs of a Literary Veteran.* 3 vols. London, 1851.

(Gillies.) Batt, M. *Contributions to the History of English Opinion of German Literature.* I. *Gillies and the Foreign Quarterly Review.* II. *Gillies and Blackwood's Magazine.* (Modern Language Notes, vol. XVII, no. 3, March 1902, and vol. XVIII, no. 3, March 1903.)

—— Zeiger, T. *Beiträge,* etc. (see General Bibliography), pp. 16 ff.

Hall, Captain Basil. *Schloss Hainfeld; or, a Winter in Lower Styria.* Edinburgh, 1836.

Hofmann, Georg. *Entstehungsgeschichte von Sir Walter Scott's Marmion.* Inaug. Diss. Königsberg i. Pr. 1913.
> One of the worst cases of wholesale uncritical allegation of influence that I have come across.

Hohlfeld, A. R. *Scott als Übersetzer.* Koch's Studien zur vergleichenden Litteraturgeschichte. 1903.
> Besides its criticism of Blumenhagen's Dissertation, it contains interesting information and careful inference.

Introductions, and Notes and Illustrations, to the Novels, Tales, and Romances of the Author of Waverley. 3 vols. Edinburgh and London.

Le Breton, Anna Letitia. *Memoir of Mrs Barbauld.* London, 1874.

(*Lenore.*) Brandl, A. *Lenore in England.* Erich Schmidts *Characteristiken.* Berlin, 1886. pp. 244 ff.

—— Greg, W. W. *English Translations of Lenore.* Modern Quarterly of Language and Literature, 1899, no. 5, and 1900, no. 1.

—— Herzfeld, G. *Zur Geschichte von Bürgers Lenore in England.* Archiv für das Studium der neueren Sprachen, vol. CVI, p. 354.

—— Roberts. *Bürger's Lenore.* Athenaeum 3823, 1901.

Lewis, M. G. *The Monk.* Gibbings and Company, 1906.

Lewis, M. G. *Tales of Wonder*. Written and Collected by M. G. Lewis, Esq., M.P., etc. In Two Volumes. London, 1801.

For M. G. Lewis, see also Margraf (*Einfluss*, pp. 10 ff.) and Sir Walter Scott (*Essay on Imitations of the Ancient Ballad* (v. infra), pp. 29 ff.), and Emerson, O. F. ("*Monk*" *Lewis and the Tales of Terror*, Modern Language Notes, vol. XXXVIII, no. 3).

Lockhart, J. G. *Memoirs of Sir Walter Scott*. 5 vols. Macmillan, 1900.

—— *The Life and Letters of John Gibson Lockhart*. By Andrew Lang. 2 vols. London, 1897.

Lorenzen, H. L. *Peveril of the Peak. Ein Beitrag zur litterarischen Würdigung Sir Walter Scotts*. (1912?)

Margraf, E. *Einfluss* etc. (see General Bibliography), pp. 12 ff.

Petri, Dr A. *Über Walter Scotts Dramen* (i. Teil). Jahresbericht über die Herzogliche Realschule zu Schmölln, S.-A. Ostern, 1909; bis Ostern, 1910. Schmölln, 1910.

Roesel, L. K. *Die litterarischen und persönlichen Beziehungen Sir Walter Scotts zu Goethe*. Leipzig, 1901.

Roesel attempts in an unusual degree to view the literary situation of the period as a whole; but on questions of detail and in his conclusions he appears to me unreliable.

Scott, Sir Walter. *Essay on Imitations of the Ancient Ballad. Minstrelsy of the Scottish Border*. Ed. by T. F. Henderson. Vol. IV. Edinburgh, London and New York, 1902.

—— *Miscellaneous Works*. Vol. VI. Edinburgh, 1870. (*Essay on Chivalry and Essay on the Drama*.)

—— *The Chase and William and Helen. Two Ballads* translated from the German of G. H. Bürger. By Walter Scott, Esq. Edinburgh, 1807.

—— *The Poetical Works*. Ed. by J. Logie Robertson, M.A. London, 1913.

—— *Journal of Sir Walter Scott* 1825–32. New Edition. Edinburgh, 1891.

Skene, J. *The Skene Papers*. Memories of Sir Walter Scott by James Skene. Ed. by Basil Thomson. London, 1909.

Wolf, Martin. *Walter Scott's Kenilworth*. Inaug. Diss. 1903.

Chapter V

Allsop, T. *Letters, Conversations and Recollections of S. T. Coleridge*. 2 vols. London, 1836.

Beddoes. *The Letters of Thomas Lovell Beddoes*. Ed. with Notes by Edmund Gosse. London and New York, 1894. (Limited edition.)

Brandl, Alois. *Samuel Taylor Coleridge und die Englische Romantik*. Strassburg, 1886.

—— *Samuel Taylor Coleridge and the English Romantic School*. English Edition by Lady Eastlake. London: Murray, 1887.

Brandl, Alois. *S. T. Coleridges Notizbuch aus den Jahren* 1795–1798. Archiv für das Studium der neueren Sprachen, Bd. xcvii, Hefte 3/4.

Breul, K. *Wallenstein*, by F. Schiller. Ed. by K. Breul. 2 vols. Cambridge University Press, 1894 and 1896.

Carré, J. M. *Quelques Lettres inédites de William Taylor, Coleridge et Carlyle à Henry Crabb Robinson sur la littérature allemande.* Extrait de la Revue Germanique de janvier–février 1912.

Carlyon, C. *Early Years and Late Reflections.* 4 vols. London, 1856–58.

Campbell. *S. T. Coleridge. A Narrative of the Events of his Life.* London, 1894.

Coleorton. *Memorials of Coleorton.* Ed. by William Knight. 2 vols. Edinburgh, 1887.

Coleridge. *The Complete Poetical Works of S. T. Coleridge.* Ed. by E. H. Coleridge. 2 vols. Oxford, 1912.

— *Biographia Literaria, or Biographical Sketches of my literary Life and Opinions.* 2 vols. London, 1817.

—— *Specimens of the Table-Talk of the late Samuel Taylor Coleridge.* Ed. by H. Nelson Coleridge. 2 vols. London, 1835.

—— *The Friend. A Series of Essays etc.*, by S. T. Coleridge. Ed. by H. Nelson Coleridge. New Edition. 2 vols. London, 1863.

—— *Anima Poetae.* From the Unpublished Notebooks of S. T. Coleridge. Ed. by E. H. Coleridge. London, 1895.

—— *Lectures and Notes on Shakspere and Other English Poets.* By S. T. Coleridge. Now first collected by T. Ashe, B.A. 1885.

—— *Letters of S. T. Coleridge.* Ed. by E. H. Coleridge. 2 vols. London, 1895. (Referred to in the notes as Coleridge, *Letters*, E. H. C.)

—— Turnbull, A. *Biographia Epistolaris, being the Biographical Supplement of Coleridge's Biographia Literaria, with Additional Letters,* etc. London, 1911.

Cottle, Joseph. *Early Recollections, chiefly relating to the late S. T. Coleridge.* 2 vols. London, 1837.

—— *Reminiscences of S. T. Coleridge and R. Southey.* London, 1847.

Dunstan, A. C. *The German Influence on Coleridge.* Modern Language Review, vol. xvii, July 1922, and vol. xviii, April 1923.

Gillman, A. W. *The Gillmans of Highgate; with Letters from S. T. Coleridge* etc. London, 1895.

Gillman, J. *The Life of S. T. Coleridge.* London, 1838.

Haney, J. L. *The German Influence on S. T. Coleridge.* Philadelphia, 1902.

This book is a valuable study of the subject, but it is difficult to obtain. It is entered in the British Museum Catalogue as *German Literature in England before* 1790, if my record is correct (this is the title of another useful study of Haney's: see General Bibliography). The Press mark is 011853.1.34.(3). I was unable to obtain a copy by advertising for it, nor have I seen it save in the British Museum. A new edition of this most useful work would be a benefit to students of Coleridge.

—— *Bibliography of Coleridge.* 1903.

Herford, C. H. *The Age of Wordsworth.* London, 1909.

(Lamb.) Lucas, E. V. *The Life of Charles Lamb.* 1905.

Machule, P. *Coleridges Wallenstein-Übersetzung.* Englische Studien, 31. Band, 1902, pp. 182–239.
    Machule's analysis of errors is much closer than Roscher's (v. infra).

Margraf, E. *Einfluss* etc. (see General Bibliography), pp. 20 ff.

Maringer, F. *S. T. Coleridges Aesthetik und Poetik.* 1. Teil. Freiburg i. Br. 1906.

Robinson, H. Crabb. *Diary, Reminiscences and Correspondence.* Ed. by Thomas Sadler. 3 vols. London, 1869.

Roscher, H. *Die Wallensteinübersetzung von S. T. Coleridge.* Inaug. Diss. Borna. Leipzig, 1905.

Sandford, Mrs Henry. *Thomas Poole and his Friends.* London, 1888.

Wordsworth.

Knight, W. *The Life of William Wordsworth.* 3 vols. Edinburgh, 1889.

Margraf, E. *Einfluss* etc., pp. 30–35.

Meusch, R. A. J. *Goethe and Wordsworth.* Publications of the English Goethe Society, no. 7, 1893.

Rea, T. *Schiller's Dramas and Poems in England.* London, 1906. pp. 18 ff.

Zeiger, T. *Beiträge* etc. (see General Bibliography), pp. 28 ff.

Southey.

Cottle, J. *Reminiscences of Samuel Taylor Coleridge and Robert Southey.* London, 1847.

Dowden, E. *Southey.* London, 1879.

Margraf, E. *Einfluss* etc. (see General Bibliography), pp. 36 ff.

Robberds, J. W. *A Memoir of the Life and Writings of the late William Taylor of Norwich.* 2 vols. London, 1843.

Southey. *Life and Correspondence of Robert Southey.* Ed. by C. C. Southey. 6 vols. London, 1849.

—— *The Poetical Works of Robert Southey.* Collected by Himself. 10 vols. London, 1840.

Zeiger, Th. *Beiträge* etc. (see General Bibliography), pp. 42 ff.

Chapter VI

Ackermann, Richard. *Quellen, Vorbilder, Stoffe zu Shelleys poetischen Werken.* Erlangen und Leipzig, 1890.

—— *P. B. Shelley. Prometheus Unbound. Erste kritische Textausgabe mit Einleitung und Kommentar von Richard Ackermann.* Heidelberg, 1908.

Ackermann, R. *Shelleys Epipsychidion und Adonais. Mit Einleitung und Anmerkungen herausgegeben von Richard Ackermann.* Berlin, 1900.
—— *Shelleys Alastor und Epipsychidion.* Inaug. Diss. Leipzig, 1890. Contains errors of fact.
Asanger, F. P. B. *Shelleys Sprach-Studien: Seine Übersetzungen aus dem Lateinischen und Griechischen.* Inaug. Diss. Bonn, 1911.
Dowden, E. *The Life of P. B. Shelley.* 2 vols. London, 1886.
Droop, A. *Die Belesenheit Percy Bysshe Shelleys.* Inaug. Diss. Jena. Weimar, 1906.
Druskowitz. *P. B. Shelley.* Berlin, 1884. (Not seen by me.)
　　Cp. J. Zupitza's review of it (Deutsche Literaturzeitung, March 1884, no. 9, pp. 315–318) for an unfavourable opinion of the book—superficial knowledge of England and English and no new information on Shelley.
Hogg, T. J. *The Life of P. B. Shelley.* 4 vols. (two published). London, 1858.
Koszul, A. *La Jeunesse de Shelley.* Paris, 1910.
Margraf, E. *Einfluss* etc. (see General Bibliography), pp. 53 ff.
Medwin, T. *The Life of P. B. Shelley.* 2 vols. London, 1847.
Middleton, C. S. *Shelley and his Writings.* 2 vols. London, 1858.
Peacock, T. L. *Peacock's Memoirs of Shelley, with Shelley's Letters to Peacock.* Ed. by H. F. B. Brett-Smith. London, 1909.
—— *The Works of T. L. Peacock.* Bentley and Son, 1875.
—— *The Life and Novels of Thomas Love Peacock.* Arthur B. Young. Norwich, 1904.
Schmitt, H. *Shelley als Romantiker.* Inaug. Diss. Marburg, 1911.
Shelley. *The Prose Works of P. B. Shelley.* Ed. by H. Buxton Forman. 4 vols. London, 1880.
—— *Note Books of P. B. Shelley, from the Originals in the library of W. K. Bixby.* Ed. by H. Buxton Forman. Privately printed. 3 vols. St Louis, 1911.
—— *The Prose Works of P. B. Shelley.* Ed. by R. H. Shepherd. 2 vols. London, 1888.
—— *The Wandering Jew.* Ed. by Bertram Dobell. London, 1887.
—— *Original Poetry of Victor and Cazire* (P. B. Shelley and Elizabeth Shelley). Ed. by R. Garnett. London and New York, 1898.
Sweet, H. A. *Source of Shelley's Alastor.* (An English Miscellany, presented to Dr Furnivall.) Oxford, 1901.
　　Attributes influence recklessly in some cases.
Zeiger, T. *Beiträge* etc. (see General Bibliography).
Zettner. *Shelleys Mythendichtung.* Inaug. Diss. Leipzig, 1902. (Not seen by me; quoted by Droop.)

Chapter VII

Ackermann, R. *Lord Byron.* 1901.

Althaus, Friedrich. *On the Personal Relations between Goethe and Byron.* Publications of the English Goethe Society, no. IV. London, 1888.

Blessington. *Conversations of Lord Byron with the Countess of Blessington.* London, 1834.

Blumenthal, F. *Lord Byron's Mystery "Cain" and its relation to Milton's "Paradise Lost" and Gessner's "Death of Abel."* Oldenburg, 1891.

The Works of Lord Byron (Poetry). Ed. by E. H. Coleridge. London, 1898.

The Works of Lord Byron (Letters and Journals). Ed. by R. E. Prothero. London, 1898.

Chew, S. C. *The Relation of Lord Byron to the Drama of the Romantic Period.* Göttingen, 1914.

Eberty, Dr Felix. *Lord Byron, ein Lebensbild.* 2. Ausgabe. Leipzig, 1879.

Eimer, M. *Byrons Beziehungen zu den Gebieten deutscher Kultur.* Anglia 1912, vol. XXXVI, pp. 313 ff., 397 ff.

Elze, K. *Lord Byron, a Biography.* London, 1872.

Fuhrmann, K. *Die Belesenheit des jungen Byron.* Friedenau bei Berlin, 1903.

Kluge, W. *Lord Byrons Werner or The Inheritance. Eine dramentechnische Untersuchung mit Quellenstudium.* Inaug. Diss. 1913.

Kraeger, H. *Der Byronsche Heldentypus.* München, 1898.

Lee, Harriet. *Kruitzner: or the German's Tale.* 5th ed. London, 1823.

Mayne, E. C. *Byron.* London, 1912.

Medwin, T. *Conversations of Lord Byron.* London, 1824.

Moore, T. *Life, Letters and Journals of Lord Byron.* London, 1838.

Schaffner, A. *Lord Byrons Cain und seine Quellen.* Strassburg, 1880.

Schiff, H. *Lord Byrons Marino Faliero.* Inaug. Diss. Marburg, 1910.

Sinzheimer, S. *Goethe und Byron.* Inaug. Diss. München, 1894.

Stöhsel, K. *Lord Byrons Trauerspiel Werner und seine Quelle.* Inaug. Diss. Erlangen, 1891.

Varnhagen, Dr Hermann. *Über Byrons dramatisches Bruchstück "Der umgestaltete Missgestaltete."* Erlangen, 1905.
    Very good, clear, careful and full of his subject.

—— *De rebus quibusdam compositionem Byronis dramatis quod Manfred inscribitur praecedentibus* etc. Erlangen, 1909.
    Careful study of the circumstances, places and dates relating to the composition of Manfred. Written in German.

GENERAL BIBLIOGRAPHY

Alford, R. G. *Goethe's Earliest Critics in England.* Publications of the English Goethe Society, no. VII. London, 1893.

Baumann, L. *Die Englischen Übersetzungen von Goethes Faust.* Halle a. S. 1907.

Beers, H. A. *A History of English Romanticism in the XVIIIth Century.* London, 1899.

Betz, L. P. *La Littérature Comparée.* Deuxième édition augmentée. Strasbourg, 1904.

Bode, W. *Die Franzosen und Engländer in Goethes Leben und Urteil.* Berlin, 1915.

Bradley, A. C. *English Poetry and German Philosophy in the Age of Wordsworth.* The Adamson Lecture, 1909. Manchester, 1909.

Brandes, G. *Der Naturalismus in England.* Leipzig, 1897.

Brandl, A. *Die Aufnahme von Goethes Jugendwerken in England.* Goethe Jahrbuch, 3. Band. 1882.

—— *Lenore in England.* In Erich Schmidt's *Charakteristiken.* Berlin, 1886. pp. 244 ff. See W. W. Greg.

—— *Goethes Verhältnisse zu Byron.* Goethe Jahrbuch, 20. Band. 1899.

Carlyle, T. *Essays.* 7 vols. Chapman and Hall.

Carré, J. M. *Goethe en Angleterre.* Paris, 1920.

C. F. L. *Deutsche Dichtungen in Englischen Übersetzungen.* Grenzboten, 28. Jahrgang, II. Semester, II. Band, p. 285.

Cooke, M. W. *Schiller's Robbers in England.* Modern Language Review, vol. XI, no. 2 (April 1916).

Fiedler, H. G. *Goethe's Lyric Poems in English Translation.* Modern Language Review, vol. XVIII, Jan. 1923.

Greg, W. W. *English Translations of Lenore.* Modern Quarterly of Language and Literature, no. 5, 1899, and no. 1, 1900.

Haney, J. L. *German Literature in England before* 1790. Americana Germanica, vol. IV.
    Haney is one of the most rational, careful and readable writers on the subject of German Literature in England.

Herford, C. H. *The Age of Wordsworth.* London, 1909.

Herzfeld, G. *Zur Geschichte der deutschen Litteratur in England.* Archiv für das Studium der neueren Sprachen, vol. CV, p. 30, and vol. CX (Nachträge), p. 109.

—— *Zur Geschichte von Bürgers Lenore in England.* Archiv für das Studium der neueren Sprachen, vol. CVI, p. 354.

Kipka. *Schillers Maria Stuart im Auslande.* Studien zur vergleichenden Litteraturgeschichte, 1905 (v).

Koeppel, Dr E. *Deutsche Strömungen in der englischen Litteratur.* Strassburg, 1910.

M. *Bürgers Lenore in England*. Beilage zur Allgemeinen Münchner Zeitung, 54, 1901.

Madden, R. R. *The Literary Life and Correspondence of the Countess of Blessington*. London, 1855.

Margraf, E. *Einfluss der deutschen Litteratur auf die englische am Ende des achtzehnten und im ersten Drittel des neunzehnten Jahrhunderts*. Inaug. Diss. Leipzig, 1901.
Uncritical, and unreliable in its statement of facts.

Möbius, H. *The Gothic Romance*. Inaug. Diss. Leipzig, 1902.

Morgan, B. Q. *A Bibliography of German Literature in English Translation*. University of Wisconsin Studies in Language and Literature, no. 16. Madison, 1922.

Omond, T. S. *The Romantic Triumph*. Edinburgh and London, 1900.

Oswald, E. *Der Einfluss des deutschen Schriftentums auf England*. Mag. für die Litteratur des Auslandes. Sept. 13, 1879.

Perry, T. S. *English Literature in the 18th Century*. New York, 1883.

—— *German Influence in English Literature*. Atlantic Monthly, Aug. 1877.

Rea, T. *Schiller's Dramas and Poems in England*. London, 1906.

Redding, C. *Yesterday and To-Day*. 3 vols. London, 1863.

Reed, Bertha. *The Influence of Solomon Gessner upon English Literature*. Philadelphia, 1905.
Tries to prove too much, and is unconvincing.

Roberts. *Bürger's Lenore*. Athenaeum 3823. 1901.

Schaible, K. H. *Geschichte der Deutschen in England*. Strassburg, 1885.

Seidensticker, O. *The relation of English to German Literature in the 18th Century*. Poet-Lore. 1890, 2.

Sellier, W. *Kotzebue in England. Ein Beitrag zur Geschichte der englischen Bühne und der Beziehungen der deutschen Litteratur zur englischen*. Leipzig, 1901.

Smiles, S. *A Publisher and his Friends. Memoir and Correspondence of the late John Murray*. London, 1891.

Stanger. *Zwei englische Faust-Übersetzer*. Archiv für das Studium der neueren Sprachen, vol. CVI, p. 355.

Stephen, Leslie. *Studies of a Biographer*, vol. II. The Importation of German.

Streuli, W. T. *Carlyle als Vermittler deutscher Litteratur*. Zürich, 1895.

Süpfle, T. *Beiträge zur Geschichte der deutschen Litteratur in England im letzten Drittel des* 18. *Jahrhunderts*. Zeitschrift für vergleichende Litteraturgeschichte. N.F. 6. Band. 1893.

Todt, W. *Lessing in England 1767–1850*. Heidelberg, 1912.

Tucker, T. G. *The Foreign Debt of English Literature*. London, 1907.
Superficial, as far as German Literature is concerned.

Turner, A. E. *Review of Carré's Goethe en Angleterre*. Modern Language Review, vol. XVI. July–October 1921.

Vaughan, C. E. *The Romantic Revolt*. Edinburgh and London, 1907.

Weddigen, F. H. *Geschichte der Einwirkungen der deutschen Litteratur auf die Litteraturen der übrigen europäischen Kulturvölkern der Neuzeit*. Leipzig, 1882.
    Rather general and diffuse, and not always correct in matters of fact. But considering its date, it is well-informed.

Weddigen, Dr Otto. *Die Vermittler des deutschen Geistes in England und Nordamerika*. Herrigs Archiv, Band 59.

Willoughby, L. A. *English Translations and Adaptations of Schiller's Robbers*. Modern Language Review, July–October 1921.

—— *Die Räuber. Ein Trauerspiel von Friedrich Schiller*. pp. 1–101. Humphrey Milford, 1922.

Zeiger, T. *Beiträge zur Geschichte des Einflusses der neueren deutschen Litteratur auf die englische*. Inaug. Diss. Leipzig. Berlin, 1901.

INDEX

For EU product safety concerns, contact us at Calle de José Abascal, 56–1°,
28003 Madrid, Spain or eugpsr@cambridge.org.

www.ingramcontent.com/pod-product-compliance
Ingram Content Group UK Ltd.
Pitfield, Milton Keynes, MK11 3LW, UK
UKHW010045140625
459647UK00012BB/1616